Microsoft® BASIC 7.1:
A Programmer's Reference

Peter G. Aitken

John Wiley & Sons, Inc.

New York • Chichester • Brisbane • Toronto • Singapore

Library of Congress Cataloging-in-Publication Data

Aitken, Peter G.
    Microsoft basic 7.1 : a programmer's reference / Peter G. Aitken.
        p. cm.
    Includes bibliographical references.
    ISBN 0-471-52901-X (alk. paper)
    1. BASIC (Computer program language) 2. Microsoft BASIC (Computer
program)   I. Title.
QA76.73.B3A377   1991
055.26'2--dc20   90-20037

Printed in the United States of America
91 92 10 9 8 7 6 5 4 3 2 1

Contents

Chapter 17:   The Date/Time, Format, and Financial Libraries 311

Chapter 18:   The User Interface Toolboxes 331

Chapter 19:   OS/2 Programming 367

Introduction

The Microsoft BASIC Professional Development System, also known as BASIC 7, is the most significant advance in BASIC programming since the introduction of the original QuickBASIC. For the first time, BASIC programmers can tackle those huge, complex programming projects that previously forced a switch to C or another "professional" language. The hundreds of thousands of experienced BASIC programmers can remain true to their language of choice.

Let's take a look at the features of BASIC 7. The following list is not anywhere near complete. Rather, I emphasize the most significant features that are of interest to anyone contemplating adopting BASIC 7 as their development system. Even if you already own BASIC 7, you may not be aware of all its features!

- The QuickBASIC Extended Environment, an integrated development environment that combines an editor, a compiler, a linker, a debugger, and a help system.

- Separate development tools for users who prefer the more traditional standalone method of programming: the Microsoft Editor; a command-line compiler; the Microsoft Overlay Linker; the CodeView debugger; and NMAKE, a program maintenance utility.

- The ability to create programs that run in real or protected mode.

- Significant improvements over earlier versions of BASIC in terms of program size and execution speed.

- Support for overlays, permitting the creation of programs as large as 16Mb in size.

- User toolboxes, including source code, for commonly needed functions such as presentation graphics, graphical fonts, pull-down menus, screen-text windows, mouse support, and matrix math.

- The Indexed Sequential Access Method (ISAM), a collection of routines for creating and manipulating data files. The ISAM routines greatly simplify the process of programming large, complex databases (up to 128Mb in size).

- The **currency** data type, an 8-byte fixed point variable type that is accurate to the ten-thousandths place and eliminates rounding errors. This new data type is faster and more memory-efficient than the Binary Coded Decimal often used to code financial applications.

- Three add-on libraries that provide functions for numeric formatting, date and time manipulation, and financial calculations.

I think you'll agree that BASIC 7 is a very impressive package. With all of its power, however, comes an unavoidable degree of complexity. Therein lies the *raison d'etre* of this book: to provide a clear, and more importantly, a *concise* reference to the BASIC 7 development system. The BASIC 7 documentation is quite good, providing a complete and reasonably clear reference to every detail of the system. It's also huge: 4 books totalling almost 2000 pages. It's sometimes difficult to find just the information you need.

In this book, I take the following approach: Rather than trying to be complete, I present the subset of information most often needed by programmers. This information is all you'll need to be up and running, creating real-world applications in BASIC 7. As your programming expertise increases, refer to the BASIC 7 documentation for information about the details.

Several typographic conventions are used in this book. For the sake of clarity, these conventions are as similar as possible to those used in the BASIC 7 documentation.

- BASIC keywords appearing in the body of the text are printed in uppercase and **boldface**.

- Words you type appear in **boldface**.

- *Italics* are used when a new term is first introduced. Italics are also used in code examples for placeholders, indicating information you must supply.

- Ellipses (...) in code examples indicate code that was omitted because it's not essential for the example.

- Square brackets ([ ]) enclose optional items.

Acknowledgments

My thanks go to Katherine Schowalter and Denise Rinaldo at John Wiley & Sons, Inc. for their help in seeing this book through to completion. I am also grateful to Ethan Winer and Irene Governale, whose careful technical editing has greatly enhanced the book's accuracy.

The QBX Environment

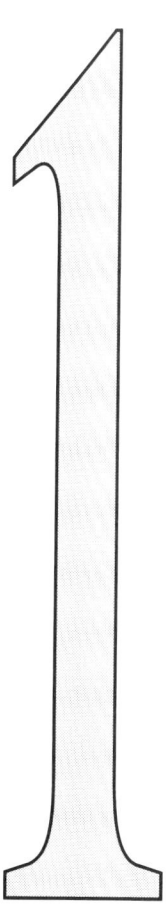

QBX stands for Quick Basic Extended, an integrated programming environment that is part of your BASIC 7 package. QBX is a wonderfully powerful and convenient tool that integrates in a single environment all of the tools that you'll need for the great majority of your programming tasks. In addition to QBX, BASIC 7 also includes a command-line compiler and a linker that provide an alternative method for program development; these will be covered in Chapter 15, Advanced Compiler and Linker Use. I suspect that most BASIC 7 programmers will use QBX almost exclusively, because it provides significant speed and convenience advantages over the command-line method of program development.

This chapter covers the use of the most important features of the QBX environment. In keeping with the book's philosophy, I make no effort to cover every nitty-gritty detail of this rich and complex programming environment. Rather, my goal is to provide the fundamental information you need to start writing programs as soon as possible. Further details can be found in the BASIC 7 documentation and the QBX on-line Help system.

Some specialized QBX functions used in structured programming are covered in Chapter 4. (If you're familiar with Microsoft QuickBASIC version 4.0 or higher, you may wish to just skim this chapter.)

Program Development Steps

Traditional program development comprises the following discrete steps, carried out in a specific order:

1. Write the BASIC source code, using a tool called an *editor*. The result of this step is a disk file with a .BAS extension, containing your program's source code.

2. Compile the source code using a tool called a *compiler*. The compiler translates the BASIC source-code file into binary instructions that the computer understands. The result of this step

is a disk file with an .OBJ extension, containing machine instructions (usually called an *object file*).

3. Link the object file with BASIC library routines, using a tool
called a *linker*. The result of this step is a complete, executable
program located in a disk file with an .EXE extension.

4. Execute the program and test to determine if it operates correctly.
If not, return to step 1 to make the needed modifications. Certain
program malfunctions may require the use of a tool called a
debugger to track down the cause of the problem.

QBX integrates all four tools—editor, compiler, linker, and
debugger—into a single, user-friendly programming environment. You
can quickly and easily switch between all needed programming functions. QBX stores intermediate information in memory rather than on
disk, so programming operations are much faster.

Starting QBX: A Quick Tour

Assuming you have installed the BASIC 7 system according to the
instructions provided and you accepted the installation defaults,
change to the \BC7\BIN directory. Start QBX by typing

```
QBX
```

at the DOS prompt. When the QBX screen appears, press the Enter
key once to clear the program title from the bottom line. Your screen
looks similar to Figure 1.1.

These are the basic components of the QBX screen:

• The *main menu* lists the first level of QBX menu commands.
Most QBX functions are performed via the main menu.

• The *View window* is where you view and edit source code. The
title of the file being edited is displayed at the top of the window. If the file hasn't been named yet, Untitled is displayed.

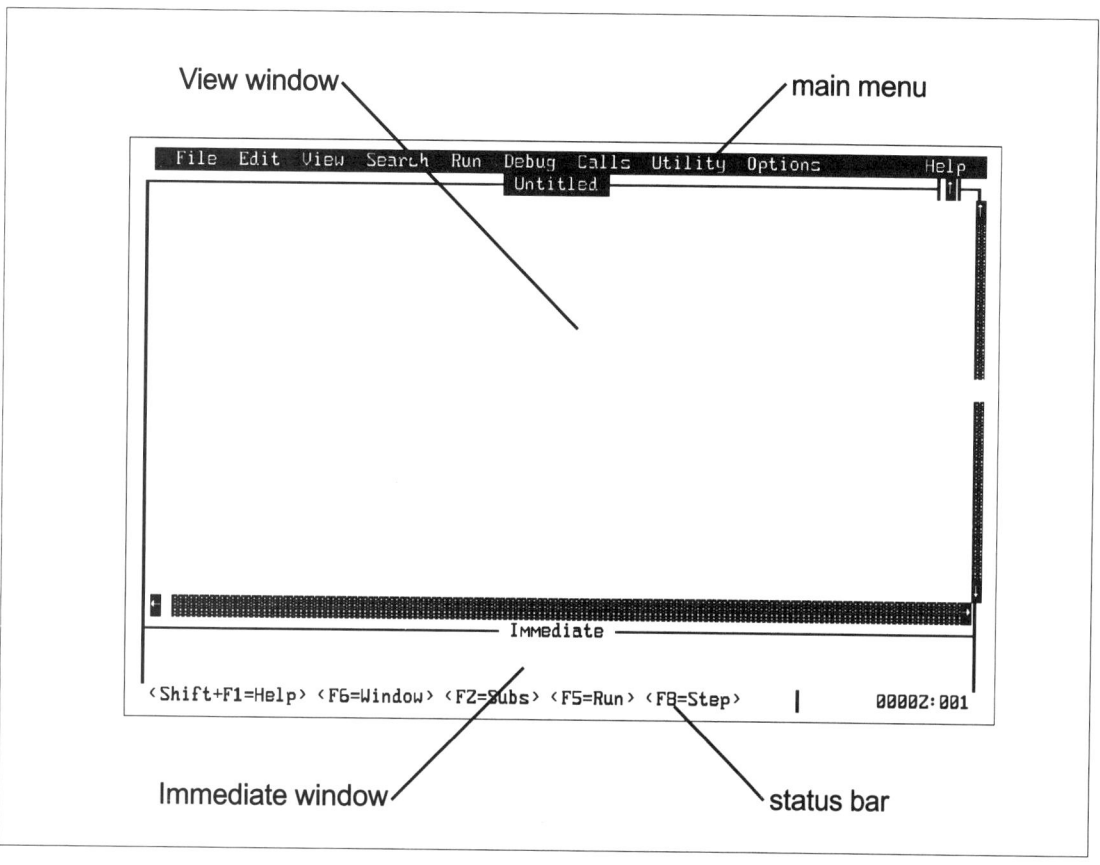

Figure 1.1. The QBX screen upon startup (with parts labeled).

- The *Immediate window* is used for directly executing short sections of BASIC code. When you enter one or more lines of code in this window and press the Enter key, each line immediately executes, and the output (if any) displays. Use the immediate window to test short sections of code before incorporating them into your program.

- The *status bar* at the bottom of the screen has two sections. On the right, it displays the row:column position of the editing cursor in the view window. On the left, it lists shortcut keys for performing certain actions. The available shortcut keys depend upon your activity at a given moment, and offer shortcuts for the most commonly needed actions. You can select shortcut keys enclosed in angle brackets by clicking with the mouse.

The QBX screen uses windows to organize information. You can display multiple windows, but only a single window can be active at one time. The active window contains a highlighted title and, if the window is large enough to need them, scroll bars. In Figure 1.1, the View window is active. To activate another window, click on the desired window with the mouse, or press F6 or Shift+F6 to cycle forward or backward through the available windows.

You can change a window's size. To expand a window to fill the entire screen, click the upward pointing arrow in the upper-right corner of the window. To return an expanded window to its original size, click the arrow again. (When a window is expanded, its arrow has two heads.) You can change the size of the active window by pressing Alt++ (plus sign) to expand it or Alt+− (minus sign) to contract it. (You must use the gray + and − keys on the numeric keypad, not those to the left of the Backspace key.) You can use the mouse as well: simply point to the border between two windows and drag it to the desired position. While you drag the border, one window expands and the other shrinks.

With a mouse, you can use the scroll bars to scroll around in a window if the contents of the window extend past its borders. To use the *vertical scroll bar* perform the following steps: To scroll up or down one line, click the arrow at the top or the bottom of the scroll bar. To scroll multiple lines, hold the mouse button down while pointing at one of the arrows.

The *elevator box* in the region between the arrows indicates your current position in the window. If you drag the elevator box to a different position, the window scrolls accordingly. If the elevator box is at the top of its travel, you're at the start of the window; if the elevator box is at the bottom of its travel, you're at the end of the window.

To scroll up or down a page at a time, click the region between the elevator box and the up or down arrow.

The horizontal scroll bar scrolls left and right in a window. Its operation is the same as that of a vertical scroll bar. You can also use the keyboard navigation keys for scrolling at any time.

Keyboard versus Mouse

QBX can be used with or without a mouse, although a mouse makes many operations faster and is highly recommended. The *mouse cursor*, the small arrow at the upper left of Figure 1.1, will be displayed only if your system has a mouse and mouse driver installed. (Depending upon the specific mouse you're using, your mouse cursor may have a different shape.) The mouse cursor moves on the screen while you move the mouse on your desk. The following terms describe how to use the mouse:

- To *click* with the mouse, point the mouse cursor at a specific screen location, and then rapidly press and release the mouse button. (Unless specified otherwise, *click* refers to the left mouse button.)

- To *double-click* with the mouse, point the mouse cursor at a specific screen location, and then rapidly press and release the mouse button twice.

- To *drag* with the mouse, point at a specific screen location, press the mouse button, and move the mouse pointer while keeping the button depressed.

QBX Menus

Most QBX functions are accessed via the main menu displayed across the top of the screen. Each main menu selection leads to a pull-down menu that contains more choices. For example, Figure 1.2 shows the pull-down menu displayed when you select View from the main menu.

QBX uses the following menu conventions:

- Ellipses (...) following a menu entry indicate that the menu choice leads to a *dialog box*, which prompts you for more information. Menu choices without ellipses are executed immediately (with a few exceptions).

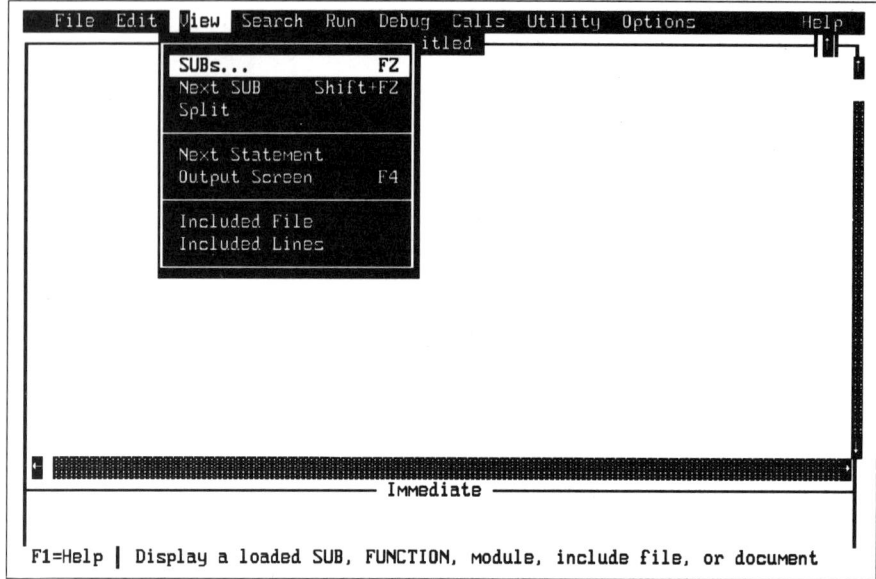

Figure 1.2. A QBX pull-down menu.

- Shortcut keys listed after a menu entry give the key or keys that you press to execute the corresponding command without utilizing the menu system. Only the most commonly used commands have shortcut keys.

- A highlighted letter indicates the key that you can press to execute the command while the menu is displayed. In Figure 1.2, for example, pressing the N key executes the Next Statement command.

- A menu entry displayed in gray text is not available at the present time (e.g., the Included File command in Figure 1.2).

You can select QBX menu commands using the mouse or the keyboard. Two methods are available for selecting menu commands with a mouse:

1. Click on a main menu command to display the pull-down menu, and then click on the desired command.

2. Point at a main menu command, and then press and hold the left mouse button to display the pull-down menu. Next, drag the pointer to the desired command and release the button.

To select a menu command with the keyboard, you must first display the appropriate pull-down menu using one of these two methods:

1. Press the ALT key (you can either hold it down or release it), and then press the key corresponding to the first letter of the desired main menu command.

2. Press and release the ALT key. Use the Left Arrow and the Right Arrow keys to move the highlight bar to the desired command, and then press the Enter key.

While the pull-down menu is displayed, select a command by pressing the highlighted letter, or use the Up Arrow and the Down Arrow keys to highlight the desired command and then press the Enter key.

Using Dialog Boxes

A *dialog box* is displayed when QBX requires additional information from you before executing a command. For example, Figure 1.3 shows the Save As dialog box (i.e., the dialog box that is displayed when you select the Save As command from the File menu), with its components labeled.

Some dialog boxes contain only a subset of these components. Each component of a dialog box is contained in its own section. To move between components, press the Tab or the Shift+Tab keys, or click with the mouse. A dialog box has the following components:

- A *text box* that you use for entering text information, such as a filename. Use the standard editing keys to enter and change information in a text box.

- A *list box* containing a list of items from which you may choose.

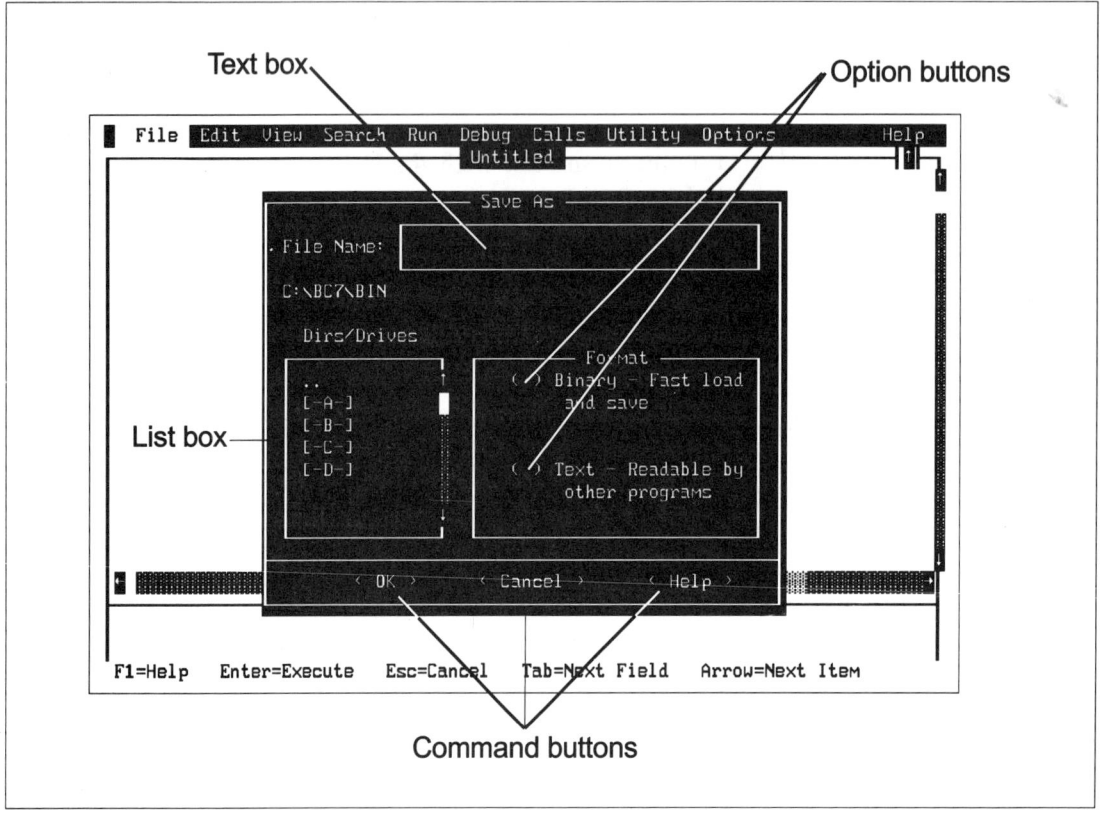

Figure 1.3. The Save As dialog box.

To select an item from a list box, double-click it with the mouse, or use the Up Arrow and Down Arrow keys to highlight it and then press the Enter key. If a list box contains more items than can be displayed at the same time, use the PgUp and PgDn keys or the scroll bar to display additional items.

- *Option buttons* for selecting predefined options. Parentheses indicate mutually exclusive options: only one of these items may be selected at a time. Square brackets (not shown in Figure 1.3) indicate nonexclusive options: more than one item may be selected. To toggle an option, click with the mouse or press the highlighted key.

- *Command buttons* that perform actions related to the dialog box. The three commands common to all dialog boxes are:

  OK, which executes the command using the information and options you entered into the dialog box.

  Cancel, which closes the dialog box without executing the command.

  Help, which displays a help screen containing information about the dialog box.

Some dialog boxes contain additional command buttons for tasks specific to those dialog boxes. To select a dialog box command, click the corresponding button, or select (highlight) the desired button by pressing the Tab or the Shift+Tab keys, and then press the Enter key. Any time a dialog box is displayed, you can press the Enter key to execute the command button whose brackets are highlighted (usually, the OK command button).

Formatting and Syntax Checking

When you enter a line of text in the View window and press the Enter key, QBX automatically scans the line. If the line is recognized as valid BASIC source code, QBX formats it according to a set of pre-defined conventions. BASIC keywords are displayed in uppercase, and the spacing between keywords, parentheses, variables, and operators is adjusted. If the line contains one or more variable names, QBX scans the entire program file for other instances of the name(s) and, if necessary, adjusts their case so that all instances of a variable match each other. For example, if you enter the line:

```
x = SIN (y)
```

and then you enter

```
PRINT X, Y
```

the first line is adjusted to read

```
X - SIN (Y)
```

This automatic formatting feature is a great help in maintaining consistent, readable source code. If the Syntax Checking selection on the Options menu is set ON, QBX also checks the syntax of each line entered. If a syntax error is found, the cursor moves to the location of the error, and a message window displays information about the error.

Editing a Program

You edit source code in the View window. When the View window is active and in edit mode, the *edit cursor* is visible in the window. The edit cursor indicates the location where editing actions, such as inserting or deleting text, will occur. Move the edit cursor by clicking on the new location with the mouse. To move it using the keyboard, follow these steps:

- Use the Up, Down, Left and Right Arrow keys to move the cursor one line or one character in the indicated direction.

- Use the Home and End keys to move the cursor to the beginning or the end of the current line.

- Use the Ctrl+Right Arrow and Ctrl+Left Arrow keys to move the cursor one word to the right or the left.

- Use the PgUp and PgDn keys to move the cursor up or down as many lines as are visible in the window.

- Use the Ctrl+End and Ctrl+Home keys to move the cursor to the end or the beginning of the program.

When you enter text, it appears on the screen at the position of the editing cursor. In the default *insert* mode, existing text to the right of the cursor is not replaced, but moves over to make room for the new text. In *overstrike* mode, new text *overwrites*, or replaces, existing text on the same line. To toggle between the insert and overstrike modes, press the Ins key. In insert mode the cursor is an underscore; in overstrike mode it is a block.

Use the following keystrokes to delete text:

- Del deletes the character under the cursor. Backspace deletes the character to the left of the cursor.

- Ctrl+Y deletes the entire current line. Ctrl+Q+Y deletes from the cursor to the end of the current line.

- Ctrl+T deletes to the end of the current word.

- Alt+Backspace is the Undo key, reversing the effect of the most recent deletion or other editing action. You can press Alt+Backspace (or select Undo from the Edit menu) multiple times to undo as many as 20 edits.

- Ctrl+Backspace is the Redo key, reversing the effect of an Undo. The Redo command is also available on the Edit menu.

Several QBX editing operations require you to mark a block of text to be operated on. A block can be any size, from a single character to an entire file. To mark a block with the mouse, point at the character at one end of the block and drag the mouse pointer until the desired block is highlighted. To mark a block from the keyboard, first move the cursor to one end of the block. Next, press and hold the Shift key and use the cursor movement keys to highlight the desired block. Once a block is marked you can perform the following operations on it:

- Copy the marked text to the *clipboard* (a temporary storage area). The marked text is not affected. To copy the text, press Ctrl+Ins, or select Copy from the Edit menu.

- Cut the marked text to the clipboard, deleting that text from the

View window. To cut text, press Shift+Del, or select Cut from the Edit menu.

- Clear, or erase, the marked text without moving it to the clipboard. To clear the text, press Del, or select Clear from the Edit menu.

- Paste text from the clipboard into the View window at the cursor position. The text remains on the clipboard and can be pasted again. To paste text, press Shift+Ins, or select Paste from the Edit menu.

The New Sub... and New Function... commands on the Edit menu will be covered in Chapter 4.

This section has covered QBX's most frequently needed editing commands. The editor offers additional capabilities that you may find useful once you have mastered the basics. For information about additional editing features, select Contents from the Help menu, and then select Editing Keys.

Saving and Retrieving Program Files

Your BASIC source code is saved in disk files that, by tradition, have the extension .BAS. The commands on the File menu save and retrieve disk files. In all of the file operations, QBX prompts you for confirmation before taking any action that might lead to data loss.

The New Program command clears the currently loaded program from memory. Use this command when you are finished working on one program and are ready to start entering a new program.

The Open Program... command reads a file from disk into the View window, replacing the original contents (if any). When you select Open Program..., the dialog box in Figure 1.4 is displayed. The File Name text box initially displays *.BAS. If you know the name of the file to be opened, enter it here. You can also select a filename from the Files list box, which lists all .BAS files in the current directory. To list .BAS files in a different disk or directory, select from the Dirs/Drives box.

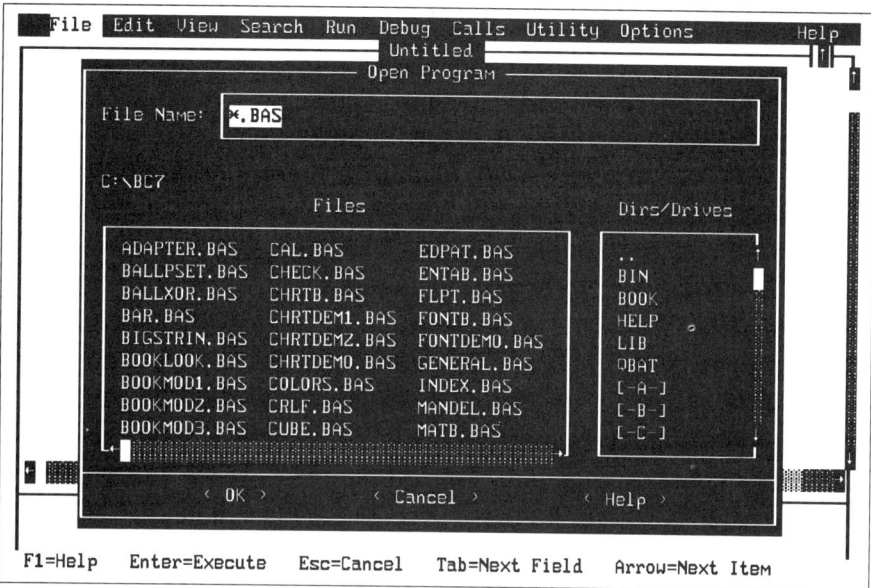

Figure 1.4. The Open Program dialog box.

The Save As... command saves the contents of the View window in a disk file with a name you specify. Use Save As... when you first save a new, unnamed program, or to save an already named file under a new name. The Save As dialog box is shown in Figure 1.5. In the File Name: text box, enter the name you wish to assign to the file. If you don't include an extension, .BAS is used. Make a selection in the Dirs/ Drives list box if you want the file saved in a different drive and/or directory. (The current drive/directory is listed above the Dirs/Drives list box.) Under Format select the format in which the file is to be saved. Binary format can be read only by QBX, but results in smaller files that can be loaded and saved faster. Text format results in larger files that can be read by other programs, such as text editors. (QBX can read Text format also.)

The Save command saves the contents of the View window under the assigned name. Use Save to update the disk copy of a file after you have assigned a filename using Save As....

The Merge... command reads a file from disk, inserting its contents into the currently loaded file at the cursor location.

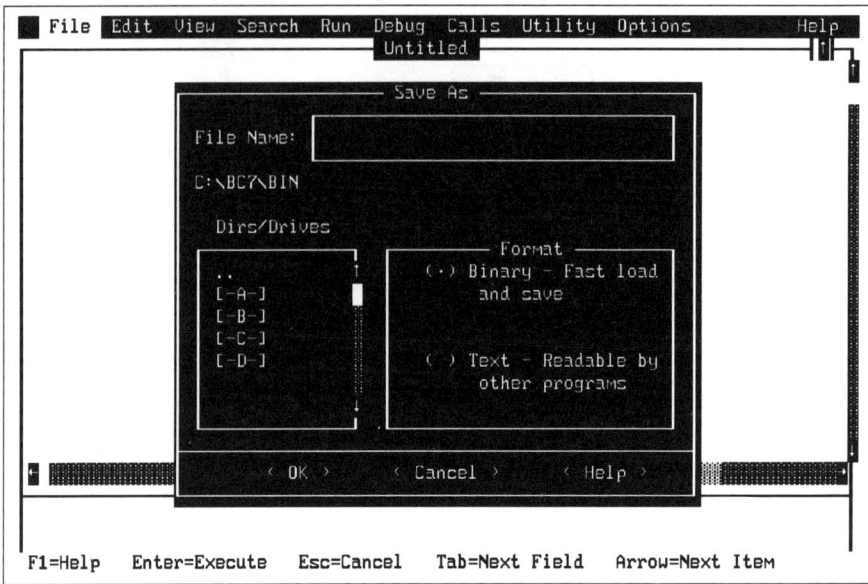

Figure 1.5. The Save As dialog box.

The Save All, Create File..., Load File..., and Unload File... commands are relevant only when you use QBX to edit multiple files. This topic is covered in Chapter 4.

Use the Print... command to send all or part of a program file to a printer or a disk file. The Print dialog box is shown in Figure 1.6. Under Send, choose the information to be printed. Choose Selected Text to print the text you have marked (highlighted). Choose Active Window to print the entire contents of the active window. Choose Current Module or All Modules to print the entire current module or all loaded modules, respectively (see Chapter 4 for information about modules). Use the options in the To box to select the print destination. You can specify one of three printer ports, or else a disk file whose name you specify.

The DOS Shell command displays the DOS prompt while keeping QBX and your program loaded in memory. Use the DOS Shell to perform tasks such as formatting diskettes. When you finish, type **EXIT** to return to QBX.

The Exit command terminates QBX and returns you to DOS.

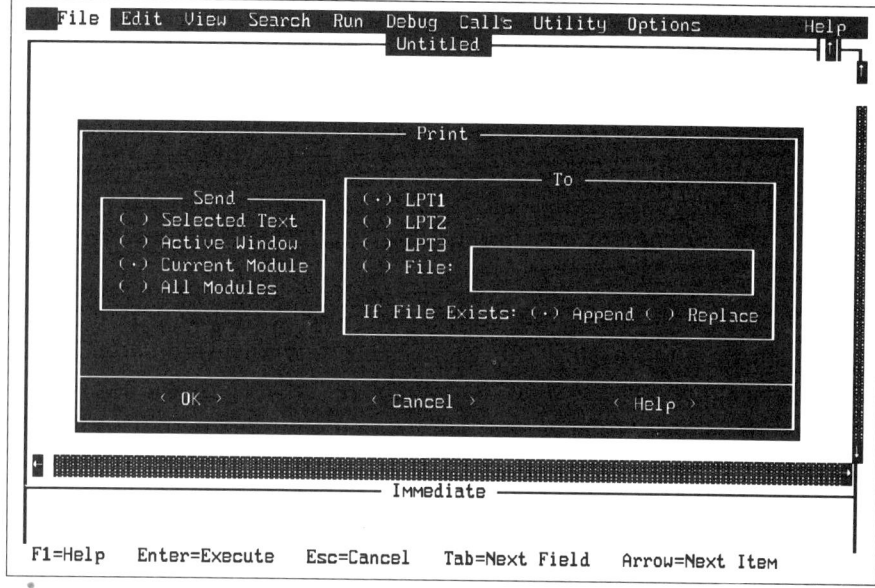

Figure 1.6. The Print dialog box.

Compiling and Running Your Program

Compiling is the process by which your BASIC source code is translated into digital instructions that the computer understands. QBX has two methods of compilation that you access via the Run menu. These methods are *compiling in memory* and *creating an .EXE file*.

Compiling in Memory

To compile in memory, select Start from the Run menu. QBX performs the following actions:

1. It compiles and links your program, storing the executable code in memory. If compilation errors occur, appropriate messages display.

2. It executes the program, allowing you to test it to see whether it is performing as intended.

3. Upon program termination, it returns you to QBX at the location in the program where you were when you issued the Start command.

In-memory compilation is very fast, and is ideal for stages of program development that consist of many repetitions of the modify-compile-test cycle.

Creating an .EXE File

Once your program is functioning properly, you will probably want to create a standalone .EXE file that can run outside of the QBX environment, be distributed to colleagues, and so forth. To create an .EXE file on disk, select Make EXE File... from the Run menu. The dialog box in Figure 1.7 is displayed.

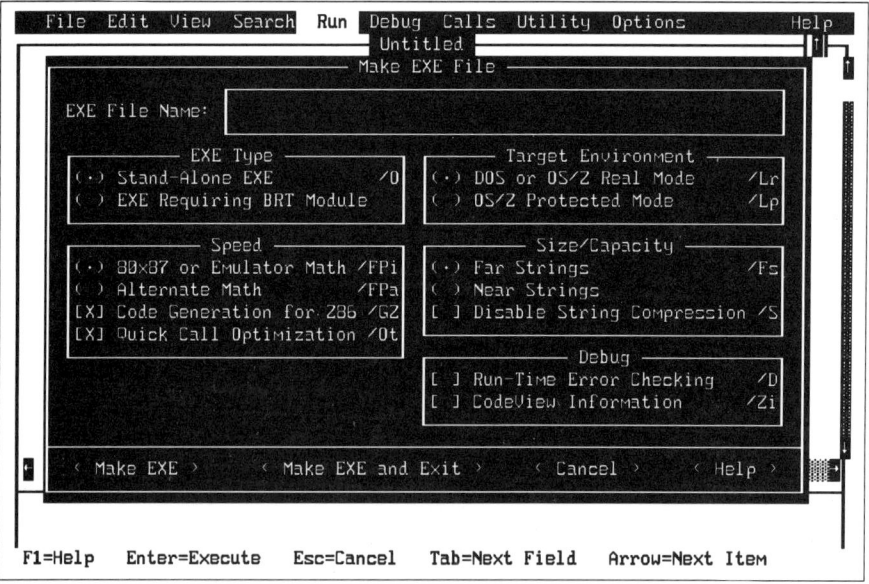

Figure 1.7. The Make EXE File dialog box.

Options in this dialog box control certain aspects of the compilation process. Some of the options may not be available, depending upon the choices you made when you installed BASIC 7. First, select the desired options (explained in the following pages). Then, select either Make EXE or Make EXE and Exit. QBX creates an executable file with the same name as your BASIC source file, and the .EXE extension.

For most programs, the default options (shown in Figure 1.7) are fine. In the Make EXE File dialog box, each option has displayed next to it the command-line switch required to activate the option when using the BC.EXE command-line compiler (covered in Chapter 15).

In the EXE Type box, specify whether the .EXE file will require the BRT module. The BRT module is a disk file supplied with the BASIC 7 package and that contains BASIC runtime routines.

- Select Stand-Alone EXE if you want to create an .EXE file linked with the BASIC runtime routines that does not require the BRT module. .EXE files compiled with this option are larger, but initialize faster and require less memory when running.

- Select EXE Requiring BRT Module to create an .EXE file not linked with the BASIC runtime routines that must access the BRT module on disk when the program executes. Programs compiled with this option are smaller, but initialize slower and require more memory when running.

Use the Speed to box select options that affect floating-point math and program speed.

- Select 80x87 or Emulator Math if you don't know whether the target system will have a numeric coprocessor installed. The resulting program uses the coprocessor if present, or else emulates the coprocessor in software. Full precision is maintained in calculations.

- Select Alternate Math if you expect the program to run on a system without a coprocessor. This option creates a smaller program that runs faster on systems lacking a coprocessor. The tradeoff is a slight loss of precision when compared to the 80x87 or Emulator Math option. This loss of precision is irrelevant for most applications.

- Select Code Generation for 286 if the program will run only on systems with an 80286, 80386, or 80486 processor. Such programs are smaller and execute faster, but cannot be run on PCs with an 8088/8086 processor.

- Select Quick Call Optimization for improved execution speed if your program doesn't use local error handling, and you're not compiling with the Far Strings (/Fs) or Runtime Error Checking (/D) options.

Use the Target Environment box to specify the operating system under which your program will run:

- Select DOS or OS/2 Real Mode to create a program that executes under the DOS operating system or in the OS/2 operating system's DOS Compatibility Box.

- Select OS/2 Protected Mode to create a program that executes in the OS/2 operating system's protected mode.

Use the Size/Capacity box to select options that affect the storage of strings:

- The Far Strings option results in maximum program storage space for string and numeric variables, at the expense of decreased space for program code. This option is permanently selected in QBX—you can't turn it off.

- The Near Strings option is not available in QBX. To use this option, you must compile your program with the BC command-line compiler. Near Strings provides maximum space for program code at the expense of decreased variable storage space.

- The Disable String Compression causes literal strings in the program code to be written to the object file instead of being stored in memory in the symbol table. Use this option if a program containing many string literals generates an Out of Memory error during compilation.

Use the Debug box to select options for program error checking and debugging information:

- Select Run-Time Error Checking to create a program that checks during execution for arithmetic overflow, array subscript out-of-bounds, and **GOSUB...RETURN** errors. If one of these errors occurs, the program halts and reports the line number nearest to the error's location. If you enable Run-Time Error Checking, you can halt your program at any time during execution by pressing Ctrl+Break. If you don't enable this option, errors are not detected and the program responds to Ctrl+Break only at **INPUT** statements. Enabling Run-Time Error Checking results in larger and slower programs.

- Select CodeView Information if you want to use the Microsoft CodeView debugger to debug the program.

Setting QBX Options

The Options selection on the main menu allows you to modify certain aspects of the QBX environment. The Options pull-down menu contains four entries:

- Select Display... to customize the QBX screen. When the dialog box is displayed, you can control screen colors, the scroll bar display, and tab stops.

- Select Set Paths... to specify the directories where QBX will look for certain types of files. (The default paths set when you installed BASIC 7 are fine for most situations.)

- Select Right Mouse... to specify the function of the right mouse button. Depending upon the selection you make here, pressing the right mouse button will either call up context-sensitive help or execute the current program up to the current line.

- The Syntax Checking option acts as a toggle. If it's ON (indicated by a bullet next to the "S" in Syntax), QBX checks the syntax of each program line as you enter it, and alerts you to errors immediately.

The Help System

The QBX on-line Help system is a valuable programming tool. It provides quick and easy access to detailed information about all aspects of QBX: the BASIC language, QBX menu selections, the editor, compiler options, and error messages. If you specified Help file installation during the setup procedure, the Help system is automatically available every time you start QBX.

The QBX Help system can be accessed in two ways: by cross references or menu commands. The Help system includes information about how to use itself—Help about Help, if you will.

Cross References

A *cross reference* is simply a link between one topic and another related topic. The QBX Help system utilizes both implicit and explicit cross references.

Implicit cross references include all BASIC keywords (statements, functions, logical operators, and metacommands), menu commands, and dialog boxes. To obtain help about an implicit cross reference, perform the following steps:

- For a command on the QBX main menu or a pull-down menu, highlight the command (do not press the Enter key) and press F1.

- For a BASIC keyword that is part of your program, put the editing cursor on (or one space to the right of) the keyword, and press F1. You can also click the keyword using the right mouse button.

- For a dialog box, display the dialog box and then press F1, or select Help from the command buttons.

For example, Figure 1.8 shows the Help screen that is displayed when you put the editing cursor on the **PRINT** keyword and press F1. Note that the View window is still the active window, although it has shrunk to a single line containing the cursor. To activate the Help window, press Shift+F6 or click anywhere in the window with the mouse.

In many ways, a Help window is like any other QBX window. While it's active, you can scroll in a Help window, change its size, and copy (but not cut) text, such as sample code to be pasted in your program. To exit Help and remove the Help window, press the Escape key.

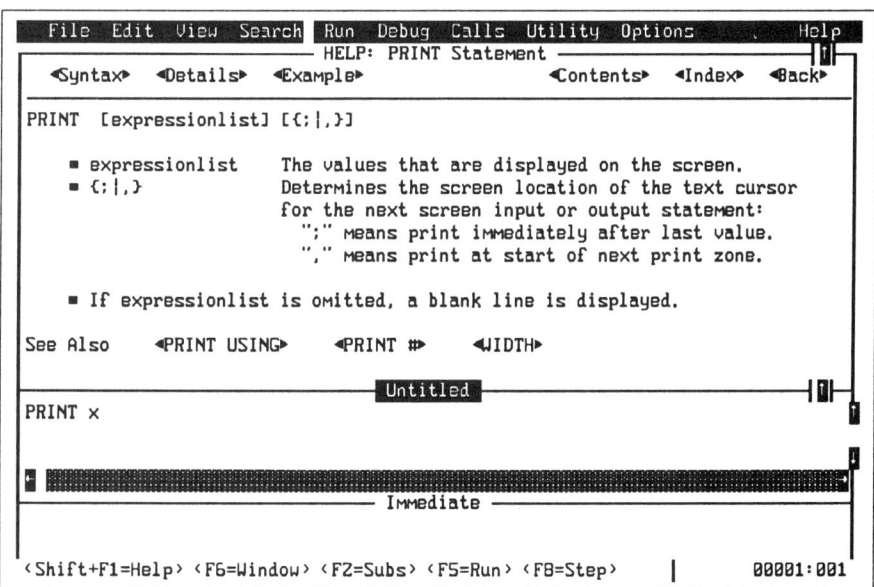

Figure 1.8. The Help screen for the **PRINT** keyword.

An *explicit* cross reference, also called a *hyperlink*, is a word or phrase in a Help window that is tied to another Help screen. Using hyperlinks, you can move among related Help screens until you find the information you want. QBX hyperlinks are bracketed by the ◄ and ► characters (e.g., the ◄Syntax►, ◄Details►, and ◄Example► hyperlinks in the top line of the Help screen in Figure 1.8).

Certain general-purpose hyperlinks are displayed on most Help screens:

- ◄Syntax► displays concise information about the syntax of a BASIC statement or function.

- ◄Details► provides more detailed information about the use of a BASIC keyword.

- ◄Example► displays a program or code fragment that illustrates the use of the statement or function.

- ◄Contents► and ◄Index► take you to the Help system table of contents or index (more about these shortly).

- ◄Back► takes you back one Help screen, to the screen you were viewing before the current one. QBX remembers the 20 most-recent Help screens. You can also move back by pressing Alt+F1.

Other more specific hyperlinks are found in the body or at the end of a Help screen (e.g., ◄PRINT USING► in Figure 1.8). To activate a hyperlink with the mouse, double-click it. With the keyboard, move the cursor to the desired hyperlink by pressing Tab or Shift+Tab and press the Enter key. (The Help window must be active.)

Help Menu Commands

The QBX on-line Help system can be accessed via the Help command on the main menu. The Help pull-down menu offers four options:

- Index displays an alphabetical index of all Help topics. Select the desired topic to display the corresponding Help screen.

- Contents displays the Help system's Table of Contents. Use the Table of Contents to locate information when you are not sure exactly where to find it.

- Topic displays Help corresponding to the BASIC keyword or symbol under the editing cursor. Selecting Topic from the Help menu has the same effect as pressing F1 while the View window is active.

- Using Help provides information about using the Help system.

Table 1.1 lists the keys used in the Help system. Remember, the Help window must be active before you can scroll on the screen, copy information, or activate hyperlinks.

Table 1.1. The Help System keys.

Key	Action
F1	Obtain context-sensitive help.
Shift+F1	Obtain help about using the Help system.
Alt+F1	Move back to the previous Help screen.
Esc	Close the Help window and return to what you were doing before you activated Help.
PgDn, PgUp	Scroll down or up in a Help window.
Tab, Shift+Tab	Select the next or the previous hyperlink in a Help screen.

Help about Program Symbols

A *symbol* is a variable, a constant, or a programmer-defined procedure name in your program. If you position the cursor on a symbol and press F1, the Help system provides information about the nature of the symbol and where it's used in the program.

Memory and QBX

You can use QBX to create moderate-sized programs on a system with only 640K of conventional memory. To create larger programs, you need extended and/or expanded memory.

Extended Memory

Extended memory can be present only on systems with an 80286, 80386, or 80486 processor. QBX can use approximately 60K of extended memory to store part of its own code, leaving that much more conventional memory for program code. For QBX to be able to use extended memory, you must install the HIMEM.SYS device driver provided with your BASIC 7 package. To do so, use an editor to place the following line in your CONFIG.SYS file:

```
device=himem.sys /HMAMIN=63
```

If the file HIMEM.SYS resides in a directory other than the root directory, include a path specification before the filename. The option **/HMAMIN=63** reserves all of the space in HIMEM for QBX. You must reboot your system for HIMEM to take effect.

Expanded Memory

Expanded memory that follows the Lotus-Intel-Microsoft 4.0 specification can be used with QBX. Expanded memory can be installed on all IBM-PC compatible computers, and usually requires an add-in memory board and a software driver. If your system has expanded memory, it can be used in several ways:

- The QBX environment can use expanded memory to store program code units (e.g., procedures) between 512 and 16K in size. The size of each procedure is listed in the Subs... dialog box, which you can view by pressing F2.

- The QBX environment can also use expanded memory to store arrays between 512 and 16K bytes in size. This applies to all array types except for variable-length string arrays.

- The ISAM database engine can use expanded memory to provide as much as 1.2Mb of expanded memory buffers. (The ISAM's use of expanded memory is covered in Chapter 14.)

- Competing procedures, such as third-party, add-on libraries or assembly language routines you write, can access expanded memory.

When you start QBX without options, it automatically has access to all available expanded memory that was not set aside for other uses. QBX uses only the expanded memory that it needs, but if some other process reserves expanded memory, none may be available for QBX to use. You can control QBX expanded memory usage with the following three startup options:

/E:mem   Reserves *mem* kilobytes of expanded memory for QBX. QBX will use no more that *mem* kilobytes, and that amount of memory will always be available to QBX.

/Es   Enables QBX to save and restore the expanded memory state. This option must be used if you have Quick Library routines that access expanded memory.

/Ea   Enables QBX to move arrays to expanded memory.

From within QBX, the **FRE(-3)** function returns the amount of expanded memory available to QBX.

Data Storage, Operators, and Expressions

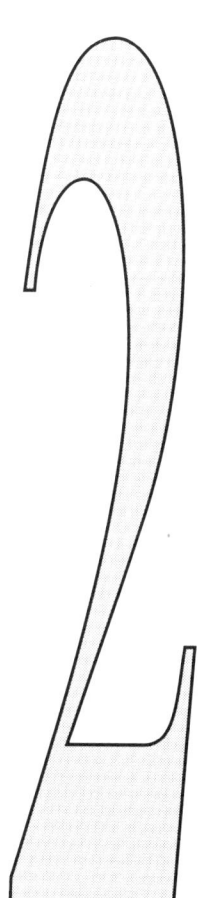

Programs work with data, and need methods for storing data in memory during program operation (disk storage is covered in Chapter 5). Programs also must be able to manipulate data in various ways. BASIC 7 offers a full range of data storage and manipulation options.

Constants

A *constant* is a data item that does not change during program execution. BASIC 7 offers two types of constants: literal and symbolic.

Literal Constants

A *literal constant* is typed directly into the program source code. A literal constant can be either *numeric* (a number value) or *string* (a series of characters enclosed in quotes). The following program statement uses both string and numeric literal constants to display a message on the screen:

```
PRINT "AJAX DATABASE PROGRAM version ";2.2
```

"AJAX DATABASE PROGRAM version " is the string constant, and **2.2** is the numeric constant. String literals are limited to 32,767 characters, and can contain any characters except the double quote. Numeric literals can be written in decimal, hexadecimal, octal, or exponential notation. Here are some examples of numeric literal constants:

1, -45.3, 0.11875   Decimal constants

&HFFFF, &h60A   Hexadecimal constants with &H or &h prefix

&O404, &o22   Octal constants, with &O or &o prefix

1.2E6, -0.3E-2   Exponential constant: a decimal number times a power of 10

Each type of numeric constant has a precision (its degree of accuracy) and a range (the largest and smallest allowed values). The BASIC 7 manual contains information on the precision and allowable ranges of numeric constants.

Symbolic Constants

As with a literal constant, a *symbolic constant* is typed directly into your program and does not change. A symbolic constant is represented by a name, or symbol, rather than by the literal value itself. The steps for using a symbolic constant are:

1. Use the **CONST** keyword to assign a literal constant to a symbolic name.

2. Use the name anywhere in your program where you want the value of the literal constant to be used.

For example:

```
CONST MONTHS = 12
DIM SALES(MONTHS)
...
FOR I = 1 to MONTHS
  PRINT SALES(I)
NEXT I
```

Multiple assignments can be included in a single **CONST** statement:

```
CONST MONTHS = 12, MYNAME = "Peter", PRIME.RATE = 0.10
```

The rules for symbolic constant names are the same as for variable names (discussed later in this chapter) with one difference. If you attach a type suffix character to a symbolic constant name when it is first declared, the type suffix is *not* part of the name. Thus,

```
CONST A% = 12
PRINT A
```

displays **12** on the screen. The major advantage of the use of symbolic constants over literal constants is that if you need to change the value of a symbolic constant, you make the change in only one location in your source code, at the place where the constant is declared. The use of constants also improves the readability of your source code.

Variables

A *variable* is a symbolic name that refers to a unit of data storage. The contents, or value, of a variable can change during program execution. A variable name can contain letters, numbers, the period, and the type declaration characters. The first character in a variable name must be a letter, and the maximum length of the variable name is 40 characters. Case does not matter. You can't use BASIC 7 reserved words as variable names. BASIC 7 offers a full range of variable types, suitable for any programming need.

Numeric Variables

As the name implies, a *numeric variable* stores a number. The *type* of a variable determines the kind of numeric information that you can store in the variable. BASIC 7's five numeric variable types can be divided into three categories:

- An *integer* variable holds a whole number (i.e., a number without a fractional, or decimal, part). BASIC 7 has two integer variable types: *integer* and *long integer*.

- A *floating-point* variable holds a number with a varying number of digits to the right of the decimal point. BASIC 7 provides two floating-point variable types: *single precision* and *double precision*.

- A *fixed-point* variable holds a number with a fixed number of digits to the right of the decimal point. BASIC 7 provides one fixed-point variable type, *currency*, which allows a maximum of four decimal places.

The permissible range of each variable type is listed in Table 2.1. This table also provides information about how you determine the type of a variable. You can specify the type of a BASIC 7 variable in three ways: using the last character of the variable's name, a **DEFtype** statement, or an **AS** statement.

To use the type suffixes, simply place the appropriate symbol as the last character in the variable name. Thus, **PROFITS@** is a currency variable, **COUNT%** is an integer variable, and **RATE#** is a double-precision variable. If no suffix is used, a variable defaults to single precision. The suffix is part of the name, so variables with the same name but different suffixes are distinct: **COUNT%** is a different variable than **COUNT!**. Note, however, that BASIC 7 treats **COUNT** and **COUNT!** as the same variable because they are both single precision (unless, of course, a previous **DEFtype** statement was used to change the default type).

Table 2.1. Basic 7 numeric variable types.

Variable type	Suffix	**AS** name	**DEFtype**	Range
Integer	%	INTEGER	**DEFINT**	-32,768 to 32,767
Long integer	&	LONG	**DEFLNG**	-2,147,483,648 to 2,147,483,647
Single precision	!	SINGLE	**DEFSNG**	+/- 3.40×10^{38}*
Double precision	#	DOUBLE	**DEFDBL**	+/- 1.79×10^{308}*
Currency	@	CURRENCY	**DEFCUR**	+/- 9.2×10^{14}*

*Approximate ranges; see BASIC data types in the QBX HELP system for more details.

Use the **DEFtype** statement to declare that variables whose names begin with certain letters of the alphabet are of a particular type, *without* using a suffix character. Here are some examples:

DEFINT A   All variables beginning with **A** are of type integer.

DEFDBL J-L   All variables beginning with **J**, **K**, or **L** are of type double.

DEFCUR A,T   All variables beginning with **A** or **T** are of type currency.

DEFtype statements affect variables only in the program module in which the statements appear. A type suffix overrides any **DEFtype** statement in effect, as illustrated here:

```
DEFINT A
APPLES = 12        ' APPLES is an integer variable
AVOCADOS! = 100    ' AVOCADOS! is a single precision variable
```

You can use the **AS** names to declare a variable type with a **DIM** statement (discussed later in this chapter), in parameter lists for subs and functions (discussed in Chapter 4), or with **COMMON**, **SHARED**, or **STATIC** statements (also discussed in Chapter 4).

String Variables

A *string variable* holds one or more characters. A character is a letter, a numeral, a punctuation mark, or another symbol such as + or %. (*String constants* are enclosed in double quotation marks, so the double-quote character can't be used in a string variable.) The following are examples of strings:

```
"Microsoft BASIC 7"
"&@^#%#&"
"123.6"
```

Note that the last string, **"123.6"**, looks very much like a number. If written without the enclosing quotation marks, it would indeed be a number and would require a numeric variable for storage. When enclosed in the quotes, it's a string, and must be stored as such.

BASIC 7 provides two types of string variables. A *variable-length* string has **$** as the last character of its name. This type of string variable holds any size string up to a maximum of 32,767 characters, and automatically expands and contracts to the required size. Thus, we can use a variable-length string in the following way:

```
NAME$ - "Joe"
PRINT NAME$
NAME$ - "Alexander Nevsky"
PRINT NAME$
```

In addition to the **$** suffix, you can use the **DEFSTR** statement (used like the other **DEFtype** statements described above), or the **STRING** name in an **AS** statement, to declare a variable-length string variable.

The second type of string variable is the *fixed-length string,* which contains a fixed number of characters. You declare a fixed-length string using a **DIM** statement, as shown here:

```
DIM varname AS STRING * n
```

where **varname** is the variable name (no special suffix is needed) and **n** is the string length in characters. For example,

```
DIM firstname AS STRING * 20
```

declares **firstname** as a fixed-length string with a capacity of **20** characters. When first declared, a fixed-length string is filled with NUL characters. Values assigned to a fixed-length string variable are left-justified if they are too short, and truncated if they are too long. This is illustrated by the following code:

```
DIM firstname AS STRING * 10
firstname - "Ed"
PRINT "..."; firstname; "..."
firstname - "ABCDEFGHIJKLMNOP"
PRINT "..."; firstname; "..."
```

which produces this output:

```
...Ed       ...
...ABCDEFGHIJ...
```

Arrays

An array is an indexed collection of variables that have the same type and name. Each individual variable in an array is called an *array element*; elements are distinguished from each other by an *array subscript*. Before you can use an array, you must dimension it using the **DIM** statement. You determine the type of an array variable in the same manner that you determine the type of other variables. Here are some examples:

```
DEFDBL A
DIM A(100)                     ' a double-precision array
DIM B(100)                     ' a single-precision array
DIM COUNT%(10)                 ' an integer array
DIM ADDRESS$(50)               ' a variable-length string array
DIM NAMES(20) AS STRING * 20 ' a fixed-length string array
```

Normally, array subscripts start at 0, so the number of elements in an array equals one more than the value with which the array was dimensioned. For example, **DIM A(5)** creates an array with 6 elements: **A(0)**, **A(1)**, **A(2)**, **A(3)**, **A(4)**, and **A(5)**. To make array subscripts start at 1, execute an **OPTION BASE 1** statement before dimensioning your arrays. You can also control both the upper and lower array limits using the **TO** keyword, as shown here:

```
DIM A(1 TO 5)    ' 5 elements, A(1) thru A(5)
DIM A(-2 TO 4)   ' 7 elements
```

The arrays described so far are *one dimensional*—they have a single subscript. You can create *multidimensional arrays* by including multiple subscripts in the **DIM** statement, as in these examples:

```
DIM COSTS(10,10)              ' 2 dimensions, 121 elements
DIM SALES(1 TO 12, 1 TO 31)   ' 2 dimensions, 372 elements
DIM X%(5,4,3,2)               ' 4 dimensions, 360 elements
```

You can use an array element anywhere you can use a nonarray variable. The subscript(s) can be either a constant or a variable, or even another array element. The maximum number of dimensions in an array is 60; the maximum number of elements per dimension is 32,767.

To change the space allocated to an array, use the **REDIM** statement. **REDIM** is used exactly like the **DIM** statement, but takes the name of an already-dimensioned array as an argument and changes the size of the array. **REDIM** cannot, however, change the number of dimensions in an array. For example,

```
DIM SalesData(10,10)
...
REDIM SalesData(20,20)          ' This is legal
REDIM SalesData(10,10,10)       ' This is not legal
```

To preserve existing data in an array, use the **PRESERVE** keyword with **REDIM**. Without **PRESERVE**, data in an array is erased when the array is redimensioned. Only dynamic arrays can be redimensioned.

BASIC 7 offers two types of array storage: *static* and *dynamic*. The storage space for a static array is allocated when a program is compiled, whereas the storage space for a dynamic array is allocated at runtime. Static arrays can be accessed more quickly, but dynamic arrays offer higher capacity. In addition, the space used by a dynamic array can be freed up for other uses while the program is running.

- An array is *static* if it's dimensioned in module-level code with constant subscripts, *implicitly dimensioned* (i.e., used with no preceding **DIM** statement), or dimensioned in a procedure declared **STATIC**.

- An array is *dynamic* if it's dimensioned using variable subscripts, or if it's dimensioned in a non-**STATIC** procedure.

You can also use the **$DYNAMIC** and **$STATIC** metacommands to control the array type. After one of these metacommands is executed, all arrays will be of the specified type, except for any implicitly dimensioned arrays (which are always static) and any arrays dimensioned in a non-**STATIC** procedure (which are always dynamic).

Individual arrays are limited to 64K in size, unless you use the /**Ah** (huge arrays) option when starting QBX or compiling the program with BC.EXE. When you use /**Ah**, a dynamic array can be as large as permitted by your system's free memory.

Operators

An operator performs a mathematical or logical operation upon one or more values. When a program adds two numbers, for example, the plus sign is the operator that tells the computer which operation to perform. BASIC 7 operators fall into five categories.

Arithmetic Operators

BASIC 7's *arithmetic operators* include the standard operators for addition, subtraction, multiplication, division, and exponentiation, plus two specialized operators for integer division and modulo. These arithmetic operators are summarized in Table 2.2.

The last two operators in Table 2.2 may need some explanation. The *integer division operator* rounds the operands to integers, performs the division, and then truncates the answer to an integer. Here are two examples:

Expression	Rounded	Answer	Truncated Integer result
14.49 \ 5	14 \ 5	2.8	2
14.51 \ 5	15 \ 5	3	3

The *modulo operator* returns the remainder of an integer division. (The *remainder*, you may remember, is the part left over: in "5 goes into 13 twice with 3 left over," the 3 is the remainder.) Following are examples of the use of the **MOD** operator:

11 MOD 3 = 2	22 MOD 7 = 1
20 MOD 7 = 6	50 MOD 5 = 0

Table 2.2. Basic 7 arithmetic operators.

Operator	Action	Example
+	Addition	X + Y (X plus Y)
−	Subtraction	X − Y (X minus Y)
*	Multiplication	X * Y (X times Y)
/	Division	X / Y (X divided by Y)
^	Exponentiation	X ^ Y (X to the Y power)
\	Integer division	X \ Y
MOD	Modulo	X MOD Y (X modulo Y)

Relational Operators

Relational operators compare two values, and are most frequently used as part of an **IF** test. Depending upon whether the comparison is true or false, the expression returns true (−1) or false (0). BASIC 7's relational operators are listed in Table 2.3.

During the process of comparing strings, the relational operators use the ASCII values of characters to determine "less than" and "greater than" relationships. Since the uppercase letters have lower ASCII values than the ASCII values of the lowercase letters, some apparently anomalous relationships can result:

Relationship	Value
"a" < "b"	true
"Z" > "A"	true
"a" < "B"	false
"Z" > "a"	false

Table 2.3. Basic 7 relational operators.

Operator	Relation	Example
=	Equal	A = B
>	Greater than	A > B
<	Less than	A < B
<>	Not equal	A <> B
>=	Greater than or equal	A >= B
<=	Less than or equal	A <= B

To enable the relational operators to correctly report alphabetical order when comparing strings, use the **UCASE$()** or **LCASE$()** function to convert strings to the same case before making the comparison. (A table of ASCII values can be found in Appendix C and the QBX on-line help system.)

Logical Operators

The *logical operators* combine multiple tests or Boolean expressions into a single true/false test. This process enables your program to make decisions based upon multiple conditions. Logical operators are sometimes called *Boolean operators*. For example, to execute program statements only if two conditions are both true, you write:

```
IF condition1 AND condition2 THEN
   ...
   (statements here)
   ...
ENDIF
```

The **AND** operator returns true only if both **condition1** and **condition2** are true. BASIC 7 provides six logical operators. With one exception, these operators all take two arguments. The actions of the six operators are explained in the following (T stands for true and F for false):

NOT Takes a single argument and returns its opposite: T if the argument is F, F if the argument is T.

AND Returns T if both arguments are T; returns F otherwise.

OR Inclusive OR. Returns F if both arguments are F; returns T otherwise.

XOR Exclusive OR. Returns F if both arguments are F or both arguments are T; returns T otherwise.

EQV Equivalence. Returns T if both arguments are F or both arguments are T; returns F otherwise.

IMP Implication. Returns T if the first argument is T and the second argument is F; returns F otherwise.

You can also use the logical operators to manipulate individual bits and to test bytes for specific bit patterns. (See your BASIC 7 documentation for details.)

Function Operators

The term *function operator* is another way of referring to BASIC 7's functions. A *function* is a predefined section of program code that performs a specific operation on data. BASIC 7 provides many built-in, or *intrinsic*, functions that you can use simply by calling them in your program such as:

```
a# - SQR(x)        ' The square root of x
b$ - SPACE$(10)    ' A string of 10 spaces
```

Intrinsic functions are described throughout this book. You'll find a complete listing in the *BASIC Language Reference* volume included with your BASIC 7 package.

BASIC 7 also allows you to define your own functions using the **FUNCTION...END FUNCTION** block. This important and powerful feature of the language is covered in detail in Chapter 4.

String Operators

BASIC 7 provides a single string operator, concatenation, which is represented by the plus sign (+). *Concatenation* combines two or more strings into a single, longer string. For example, the statements

```
version$ - "7.1"
A$ - "BASIC " + "version " + version$
```

assign the value **"BASIC version 7.1"** to the variable **A$**.

Expressions

An *expression* is any BASIC code that can be evaluated to a specific value. In other words, an expression is anything that can be placed on the right side of a equal sign. Here are some examples of expressions:

```
8
RIGHT$("Microsoft BASIC", 4)
ABS(X) + ARRAY%(3)
(ARRAY(n) < ARRAY(n+1))
(12000/7)*0.3 + SIN(.5)
```

BASIC 7 expressions fit into three categories: numeric, string, and Boolean. A *numeric expression* evaluates to a numeric value and a *string expression* evaluates to a string. When using numeric or string expressions in assignment statements, you must be sure to match variable types so that you assign string expressions to string variables and numeric expressions to numeric variables. Otherwise, you will get a **Type Mismatch** error.

Boolean expressions use the relational operators and often use the logical operators as well. A *Boolean expression* evaluates as true if the relationship it expresses is true, and evaluates as false if the relationship is false, as shown in these examples:

(X < Y)   True if X is less than Y; false if X is less than or equal to Y.

(X < Y AND A > B)   True if X is less than Y and A is greater than B; false otherwise.

Strictly speaking, a Boolean expression is a numeric expression because BASIC 7 uses the values −1 and 0 to represent true and false, respectively. This can be illustrated by executing the following statements:

```
x = 1
y = 2
PRINT x > y
PRINT x < y
```

The output is:

```
0
-1
```

You could assign the result of a Boolean expression to a numeric variable, such as **x% = (a = b)**. Remember that while BASIC 7 evaluates a true Boolean expression as -1, any nonzero value is considered true when used in a decision statement. For example, the code

```
x = 12
IF x THEN BEEP
```

causes the computer to beep.

Operator Precedence and Parentheses

When BASIC 7 evaluates an expression that contains more than one operator, it follows a strict order in performing the operations: certain operators are evaluated before other operators.

Arithmetic operations are performed first, in the following order:

1. Exponentiation (^)
2. Negation (–)
3. Multiplication and division (*, /)
4. Integer division (\)
5. Modulo arithmetic (MOD)
6. Addition and subtraction (+, –)

Relational operations are performed next. All relational operators have the same precedence, and are performed in left-to-right order.
Logical operations are performed last, in the following order:

1. **NOT**
2. **AND**
3. **OR**
4. **XOR**
5. **EQV**
6. **IMP**

Operations with the same precedence are performed in left-to-right order. Operator precedence can cause unexpected results if you are not careful. For example, let's say you wanted to add 5 and 6 and then multiply the resulting sum by 10. You might write:

```
5 + 6 * 10
```

Since the * operator has higher precedence than +, the multiplication is performed first, and the above expression incorrectly evaluates to $5 + 60 = 65$, not to $11 * 10 = 110$ (which is what you intended). You can override operator precedence by using parentheses and forcing the operators in an expression to evaluate in any order you desire. When an expression contains one or more pairs of parentheses, it is evaluated "from the inside out." The process of evaluation starts with the contents of the innermost set of parentheses, and works outward until the entire expression has been evaluated. In this example, an expression is evaluated both without and with parentheses (constants are used here for clarity, but the process is the same with variables):

Without parentheses:

Expression: $2 \wedge 2 + 1 * 2$
Step 1 $(2 \wedge 2)$: $4 + 1 * 2$
Step 2 $(1 * 2)$: $4 + 2$
Result: 6

With parentheses:

Expression: $2 \wedge ((2 + 1) * 2)$
Step 1 $(2 + 1)$: $2 \wedge (3 * 2)$
Step 2 $(3 * 2)$: $2 \wedge 6$
Result: 64

When you don't need to use parentheses to modify the order in which operations are performed, you can still use parentheses to improve the clarity of complicated expressions. This method makes no difference in how the expressions are evaluated, but makes it easier for you to understand them.

The BASIC Language: Program Control

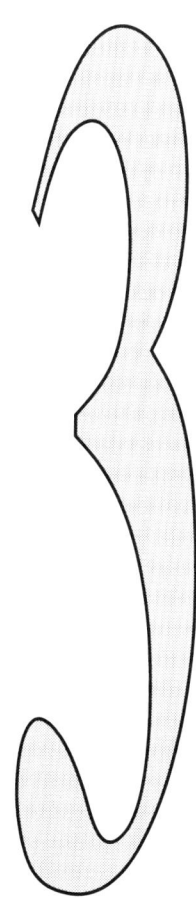

A *BASIC program* consists of a series of statements that instruct the computer to perform certain actions. By default, statements are executed in *top-down order*: they are executed in the same order that they exist in the source-code file. Here's a simple example:

```
INPUT "Enter two numbers: "; X, Y
Z = X + Y
PRINT "The sum is "; Z
END
```

The first line inputs two numbers from the user, the second line adds them, the third line displays the result, and the fourth line ends the program. For this and other simple programs, a top-down execution order is fine. For any real-world programming, however, you need to be able to control program execution: which statements are executed, and when? In this chapter, we'll look at *flow control statements*, the BASIC statements that control program execution.

Line Labels

You can label individual lines in a BASIC program with either an alphanumeric line label or a line number. Such labels allow other parts of the program to refer to specific locations within the code.

A *line label* starts with a letter and ends with a colon; it can contain from 1 to 40 characters (letters and numerals). Case is not significant. A *line number* can be any integer between 1 and 65529. (A line number of 0 is permitted but not recommended because the statement **ON ERROR GOTO 0** disables error trapping.) A line label or line number must be the first item (other than spaces or tabs) on a line of source code. You can also place a line label or line number alone on its own line. The following are all valid line labels.

```
DRAWBOX:
CalcInterest:
Sub10:
Sub2Part3:
```

Use the **GOTO** or **GOSUB** statements to direct program execution to a statement identified with a line label or line number. For example, here's one way to pause program execution until a key is pressed:

```
...
100   K$ - INKEY$
         IF K$ - "" THEN GOTO 100
...
```

This example shows how to use a line label:

```
...
INPUT "Clear screen (Y or N)?", answer$
IF UCASE$(answer$) <> "Y" THEN GOTO NoClear
CLS
NoClear:
...
```

For reasons discussed later in this chapter, I advise against using any **GOTO** or **GOSUB** statements in your programs. If you follow this advice, you'll use line numbers primarily to perform error trapping. (In error trapping, line numbers are used with the **ERL** statement to identify the location in the code where an error has occurred. See Chapter 13.)

Unlike earlier versions of BASIC, line numbers in BASIC 7 don't determine the order of execution. Line labels and line numbers are optional, and the use of unnecessary line labels or numbers decreases program execution speed. To remove all extraneous line labels from your BASIC source file, use the program REMLINE.BAS (included with your BASIC 7 package).

GOTO and GOSUB Statements

BASIC 7 supports four flow control statements that are holdovers from earlier versions of BASIC: **GOTO**, **GOSUB**, **ON...GOTO**, and **ON...GOSUB**. The problem with these statements is that they defeat the significant advantages of structured programming. Fortunately, modern BASIC compilers provide other control statements that perform the same tasks while allowing you to follow the principles of structured programming. These statements and the advantages of structured programming are discussed in Chapter 4.

Be aware that the **GOTO** and **GOSUB** statements are faster and create less code that the other statements. If you're trying to squeeze every iota of speed from your program, you may want to use **GOTO** and **GOSUB** (carefully!) in time-critical portions of your code. (For more information, refer to your BASIC 7 documentation of the on-line HELP system.)

Loop Structures

The statements in a loop structure execute 0, 1, or more times. Loop execution continues until one of three things happens:

1. A predefined number of loop executions occurs.

2. A specific logical condition is met.

3. A statement within the loop terminates execution.

Depending upon the type of loop, the decision whether to execute the loop again may be made at the end of the loop or at the beggining of the loop. When the decision is made at the end of the loop, the loop always executes at least once. When the decision is made at the beginning of the loop, the loop may never execute. These differences are illustrated in the next discussion.

DO...LOOP Loops

The **DO...LOOP** structure is the most flexible of BASIC's loop structures. It allows loop execution to repeat until a specified condition is either true or false, and it allows the condition to be evaluated at either the beginning or the end of the loop. The following example shows how to write a loop that executes while a condition is true:

```
DO WHILE condition
.
(statements here)
.
LOOP
```

When program execution first reaches the **DO** statement, *condition* is evaluated. If *condition* is false, execution passes to the statement immediately following the **LOOP** statement. If *condition* is true, the statements between the **DO** and the **LOOP** statements are executed, execution passes back to the **DO** statement, and *condition* is evaluated again. To execute the loop while *condition* is false, replace the **WHILE** keyword with **UNTIL**:

```
DO UNTIL condition
...
(statements here)
...
LOOP
```

The statements in the loop execute as long as *condition* is false (which is the same as saying until *condition* is true).

Let's look at a couple of examples. The following two code fragments perform the same action: print the elements of a string array, stopping when an empty array element is found. The first code example uses **UNTIL**, and the second uses **WHILE**.

```
COUNT% = 1
DO UNTIL ARRAY$(COUNT%) = ""
  PRINT ARRAY$(COUNT%)
  COUNT% = COUNT% + 1
LOOP

COUNT% = 1
DO WHILE ARRAY$(COUNT%) <> ""
  PRINT ARRAY$(COUNT%)
  COUNT% = COUNT% + 1
LOOP
```

In some situations, you want the loop test performed at the end of the loop, rather than at the beginning. To do so place the **WHILE** or

UNTIL keyword in the **LOOP** statement, rather than in the **DO** statement. Here are two examples:

```
DO
  K$ - INKEY$
LOOP WHILE K$ - ""

DO
  K$ - INKEY$
LOOP UNTIL K$ <> ""
```

Both of these code fragments loop until a key is pressed. (They are used for illustration only; in a real program, you would preferably use the **SLEEP** statement to pause until a key is pressed.) Note that by placing the loop test at the end of the loop, you insure that the loop executes at least once. If the loop test is placed at the beginning of the loop, the loop statements may never execute (depending upon the initial evaluation of *condition*).

Alternately, you can exit a **DO...LOOP** structure by using the **EXIT DO** statement. When an **EXIT DO** statement executes within a **DO...LOOP**, program execution passes immediately to the first statement following the **LOOP** statement at the end of the loop. You can place **EXIT DO** statements only within **DO...LOOP** structures, and a given **DO...LOOP** can contain as many **EXIT DO** statements as needed. The following example uses a **DO...LOOP** to assign keyboard input to successive elements of a string array. When an empty line is input, an **EXIT DO** statement terminates the loop. The loop test statement terminates the loop if the end of the array is reached.

```
elements - 20
DIM array$(elements)

count - 0

DO
  INPUT array$(count)
  IF array$(count) - "" THEN EXIT DO
  count - count + 1
LOOP UNTIL count > elements
```

FOR...NEXT Loops

Use a **FOR...NEXT** loop when you know in advance how many times the loop should be repeated. Write a **FOR...NEXT** loop in this manner:

```
FOR count = start TO stop
...
(statements)
...
NEXT count
```

When the **FOR** statement is first reached, **count** is set equal to **start** and the statements up to **NEXT** are executed. **count** is then incremented by 1 and compared to **stop**. If **count** > **stop**, the loop terminates and execution passes to the statement after **NEXT**. If **count** <= **stop**, the loop repeats. **start** and **stop** can be either constants or variables. The following example simply prints the numbers 1 to 10 on the screen:

```
FOR I% = 1 TO 10
  PRINT I%
NEXT I%
```

The default **FOR...NEXT** increment is 1, but you can specify any increment by including the optional **STEP** keyword. For example, the following code prints the numbers 1, 1.1, 1.2, 1.3, and so on:

```
FOR I = 1 TO 10 STEP .1
  PRINT I
NEXT I
```

Note that the type of the **count** variable must be appropriate. In the first example, you can use the integer variable **I%** because both the **start** and increment values are integers. In the second example, the single precision variable **I** is used because of the noninteger increment value. When possible, use an integer variable for the **FOR...NEXT** counter because program execution is faster. If you use an integer counter variable where a single- or double-precision variable is needed, the program will compile and run, but you will get unpredictable results.

A **FOR...NEXT** loop performs its test at the beginning of the loop. As a result, conditions can exist that prevent the loop from executing at all. These conditions occur if the **STEP** value is positive and **start** > **stop**, or if the **STEP** value is negative and **start** < **stop**.

To exit a **FOR...NEXT** loop before the counter variable reaches the **stop** value, place an **EXIT FOR** statement inside the **FOR...NEXT** loop. A **FOR...NEXT** loop can contain multiple **EXIT FOR** statements and **EXIT FOR** statements must be located inside a **FOR...NEXT** loop. Here's an example:

```
DIM ARRAY$(500)
...
...
FOR I% = 0 TO 500
  IF ARRAY$(I%) = "" THEN EXIT FOR
  IF INKEY$ <> "" THEN EXIT FOR
  PRINT ARRAY$(I%)
NEXT I%
```

Strictly speaking, the **NEXT** statement does not have to include the counter variable. A **NEXT** statement by itself automatically refers to the most recent **FOR** statement that does not already have a matching **NEXT**. Thus, the following code is legal:

```
DIM ARRAY$(10,20)
...
...
FOR I% = 0 TO 10
  FOR J% = 0 TO 20
    PRINT ARRAY$(I%,J%)
  NEXT                 ' refers to the j% loop
NEXT                   ' refers to the i% loop
```

I suggest, however, that you develop the habit of always including the counter variable in each **NEXT** statement. This makes the code easier to read, particularly when you use long loops or, as in this example, you nest loops.

WHILE...WEND Loops

A **WHILE...WEND** loop executes as long as a condition is true. It is written as follows:

```
WHILE condition
...
(statements)
...
WEND
```

A **WHILE...WEND** loop functions in exactly the same manner as the following variant of the **DO...LOOP** structure:

```
DO WHILE condition
...
(statements)
...
LOOP
```

You can write all of your programs without ever using a **WHILE...WEND** loop. Many existing BASIC programs contain **WHILE...WEND** loops because earlier versions of BASIC did not support **DO...LOOP** structures. The following code fragment loops until you press a key:

```
WHILE INKEY$ = ""
WEND
```

Nested Loops

A *nested loop* is one that is contained inside another loop. There is no limit to the *nesting depth* (the number of loops that can be placed consecutively, each within the previous loop). The only restriction is that each inner loop must be entirely contained in its outer loop with no overlapping. The following nesting structure is illegal because the **FOR...NEXT** loop is not contained entirely within the **DO...LOOP**:

```
DO WHILE condition
FOR i = 1 TO 10
LOOP
NEXT i
```

The following structure is legal because each inner loop is contained entirely within its outer loop:

```
DO WHILE condition

  FOR i = 1 TO 10
    ...
    ...
  NEXT i

  FOR j = 10 TO 100
    ...
    WHILE INKEY$ = ""
    WEND
    ...
  NEXT j

LOOP
```

Note the indentation pattern used in this example: the code statements in a loop are indented one tab stop to the right with respect to the statements defining the beginning and the end of that loop. This method of formatting your source code is not required, but it improves the readability of your code. Indenting a loop makes it clear where the loop begins and ends, and which statements belong to which loop.

Infinite Loops

As its name implies, an *infinite loop* executes forever. These loops result from improper program logic, such as forgetting to increment a counter in a **DO...LOOP** structure. An infinite loop can also occur if your program receives unexpected input. This short program may get caught in an infinite loop:

```
CLS
PRINT "Prints the tangent of values between 1 and 2, with"
PRINT "a user-specified increment."
INPUT "Enter desired increment: ", increment#
value# = 1

DO
  PRINT "The tangent of "; value#; " is "; TAN(value#)
  value# = value# + increment#
LOOP UNTIL value# > 2

END
```

If you enter an increment value of 0, the **DO...LOOP** repeats end-lessly because **value#** will never be greater than 2. To avoid this prob-lem, your programs must always check their input to be sure that appropriate values are entered. The previous program could verify input by replacing the **INPUT** statement with the following code:

```
increment# = 0

DO
  INPUT "Enter desired increment: ", increment#
LOOP UNTIL increment > 0
```

Decision Structures

A *decision structure* is a programming construct that lets your program control its own execution. Based upon the evaluation of an expression, one or more program statements within the decision struc-ture are either executed or not executed. BASIC 7 provides two pri-mary types of decision structures: the **IF...THEN...ELSE** block and the **SELECT CASE** statement.

IF...THEN...ELSE Block

The **IF...THEN...ELSE** block tells your program: "If a certain condi-tion is true, execute these statements; if the condition is not true, execute these other statements." It's an extremely powerful programming tool that you'll use frequently. The structure of an **IF...THEN... ELSE** block is as follows:

```
IF condition1 THEN
   statementblock1
ELSEIF condition2
   statementblock2
ELSE
   statementblock3
ENDIF
```

The arguments *condition1* and *condition2* are either numeric or Boolean expressions. A condition is considered false if it evaluates to 0, and true if it evaluates to a nonzero value. Each statement block consists of one or more BASIC statements. There are no limitations on the number or the type of BASIC statements that you can include within an **IF...THEN...ELSE** block.

An **IF...THEN...ELSE** block can contain multiple **ELSEIF** statements, each with its associated condition and statement block. The block can contain only one **IF** and one **ELSE**, and they must be located (respectively) before and after any **ELSEIF**s. The only required components of an **IF...THEN...ELSE** block are the **IF** and **ENDIF** statements; the **ELSEIF** and **ELSE** statements are optional. Let's look at some examples.

The following code contains only an **IF** statement:

```
IF SALES < COSTS THEN
   PRINT "You are in the red!"
ENDIF
```

This example contains an **IF** statement with an **ELSE** statement:

```
IF SALES < COSTS THEN
   PRINT "You are in the red!"
ELSE
   PRINT "You are in the black."
ENDIF
```

This code contains an **IF** statement with **ELSEIF** and **ELSE**:

```
IF SALES < COSTS THEN
   PRINT "You are in the red!"
ELSEIF SALES - COSTS < 100 THEN
   PRINT "You made a small profit."
ELSE
   PRINT "You made a large profit."
ENDIF
```

When an **IF...THEN...ELSE** block is encountered during program execution, the first condition (which follows the **IF** statement) is evaluated. If this condition is true, then the statements in the associated statement block are executed. Next execution passes to the first statement after **ENDIF** (unless, of course, execution was branched out of the **IF...THEN...ELSE** block by a statement in the block).

If the first condition is false, any additional conditions (those following **ELSEIF**s) are evaluated in top-to-bottom order. When a true condition is found, the associated statements execute and then execution passes to the first statement following the **ENDIF**. If no true condition is found, the statements after **ELSE** execute or, if there is no **ELSE**, execution passes to the first statement after **ENDIF**.

IF...THEN...ELSE blocks can be nested:

```
IF X > 0 THEN
  IF Y > 0 THEN
    PRINT "X and Y are both greater than zero."
  ELSE
    PRINT "X is greater than zero but Y is not."
  ENDIF
ENDIF
```

Remember that only a single block of statements within an **IF...THEN...ELSE** structure executes. Even if more than one condition is true, only the statements associated with the first true condition execute.

In addition to the **IF...THEN...ELSE** block, BASIC 7 supports the single-line **IF...THEN...ELSE** statement (familiar to anyone who has programmed with the old BASICA interpreter). This statement places the entire **IF...THEN...ELSE** structure on a single line:

```
IF X > 0 THEN PRINT X ELSE PRINT Y
```

There are two reasons to avoid the single-line form in favor of the
IF...THEN...ELSE block: The single-line statement doesn't support
ELSEIF, and it makes your source code harder to read.

SELECT CASE Block

The **SELECT CASE** block controls program execution based on the
value of a variable or expression. **SELECT CASE** evaluates a single
variable or expression, and matches it against a number of templates.
If a match is found, the statements associated with the matching template execute. The structure of a **SELECT CASE** block is as follows:

```
SELECT CASE expression
  CASE template1
     statementblock1
  CASE template2
     statementblock2
  CASE ELSE
     statementblock3
END SELECT
```

When a **SELECT CASE** block is encountered, *expression* is evaluated and compared with *template1*. If they match, *statementblock1*
executes, and then execution passes to the first statement after the
END SELECT statement (unless a statement in *statementblock1*
routes program execution elsewhere).

If the first template does not match, comparisons are made with
additional templates in top-to-bottom order. When a match is found,
the associated statement block executes, and execution passes to the
first statement after **END SELECT**. If no match is found, the statements after **CASE ELSE** execute. **CASE ELSE** is optional: If it's not
included and no match is found, then none of the statements within the
SELECT CASE block are executed. Here's a simple example:

```
INPUT "Enter a value between 1 and 3"; X
SELECT CASE X
  CASE 1
    PRINT "You entered 1"
```

```
      CASE 2
        PRINT "You entered 2"
      CASE 3
        PRINT "You entered 3"
      CASE ELSE
        PRINT "That's not between 1 and 3!"
    END SELECT
```

The template after each **CASE** statement can contain a single template (as in the previous example), or several individual templates. In the case of multiple templates, each template must be separated by commas and can be one of the following:

- A numeric or string expression

- A range of numeric or string expressions that use the **TO** keyword

- A range of numeric or string expressions that use the **IS** keyword and a relational operator

All of the templates must be of the same type (i.e., numeric or string) as the expression being evaluated. Let's look at some multiple templates:

CASE statement	Matches
CASE 1, 2, 3	The values **1**, **2**, or **3**
CASE 5, X	The value **5** or the value stored in variable **X**
CASE "A", "B"	The strings **"A"** or **"B"** (but not "a" or "b")
CASE IS > XYZ$	Any string greater than the string in variable **XYZ$**
CASE 1 TO 3	Any value between **1** and **3**, inclusive
CASE IS < 10	Any value less than **10**
CASE IS > 20, IS < –20	Any value greater than **20** or less than **–20**

When you use the **TO** keyword in a **CASE** statement, you must list the lower value first. This is true for both numeric and string expressions.

This example presents a valid use of the **TO** keyword in a **CASE** statement:

```
CASE 1 TO 5
CASE -100 TO -10
CASE "A" to "Z"
```

In contrast, this code demonstrates an invalid use:

```
CASE 5 TO 1
CASE -10 TO -100
CASE "Z" TO "A"
```

Structured and Modular Programming

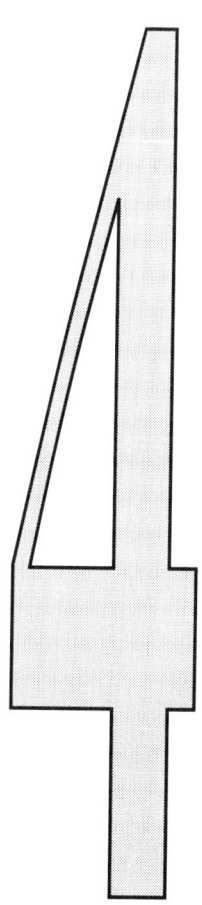

Structured programming and modular programming are two techniques of central importance in today's world of ever larger, more complex programs. BASIC 7 provides full support for both techniques.

Structured Programming

Structured programming is the principle of program design that implements individual parts of a program as functionally independent sections of code. Structured programming offers several significant advantages:

- A structured program is easier to write because you break the entire project down into a number of smaller tasks that are easier to solve individually rather than tackling the entire project at once.

- A structured program is easier to debug because you can localize a problem to a specific section of code more easily.

- A structured program is easier to maintain because modifications you make to one part of the program are less likely to cause problems in another part.

BASIC 7 implements structured programming by means of procedures. A *procedure* is an independent section of code that the main program can call. Code within a procedure is called *procedure-level* code; code outside of a procedure is called *module-level* code. BASIC 7 provides two types of procedures: *functions* and *subprograms*. Functions and subprograms are almost identical to each other, but a function returns a value to the calling program, while a subprogram does not. Also, you invoke a subprogram by using the **CALL** command, and you invoke a function by referring to it anywhere a variable could be used (such as in an assignment or **PRINT** statement).

Defining a Procedure

To define a new function or subprogram in QBX, select NEW SUB...
or NEW FUNCTION... from the Edit menu. QBX prompts you for the
procedure name, and then opens a window with the bare-bones structure of the definition already filled in. You can also type **FUNCTION
FuncName** or **SUB SubName** (where **FuncName** or **SubName** is the
name of the procedure) into the program, and then press the Enter
Key. Next, You complete the definition.

To complete the definition for a function, follow this format:

```
FUNCTION funcname [parmlist] [STATIC]
  [STATIC varlist]
  .
  . (BASIC statements)
  .
END FUNCTION
```

To complete the definition for a subprogram, follow this format:

```
SUB subname [parmlist] [STATIC]
  [STATIC varlist]
  .
  . (BASIC statements)
  .
END SUB
```

funcname or *subname* is the name that identifies the procedure.
This name can be up to 40 characters long, and follows the same rules
as those for regular BASIC variables. Function names (but not subprogram names) are associated with a data type (integer, string, etc.) that
is the type of the value that the function returns to the calling program.
The rules for assigning a type to a function name are the same as the
rules for assigning a type to a regular BASIC variable (see Chapter 2).
Procedure names must be unique; they cannot duplicate another procedure or variable name.

parmlist is an optional list of one or more variables. These variables indicate the number and type of the arguments passed to the
function by the calling program.

STATIC is an optional keyword that applies to *local variables* (those used within the function). To make all local variables **STATIC**, place the keyword at the end of the first line in the function. To make selected local variables **STATIC**, place the keyword on the second line of the function, followed by a list of variables. *varlist* is a list of variables (separated by commas) to be made **STATIC**.

Statements in Procedures

There's no limit to the number of BASIC statements that you can include in a procedure. It's good programming practice to keep procedures to a small or moderate size by splitting complex tasks into several procedures, rather than creating one huge procedure. You can include any BASIC statement in a procedure, with these exceptions:

DEF FN...END DEF
FUNCTION...END FUNCTION
SUB...END SUB
COMMON
DECLARE
DIM SHARED
OPTION BASE
TYPE...END TYPE
DATA
REDIM (referring to an array passed as a parameter).

Returning a Value From a Function

To return a value from a function, you assign a value to the function name before execution returns to the calling program. This is done using a simple assignment statement: *funcname* = *expression*. You can make multiple assignments to *funcname* in the function; when more than one assignment is executed, the most recent value is returned. The following function accepts two numeric arguments and returns the smaller value.

```
FUNCTION Smaller(x,y)

  IF x < y THEN
    Smaller = x
  ELSE
    Smaller = y
  END IF

END FUNCTION
```

The data type of the function name (integer, string, etc.) must agree with the value assigned to the function name. If no value is assigned to the function name, it returns 0 or the null string.

Exiting Procedures

When program execution reaches the **END SUB** or **END FUNCTION** statement at the end of a procedure, execution passes back to the calling program immediately after the point where the procedure was called. You can also exit a procedure at any other point using the **EXIT SUB** or **EXIT FUNCTION** statements, which have the same effect as if execution had reached the end of the procedure. The following function illustrates **EXIT FUNCTION**:

```
DEFINT A-Z
FUNCTION largest.divisor (x)
' Returns the largest integer divisor of a positive integer
' argument. Returns 0 if the argument is a prime number.

FOR i = x - 1 TO 2 STEP -1

  IF x \ i = x / i THEN
    largest.divisor = i
    EXIT FUNCTION
  END IF

NEXT i

largest.divisor = 0
END FUNCTION
```

There's no limit to the number of **EXIT FUNCTION** or **EXIT SUB** statements you can place in a procedure, but only the first executed statement has any effect.

Variables In Procedures

A variable used in a procedure is called a *local* variable. Local variables are totally independent of any other variables with the same name that may be defined in other procedures or in module-level code. By default, all local variables are *automatic*: they are initialized to zero (for numeric variables) or to the null string (for string variables) each time the procedure is called. To make a local variable retain its value between calls to the procedure, you must declare it as **STATIC**.

To use a local array in a procedure, dimension the array at the start of the procedure. To make an array **STATIC**, include the array name followed by empty parentheses in the **STATIC** statement, before the **DIM** statement. For example, look at the following code fragment:

```
SUB Calculate
  STATIC First()
  DIM First(20), Second(20)
...
END SUB
```

This code declares **First()** to be **STATIC** and **Second()** to be automatic. Elements of **First()** retain their values between calls to the procedure, and all elements of **Second()** are reset to 0 each time the procedure is called.

Declaring Procedures

Declare each procedure in your program using the **DECLARE** statement. Place procedure declarations at the very beginning of your program, or in an include file read by an **$INCLUDE** metacommand at the beginning of the file. QBX automatically generates **DECLARE** statements and inserts them into your program each time the file is saved.

The syntax of a **DECLARE** statement is:

```
DECLARE FUNCTION funcname [parmlist]
DECLARE SUB subname [parmlist]
```

In a **DECLARE** statement, the *funcname* or *subname* and the optional *parmlist* are identical to the first line of the procedure definition. Note the distinction between a procedure *definition* and a procedure *declaration*: the definition contains the BASIC code executed when the procedure is called, and the declaration is a single line that contains information about the procedure's name and parameters.

Procedure declarations serve two purposes. First, they resolve external and forward references. An *external reference* occurs when a program calls a procedure defined in another module or in a library. A *forward reference* occurs when a call to a procedure is located before the procedure definition in the source code. (It's customary to place all procedure definitions at the end of the source code file, so forward references are the norm.) The procedure declaration tells the compiler that the procedure is defined somewhere else.

The second purpose of procedure declarations is to permit *type checking* of arguments. Each time a procedure is called, its arguments are checked against the *parmlist* in the **DECLARE** statement to insure that the correct number and type of arguments are being passed.

QBX does not automatically generate **DECLARE** statements for procedures in a different module or in a Quick Library. In these situations, you must add the **DECLARE** statement yourself.

Calling Functions

To call a function simply use its name in an expression. This is the same method that you use for calling BASIC 7's intrinsic functions. For example, this short function returns the square of its one argument:

```
FUNCTION Squared(x)
  Squared = x * x
END FUNCTION
```

The following are all valid methods of calling the function from the main program:

```
y = Squared(12)

x = Squared(Squared(2))

PRINT Squared(4) * Squared(3)

IF Squared(j) < 1400 THEN
```

Calling Subprograms

To call a subprogram that takes no arguments put its name in a **CALL** statement, or use the name itself as a statement:

```
CALL GetData
GetData
```

You call a subprogram that takes arguments in the same way. If you use the **CALL** statement, the arguments must be enclosed in parentheses. If you omit the **CALL** statement, omit the parentheses:

```
CALL SortData (X, Y, Z)
SortData X, Y, Z
```

If your program calls a subprogram without using the **CALL** statement, the subprogram must be declared using a **DECLARE** statement. Otherwise, a declaration is optional (but highly recommended).

Parameters and Arguments

It's important to understand the distinction between a parameter and an argument. A *parameter* is a variable in a procedure definition or declaration and serves as a placeholder for an argument. An *argument* is a value (a constant, variable, or expression) that is passed to the procedure when the procedure is called. Inside the procedure, each parameter variable has (at least initially) the value of the corresponding argument passed to the procedure. The following short program illustrates this:

```
DECLARE SUB Display (a!, b$)

i - 1
x$ - "hello"

CALL Display(i, x$)

CALL Display(3 - 1, "goodbye")

END


SUB Display (a, b$)
  PRINT a, b$
END SUB
```

The output of this program is:

```
1           hello
2           goodbye
```

In the definition and the declaration of the subprogram **Display**, the variables **a!** and **b$** are parameters. In the first **CALL** statement, the variables **i** and **x$** are the arguments. In the second **CALL** statement, the expression **3 − 1** and the constant **"goodbye"** are the arguments.

Passing Records and Arrays as Arguments

BASIC 7 lets you pass entire arrays or user-defined records as arguments to procedures.

This example shows how to pass an entire array:

```
DECLARE SUB Sub1 (x() AS DOUBLE)
DIM array(50) AS DOUBLE
...
```

```
CALL Sub1(array())
...
END

SUB Sub1 (x() AS DOUBLE)
...
END SUB
```

This example shows how to pass a user-defined record. Note the use of the **ANY** keyword in the procedure declaration, which disables type checking for that parameter.

```
DECLARE SUB Sub1 (a AS ANY)

TYPE SalesData
  SalesPerson AS STRING * 20
  amount AS CURRENCY
END TYPE

DIM x AS SalesData
...
CALL Sub1(x)
...
END

SUB Sub1 (a AS SalesData)
...
END SUB
```

This example shows how to pass an array of user-defined records:

```
DECLARE SUB Sub2 (x() AS ANY)

TYPE SalesData
  SalesPerson AS STRING * 20
  amount AS CURRENCY
END TYPE

DIM array(20) AS SalesData
...
CALL Sub2(array())
...
END
```

```
SUB Sub2 (x() AS SalesData)
...
END SUB
```

When you pass an entire array as an argument, the procedure has no direct way to know the size of the array (unless you pass the size as another argument). You can use the **LBOUND()** and **UBOUND()** functions to determine array size inside a procedure, as shown in this example:

```
DECLARE SUB sub1 (x())
DIM a1(100)
DIM a2(-200 TO 200)

CALL sub1(a1())
CALL sub1(a2())

END

SUB sub1 (x())
PRINT LBOUND(x), UBOUND(x)
END SUB
```

The following output results:

```
0        100
-200     200
```

Passing Arguments by Value or by Reference

When your program passes a variable to a procedure, QBX's default is to pass the variable *by reference*: the procedure is passed the address where the variable is stored in the computer's memory. When the procedure knows the address, it can retrieve the value stored there. The procedure can also modify the value, which can be desirable in that it permits a subprogram to "return" a value, or a function to "return" multiple values. Here's an example:

```
DECLARE SUB Sub1 (z)
```

```
a - 1
PRINT "a ="; a

CALL Sub1(a)

PRINT "a ="; a

END

SUB Sub1 (z)
z - 9999
END SUB
```

The output of this program is:

```
a - 1
a - 9999
```

This demonstration shows that by changing the value of the parameter **z**, which was passed by reference, the procedure modifies the value of the argument **a**.

To make it impossible for a procedure to change the value of variables passed as arguments, use the method called passing *by value*. When a variable is passed by value, a copy of the original variable is made and the address of the copy is passed to the procedure. The procedure has access to the value of the argument, but not to the original argument variable itself. To pass by value, place parentheses around the variable name. Modify the **CALL** statement in the previous example to read

```
CALL Sub1((a))
```

and then run the program again. You'll see that the procedure doesn't change the value of the variable **a**.

This method is called passing by value in the BASIC 7 documentation, but it would be more accurately called passing *by copy* because the address of a copy of the argument is passed to the procedure. When an argument is truly passed, the value of the argument itself—not its address or the address of a copy—is passed to the procedure. To do this in BASIC 7, use the **BYVAL** keyword in the argument list. **BYVAL** is useful primarily when calling nonBASIC procedures, and can't be used with string arguments. (See BASIC 7 on-line help for more details.)

Shared Variables

BASIC 7's default is for local variables within each procedure to be independent both from *global variables* (those defined in the module-level code), and from local variables defined in other procedures. This arrangement is fine in most circumstances because the segregation of local and global variables is an important factor in the power of structured programming. At times, however, a procedure needs access to one or more global variables without having those variables passed as arguments. To make this possible, use the **SHARED** keyword.

To make a global variable accessible in selected procedures, put the variable name in a **SHARED** statement at the start of each procedure definition. List array names followed by empty parentheses. If you initially assigned the variable's type using the **AS** keyword, you must also use the **AS** keyword in the **SHARED** statement.

To make a global variable accessible in all procedures, use the **SHARED** keyword in a **DIM**, **COMMON**, or **REDIM** statement in the module-level code. If a variable is declared **STATIC** in a procedure, this declaration overrides the effect of a module-level **SHARED** statement. This situation applies only if the variable is specifically included in a **STATIC** statement, not if **STATIC** is placed at the end of the first line in the procedure definition. The following code demonstrates how to use **SHARED**:

```
DECLARE SUB Sub1 ()
DECLARE SUB Sub2 ()
DECLARE SUB Sub3 ()

DIM SHARED SalesData(10), InterestRate AS SINGLE
DIM TaxData(10)
```

```
      InterestRate = .1
      SalesData(1) = 100
      TaxData(1) = 200
      TaxRate = .18

      CLS

      CALL Sub1
      CALL Sub2
      CALL Sub3

      END

      SUB Sub1

      ' In this procedure, TaxRate and TaxData() are SHARED because
      ' of the procedure-level SHARED statement, and InterestRate
      ' and SalesData() are shared because of the module-level
      ' SHARED statement.

      SHARED TaxRate, TaxData()

      PRINT
      PRINT "In Sub1:"
      PRINT "InterestRate ="; InterestRate
      PRINT "SalesData(1) ="; SalesData(1)
      PRINT "TaxData(1) ="; TaxData(1)
      PRINT "TaxRate ="; TaxRate

      END SUB

      SUB Sub2

      ' In this procedure, InterestRate and SalesData() are SHARED
      ' because of the module-level SHARED statement, and TaxData()
      ' and TaxRate are local.

      DIM TaxData(15)

      PRINT
      PRINT "In Sub2:"
```

```
PRINT "InterestRate ="; InterestRate
PRINT "SalesData(1) ="; SalesData(1)
PRINT "TaxData(1) ="; TaxData(1)
PRINT "TaxRate ="; TaxRate

END SUB

SUB Sub3 STATIC

' In this procedure, all variables are local because the STATIC
' statement overrides the module-level SHARED statement.

STATIC SalesData(), InterestRate
DIM TaxData(20), SalesData(5)

PRINT
PRINT "In Sub3:"
PRINT "InterestRate ="; InterestRate
PRINT "SalesData(1) ="; SalesData(1)
PRINT "TaxData(1) ="; TaxData(1)
PRINT "TaxRate ="; TaxRate
END SUB
```

This program produces the following output:

```
In Sub1:
InterestRate = .1
SalesData(1) = 100
TaxData(1) = 200
TaxRate = .18

In Sub2:
InterestRate = .1
SalesData(1) = 100
TaxData(1) = 0
TaxRate = 0

In Sub3:
InterestRate = 0
SalesData(1) = 0
TaxData(1) = 0
TaxRate = 0
```

Editing Procedures in QBX

The QBX editor simplifies the process of working with procedures. As mentioned earlier, you can select New Sub... or New Function... from the Edit menu to automatically create the skeleton of a new subprogram or a function. You then fill in the details as needed. Procedure declarations are also generated automatically each time you save the file.

Both module-level code and procedure-level code are contained in the same *module*, or file. The QBX editor keeps them separated, and allows you to view only module-level code or a single procedure in the View window at one time. To move between program elements, select Subs... from the View menu. A list of modules and procedures displays, as shown in Figure 4.1.

Select the desired procedure from the list. Next select a command using the following command buttons:

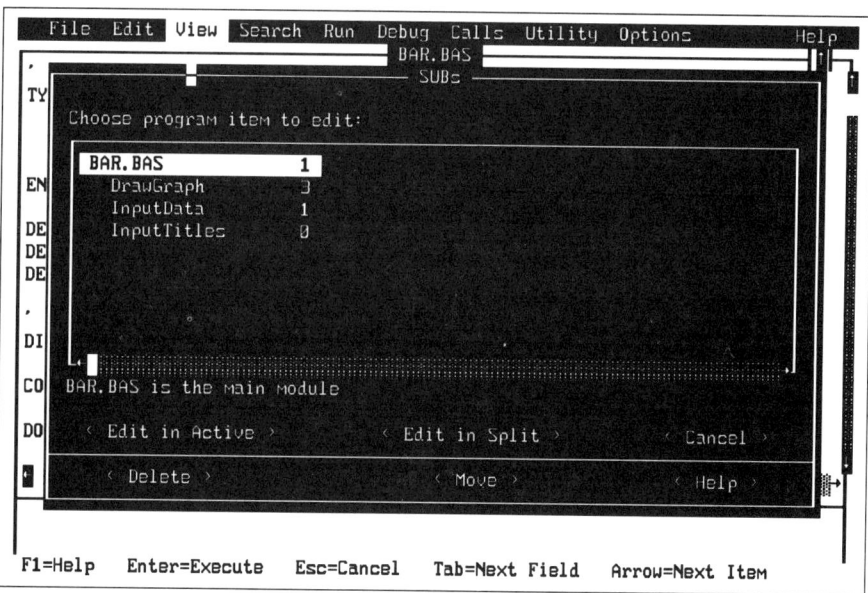

Figure 4.1. The SUBs dialog box lists currently loaded modules and procedures.

- Edit in Active displays the selected procedure in the View window, where you can edit it.

- Edit in Split divides the View window into two windows. The selected procedure is displayed in one window, and the original contents of the View window is displayed in the other.

- Delete erases the procedure from the program.

- Move lets you move the procedure to another module.

The number next to each program element name provides the size of that element, measured in kilobytes.

Modular Programming

Modular programming is the program-development technique that places a program's source code in two or more separate disk files. The primary reason to use modular programming is that you can reuse tested and debugged sections of source code in multiple programs, without having to re-key the statements.

A *module* is a disk file that contains executable BASIC statements. QBX lets you work with multiple modules at the same time. The *main module* contains the first program statement to be executed. This module always contains module-level code (because execution cannot start in a procedure), and may also contain procedure-level code. Many BASIC programs, particularly small to medium-sized ones, utilize only a main module.

A *secondary module* is a module other than the main module that is loaded into QBX. A secondary module can contain module-level code, procedure-level code, or a combination of both.

QBX Module Commands

You'll find the commands for creating, saving, and loading secondary modules on the File menu.

To begin writing a new secondary module select Create File.... In the Create File... dialog box, enter the desired filename (the .BAS extension is automatically added), and select Module as the file type. When a new View window opens, enter the code for the secondary module.

To load a secondary module from disk, select Load File.... In the Load File... dialog box, select the file to load, and select Module as the file type. The specified file is loaded into a new View window.

To save the module file when a secondary module appears in the active view window, select Save or Save As.... Select Save All to save all currently loaded modules.

When two or more modules are loaded, use the Subs... command on the View menu to move between modules and their components. The SUBs dialog box lists each module name (the name of the module file). Under each module name, the procedures (if any) contained in the module are listed. See Figure 4.2 for an example.

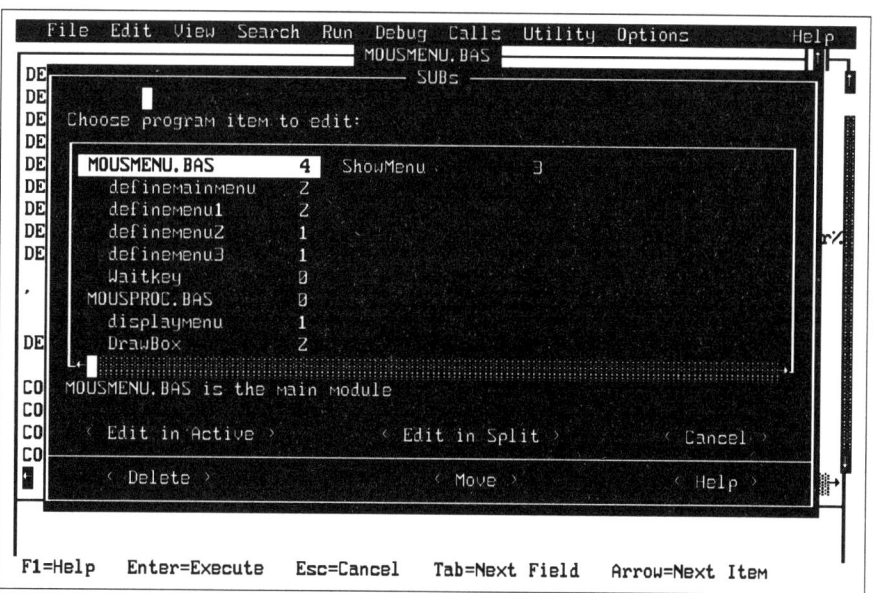

Figure 4.2. The SUBs dialog box lists multiple modules and their component procedures.

Using Secondary Modules

You can use secondary modules to their best advantage when they contain only procedure-level code. You can access procedures in a secondary module in the same way that you access procedures in the main module. By placing each set of related procedures (e.g., screen display, disk output) in its own module, you can quickly and easily use the sets in different programs.

When you store procedures in a separate module, you need to declare them in a **DECLARE** statement in the main module. The **DECLARE** statements that QBX automatically generates are placed into the secondary module that contains the procedures, not into the main module. Use the QBX editor's cut-and-paste feature to move the **DECLARE** statements from the secondary module to the main module. You can also put the **DECLARE** statements into a separate include file, and then use the **$INCLUDE** metacommand to read them into the main module at compile time.

Another concern when using secondary modules is data visibility. Normally, variables defined in one module are not accessible in other modules. This is true even if you declare the variables **SHARED** because **SHARED** only operates within a single module. To share variables across modules, use the **COMMON** statement. You must include a **COMMON** statement in the module-level code of each module that will access the variables. Use this syntax:

```
COMMON [SHARED] [/blockname/] varlist
```

varlist is a list of one or more variables, separated by commas, that are to be shared between modules. The variable names need not be identical in the different modules' **COMMON** statement, but the order and the data type of the variables must match.

The optional **SHARED** keyword causes all of the variables in *varlist* to be available to all of the procedures in the module containing the **COMMON** statement. Otherwise, these variables are available only in the module-level code, or in procedures that specifically declare the variables as **SHARED**.

/blockname/ is an optional name that causes the variables in *varlist* to be placed in a named common block. **blockname** can be be-

tween 1 and 40 characters long, following the same rules as other
BASIC variables. Named common blocks allow variables to be shared
selectively with various modules. If **/blockname/** is omitted, common
variables are placed in a blank common block, and must be shared *en
masse*.

The following code example demonstrates how to use the **COM-
MON** statement to share variables between modules.

```
' This code is the main module.

DECLARE SUB Sub1 ()
DECLARE SUB Sub2 ()

COMMON /first/ w, x
COMMON /second/ y, z

CLS

w = 1: x = 2: y = 3: z = 4

CALL Sub1
CALL Sub2

END

' This code is secondary module A.

COMMON SHARED /first/ a, b
END

SUB Sub1
   PRINT a, b
END SUB

' This code is secondary module B.

COMMON SHARED /second/ a, b
END

SUB Sub2
   PRINT a, b
END SUB
```

If you load these three modules into QBX and run the program, the following output results:

```
1        2
3        4
```

In module A, the variables **a** and **b** have the values assigned to the main module variables **w** and **x**, respectively. In module B, the variables **a** and **b** have the values assigned to the main module variables **y** and **z**, respectively.

DEF FN and ON...GOSUB

BASIC 7 supports the **DEF FN** and **ON...GOSUB** statements. These statements date from older interpreted BASICs, and provided a rudimentary degree of structured programming. With BASIC 7's procedures and functions, you'll never need to use **DEF FN** and **ON... GOSUB**.

Working with Disk Files

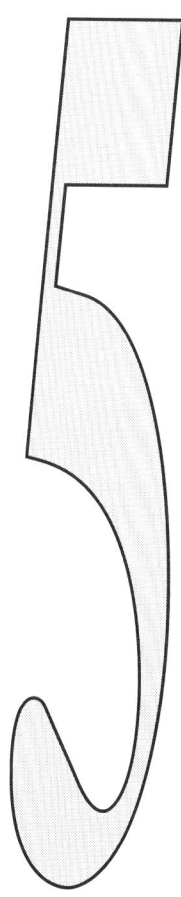

Most BASIC programs that you write, whether multimegabyte databases or small program configuration files, will use disk files to store
data. BASIC 7 supports four different types of disk files. Each type of
file is suited for specific tasks. Three file types are covered in this
chapter, and the fourth type (ISAM data files) is covered in Chapter 14.

Opening Disk Files

Before you can use any type of file, you must open it. To open files,
use the **OPEN** statement. The details of the **OPEN** statement depend
upon the type of file being opened, and upon what you want to do with
the file. The basic syntax of the **OPEN** statement is:

```
OPEN filename$ [FOR mode] AS [#]filenum% [LEN=reclen%]
```

where *filename$* is the name of the disk file being opened.

In this statement, *mode* specifies the file mode. There are 5 possible
modes:

- *random* opens a random-access file for reading or writing.

- *binary* opens a binary file.

- *input* opens a sequential file for reading.

- *output* opens a sequential file for writing. If the file specified by
  filename$ already exists, it is replaced by the new file.

- *append* opens a sequential file for writing. If the file specified
  by *filename$* already exists, new data is added at the end of the
  existing file.

If you omit the *mode* argument, the file is opened in **random** mode.

In the **OPEN** statement, *filenum%* is an integer expression with a
value between 1 and 255. *reclen%* is an integer expression that specifies the record length for random-access files, or the buffer size for
sequential files.

Examples showing how to use the **OPEN** statement are provided later in this chapter in the sections about the individual file types.

Filenames

The *filename$* in an **OPEN** statement follows the same rules as DOS filenames. It can consist of uppercase and lowercase letters, the numerals 0-9, and the symbols ()@#$%^&!-_'~. The filename itself consists of 1 to 8 characters, optionally followed by a period and a 1 to 3-character extension. *filename$* can also include drive and/or path information (see your DOS manual for information about specifying paths). Here are some examples of valid *filename$* expressions.

```
SALES.DAT
c:\bc7\april_10.txt
..\X12^5!!
```

Filenames are not case sensitive, so the strings **SALES.DAT** and **sales.dat** refer to the same file.

File Numbers

When a file is opened, a unique file number is associated with it. This is the number given by the *filenum%* argument to the **OPEN** statement. Use a file number to refer to a specific file when data is read from and/ or written to the file. When the file is closed, the file number is freed and can be used for another file. BASIC 7 allows you to have more than one file open at a time. The maximum number of simultaneous open files is limited by the **FILES=** statement in your CONFIG.SYS file.

When your program executes an **OPEN** statement, the *filenum%* argument cannot be a value already in use by another open file. To obtain an unused file number, use the **FREEFILE** function, which returns the lowest unused file number:

```
...
FileNum% = FREEFILE
```

```
OPEN "SALES.DAT" FOR APPEND AS #FileNum%
...
```

Closing Disk Files

When you're finished using a file, you must close it. Closing a file clears the file's buffer (a temporary storage area in memory), insuring that all data has actually been written to disk. It also frees up the file number associated with that file. To close a specific file or files, execute the **CLOSE** statement with the file number(s) as arguments. To close all open files, execute **CLOSE** with no arguments:

```
CLOSE #1
CLOSE #1, #2
CLOSE
```

All open files are automatically closed when a BASIC 7 program terminates.

Sequential Files

A *sequential file* stores ASCII text data in a series of records. The name *sequential* reflects the fact that you must always read a sequential file from the beginning—to read record 10, you must first read records 1 to 9. You can't easily jump directly to a record in the middle of the file.

Records in sequential files have the following characteristics:

- Each record is a line of text whose length may vary. The end of the record is marked by a carriage return-line feed (CR-LF) character.

- Each record consists of one or more pieces of data, called *fields*. Each record usually contains the same number of fields, in the same order.

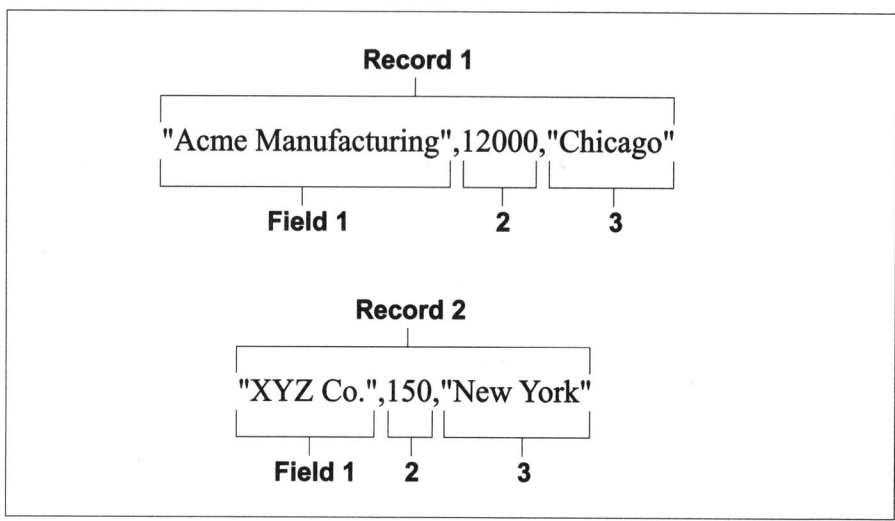

Figure 5.1. Record structure in a sequential file

- Records in a sequential file can be of different lengths. Fields in different records can also be of different lengths.

Figure 5.1 illustrates the structure of sequential file records. Note the use of commas and double quotation marks to delimit the fields in a sequential file.

Writing Data to a Sequential File

To write data to a sequential file, you must first open the file using **OPEN**, with either **FOR OUTPUT** or **FOR APPEND** as the mode argument. If the specified file does not already exist, these two modes have the same effect: a new file is created. If the specified file does exist, **FOR OUTPUT** deletes the old file and puts output into a new file. Alternatively, **FOR APPEND** preserves the old file and adds output to the end of that file.

One way to write data to a sequential file is by using the **WRITE #** statement with the same file-number argument that was used to open the file. **WRITE #** writes a single record to the file. If you are writing multiple fields, separate them by commas. Here are some examples:

```
WRITE #1, Address$    ' Write a record with one field
WRITE #1, x, y, z     ' Write a record with three fields
```

You can also put data into a sequential file using the **PRINT #** statement. Unlike **WRITE #**, **PRINT #** doesn't delimit fields with commas, or enclose strings in double quotes. Instead, it writes data to the file in the exact same format as if the data had been displayed on the screen using **PRINT**. If you execute these statements,

```
WRITE #1, "Microsoft", "BASIC", 7
PRINT #1, "Microsoft", "BASIC", 7
```

the file contains these lines:

```
"Microsoft","BASIC",7
Microsoft      BASIC           7
```

If you plan read a sequential file with **INPUT #**, use the **WRITE #** statement. Use **PRINT #** only for special applications—sequential file records written using the **PRINT #** statement can't be properly read with the **INPUT #** statement because the fields are not delimited.

Reading Data from a Sequential File

The most common method of reading data from a sequential file is by using the **INPUT #** statement. **INPUT #** reads one or more fields from the input file and assigns them to variables in its argument list. Remember that sequential files must be read sequentially, starting with the first field in the first record. Here's a brief example:

```
...
OPEN FileName$ FOR OUTPUT AS #1

WRITE #1, "Apples", 10
WRITE #1, "Peaches", 20

CLOSE #1

OPEN FileName$ FOR INPUT AS #1
```

```
INPUT #1, A$, x
INPUT #1, B$, y
...
```

After this code executes, **A$ = "Apples"**, **x = 10**, **B$ = "Peaches"**, and **y = 20**. If you close file **#1** and reopen it **FOR INPUT**, input starts at the beginning of the file.

The way in which **INPUT #** breaks records into fields depends upon the type of variable (in the **INPUT #** statement's argument list) into which the field is being read. If the field is being read into a string variable, the end of a field is marked by one of the following:

- Double quotation marks, if the field begins with double quotation marks

- A comma, if the field does not begin with double quotation marks

- A carriage return-line feed (CR-LF), if the field is the last field in a record

If the field is being read into a numeric variable, the end of the field is marked by one of the following:

- A comma

- One or more spaces

- CR-LF

It's important to synchronize your **WRITE #** and **INPUT #** statements in terms of the type, the order, and the number of fields in each record. A loss of synchrony can cause problems in two ways. First, if you **INPUT** a field into a variable of a different type, no error occurs but you can get unexpected results. For example, when you read a numeric field into a string variable, the string representation of the number results, but if you read a string field into a numeric variable, the result depends upon the string. If the string starts with a non-numeric character, the result is the value of 0. If the string starts with one or more numeric characters, the result is the value of those characters.

The second way in which a loss of synchrony can cause problems affects the **INPUT #** statement. The **INPUT #** statement counts fields (not records) in the file. If an **INPUT #** statement reads fewer fields than the number of fields contained in a record, the next **INPUT #** statement starts with the next field, not with the next record. This is illustrated by the following code fragment:

```
. . .
OPEN FileName$ FOR OUTPUT AS #1
WRITE #1, "A", "B", "C", "D"
WRITE #1, "E", "F", "G", "H"
CLOSE #1
. . .
OPEN FileName$ FOR INPUT AS #1
INPUT #1, X1$, X2$, X3$
INPUT #1, X4$, X5$, X6$
. . .
```

The result is that **X4$ = "D"**, **X5$ = "E"**, and **X6$ = "F"**. The second **INPUT #** statement started reading at the fourth field in the first record, not at the first field in the second record.

You can also read data from a sequential file using the **LINE INPUT #** statement or the **INPUT$()** function. **LINE INPUT #** reads an entire line, or record, from the file without regard for field delimiters, and assigns the record to a string variable. **INPUT$()** reads a specified number of bytes from the file, including CR-LF characters, and assigns them to a variable. The syntax of these statements is:

```
LINE INPUT [#] filenum%, var$

var$ = INPUT$(n%, filenum%)
```

In these statements, *filenum%* is the number assigned to the file when it was opened, *var$* is the variable to receive the input from the file, and *n%* is the number of bytes to be read.

The following program demonstrates the use of **INPUT$()** and **LINE INPUT #**.

```
' Demonstrates LINE INPUT # and INPUT$().

CLS
FileName$ = "TEST.TXT"

OPEN FileName$ FOR OUTPUT AS #1

WRITE #1, "Microsoft", "Basic", 7
WRITE #1, "Programming", "Language"
CLOSE #1

OPEN FileName$ FOR INPUT AS #1
x$ = INPUT$(32, #1)
PRINT "Using INPUT$(): ", x$
CLOSE #1

PRINT

OPEN FileName$ FOR INPUT AS #1
LINE INPUT #1, x$
PRINT "Using LINE INPUT: ", x$

CLOSE #1
KILL FileName$

END
```

The output of this program is:

```
Using INPUT$():
"Microsoft","Basic",7

"Programm

Using LINE INPUT:
"Microsoft","Basic",7
```

In this program, the **INPUT$()** function read 32 bytes, up to the second "m" in **"Programming"**. Because the CR-LF is part of the string assigned to **x$**, the **PRINT** statement outputs **x$** on two screen lines. **LINE INPUT** # read the entire first record, up to—but not including—the CR-LF.

Detecting End of File (EOF)

To detect the end of a sequential file, use the **EOF()** function. **EOF()** returns −1 (true) if the last record in the file has been read, or 0 (false) if it has not yet been read. To read an entire sequential file, use **EOF()** in a loop:

```
...
WHILE NOT EOF(1)
  INPUT #1, ...
WEND
...
```

A Sequential File Example

The following short program demonstrates the use of a sequential file to store text and number information.

```
' Demonstrates writing and reading sequential file data.
CLS
DIM Amount AS CURRENCY
FileName$ = "address.txt"

' Open the file for output.
OPEN FileName$ FOR OUTPUT AS #1

DO
  ' Input the first data item from the keyboard.

  INPUT "Enter name (a blank to quit): ", Name$

  ' Exit loop if Name$ is blank.

  IF Name$ = "" THEN EXIT DO
```

```
    ' Input other data items.

    INPUT "Enter city: ", City$
    INPUT "Enter amount: ", Amount
    PRINT

    ' Write record to file.

    WRITE #1, Name$, City$, Amount

LOOP

' Close the file.

CLOSE #1
CLS
INPUT "Display data (y or n)? ", a$

IF UCASE$(a$) = "Y" THEN

   ' Clear screen and open file for input.

   CLS
   OPEN FileName$ FOR INPUT AS #1

   ' Loop until the end of file is reached.

   WHILE NOT EOF(1)

      ' Input a record and print the fields.
      INPUT #1, Name$, City, Amount
      PRINT "Name: ", Name$
      PRINT "City: ", City$
      PRINT "Amount: ", Amount
      PRINT

   WEND

   CLOSE #1

END IF

END
```

Random-Access Files

A *random-access* file stores data in a series of numbered records. Records in a random file are numbered sequentially from 1 to a maximum of 2,147,483,647. The name *random* reflects the fact that you can directly access each record, without having to first access previous records. In a 500-record file, for example, you could access record 412, then record 10, and finally record 300 without accessing any other records.

Records in a random-access file have the following characteristics:

- Each record consists of a fixed number of characters. All of the records in a random-access file have the same size.

- Each record consists of one or more pieces of data, called *fields*. Each record always contains the same number of fields, in the same order.

- Each field within a record consists of a fixed number of characters. The number of characters is the same for all records in the file.

Unlike sequential files, random-access files don't use delimiters to separate fields and records. The fixed lengths of the fields and records are used to determine where each field or record begins and ends. The structure of records in a random-access file is diagrammed in Figure 5.2.

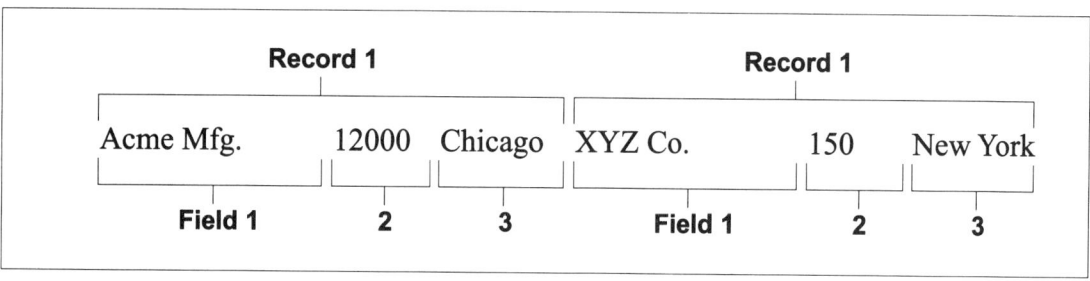

Figure 5.2. Record structure in a random-access file.

Note that many fields contain blanks, which is necessary because of the fixed field length. Data items must be adjusted to fit the field they are stored in. If a data item is too short, it is padded with spaces to fill the field. If a data item is too long, it is truncated.

Defining Random-Access File Records

Before you can use a random-access file, you must define the record structure and field lengths. This is most easily done by using the **TYPE...END TYPE** statement to create a user-defined data type. Then, use **DIM** to declare a variable of the user-defined type, and use the **LEN** function in the **OPEN** statement to determine record length. The maximum allowed record length is 32,767 bytes. For example the following code defines a record structure containing three fields, then opens a random-access file using the defined structure:

```
TYPE DataRecord
  Name AS STRING * 20
  City AS STRING * 12
  Amount AS CURRENCY
END TYPE

DIM UserData AS DataRecord

OPEN FileName$ FOR RANDOM AS #1 LEN = LEN(UserData)
```

Note that the **LEN** function must refer to a variable name, not to the type name. In the previous example, **LEN(DataRecord)** would not work.

BASIC 7 also supports the old-fashioned way of defining records, using the **FIELD** statement. This older method is more complicated, but offers one advantage: you can write a program that allows the user to define the structure of random-access file records at runtime. With **TYPE...END TYPE**, random-access file structure must be determined when the program is compiled (i.e., field structure is hard-coded in the source code). The QBX on-line help system contains information about using the **FIELD** statement.

Writing Data to Random-Access Files

To write data to a random-access file, use the **PUT** statement:

```
PUT [#] filenum%,[recordnum&],var
```

In this statement, *filenum%* is the number of the random-access file, and *recordnum&* is the record number where the data is to be placed. If *recordnum&* is omitted, the next record (the record after the last **GET** or **PUT**) is used. *var* is a variable of the user-defined type.

Continuing with this example, the statement to write a single record of data to the first record in the file is:

```
PUT #1, 1, UserData
```

If you are creating a new random-access file, you can start *recordnum&* at 1 and increment it for each successive **PUT** statement. When you're adding records to an existing file, you must add new records at the end of the file to avoid overwriting existing records. For a file containing *n* records, start adding new records at *n + 1*. The expression

```
LOF(n) \ LEN(DataType)
```

returns the number of records in file *n*. By adding 1, you obtain the starting location where new records are to be added. To obtain the number of the next record to be read or written, use the **SEEK** function. The **LOC** function returns the number of the last record read or written.

```
NextRecord& = SEEK( filenum%)
LastRecord& = LOC( filenum%)
```

Reading Data from Random-Access Files

To read data from a random-access file use the **GET** statement:

```
GET [#] filenum%,[recordnum&],var
```

filenum% is the number of the random file, and *recordnum&* is the record number where the data is to be placed. If *recordnum&* is omitted, the next record (the record after the last **GET** or **PUT**) is used. *var* is a variable of the user-defined type.

Continuing on with the earlier example, the statement that read the first record from a random-access file is:

```
GET #1, 1, UserData
```

To sequentially read all records from a random-access file, use a loop that starts with the first record and increments *recordnum&* until the end of the file is reached. To detect the end of the file, use the **EOF()** function in the same manner as shown for sequential files earlier in this chapter. You can also calculate the number of records in the file by dividing the file length by the record length:

```
NumberOfRecords& = LOF(1) \ LEN(UserData)
```

A Random-Access File Example

The following short program demonstrates the use of random-access files.

```
' Demonstrates random-access files.

CLS
FileName$ = "Random.txt"

' Define a data type.

TYPE DataRecord
  Name AS STRING * 20
  City AS STRING * 12
  Amount AS CURRENCY
END TYPE

DIM UserData AS DataRecord

' Open the file.
```

```
OPEN FileName$ FOR RANDOM AS #1 LEN = LEN(UserData)

' Determine the next record number. This avoids writing over
' existing records if the file already exists.

nextrec& = LOF(1) \ LEN(UserData) + 1

DO

   ' Accept data from keyboard.

   INPUT "Enter name: ", Temp$

   IF Temp$ = "" THEN
     EXIT DO
   END IF

   UserData.Name = Temp$
   INPUT "Enter city: ", UserData.City
   INPUT "Enter amount: ", UserData.Amount
   PRINT

   ' Write data to file and increment record number.

   PUT #1, nextrec&, UserData
   nextrec& = nextrec& + 1

LOOP
CLOSE #1

CLS

INPUT "Display records (y or n): ", a$
IF UCASE$(a$) = "Y" THEN

   OPEN FileName$ FOR RANDOM AS #1 LEN = LEN(UserData)

   ' Determine the number of records in the file.

   maxrec& = LOF(1) \ LEN(UserData)

   ' Loop, reading each record and displaying it.
```

```
    FOR recnum& = 1 TO maxrec&
      GET #1, recnum&, UserData
      PRINT
      PRINT "Name: "; UserData.Name
      PRINT "City: "; UserData.City
      PRINT "Amount: "; UserData.Amount
    NEXT recnum&

    CLOSE #1

  END IF

  END
```

Access by Record Number

The major advantage of using random-access files rather than sequential files is that you can directly access any record in a random-access file by using its record number in a **GET** or **PUT** statement. The previous example used only sequential access to a random-access file, which is perfectly legitimate but ignores much of the power of this file type.

To use true random access in a random-access file, you must know what you're looking for. The ability to directly access Charlie Smith's record is not much help unless you know his record number! One technique for keeping track of a random file's contents is to use an *index*. The BASIC 7 documentation contains information about creating an index (plus a sample index program) in the chapter on File and Device I/O.

Binary Files

Binary-file access allows you to access the individual bytes of a file. It's not limited to ASCII text or BASIC variables. You can use binary-file mode to read and modify non-ASCII files, such as word processor and spreadsheet files.

A *binary* file has no records or other structure; it is simply treated as an unformatted sequence of bytes. Binary files can be used to store program variables and other data, but because of the lack of formatting, the program is completely responsible for keeping track of what is stored where. To open a binary file for both reading and writing, use the **FOR BINARY** argument in an **OPEN** statement

The File Pointer

Each binary file is associated with a *file pointer*. The file pointer indicates the position in the file where read and write operations will occur. Positions in a file are numbered from 1 through *n*, where *n* is the length of the file in bytes. The following statements and functions change and query the file pointer.

Use this statement to move the file pointer to a new position in the file, without performing any input or output:

```
SEEK [#] filenum%, newposition&
```

Use these statements to determine the current file-pointer position:

```
pos& = SEEK( filenum%)
pos& = LOC( filenum%)
```

SEEK() returns the position of the next byte to be read or written, while **LOC()** returns the position of the last byte that was read or written. Unless you explicitly move the pointer, the value of **LOC()** is 1 less than the value of **SEEK()**.

Writing and Reading Binary Files

Binary files use the same statements for reading and writing that random-access files use: **GET** and **PUT**. BASIC knows which mode the file was opened in, and interprets the **GET** or **PUT** statement appropriately. The syntax for binary files is:

```
GET [#] filenum%,[position%],variable
PUT [#] filenum%,[position%],variable
```

In these statements, *filenum%* is the number under which the file was opened in **FOR BINARY** mode. *position%* is the starting byte position for the write or read position. If *position%* is omitted, **GET** or **PUT** acts at the current file-pointer position. The file pointer is incremented by the number of bytes read or written. *variable* can be any type of BASIC variable, including user-defined types and variable length strings. The **GET** or **PUT** operation automatically reads or writes the number of bytes contained in *variable*.

You can also read data from a binary file using the **INPUT$()** function, which was described earlier in this chapter in the section about sequential files.

A Binary File Example

Binary files are not as useful for saving BASIC program data as are either sequential or random-access files. Rather, they are useful primarily for manipulating other types of disk files, such as word processor files. The following example inputs a word processor file (or any other kind of file), removes characters with ASCII value below 32 or above 130, and writes the result to a new file.

```
' Demonstrates binary-file access.
' Inputs a file and filters out all characters with ASCII
' value less than 32 or greater than 130.

CLS

' Get the filenames and open the files.

INPUT "Enter input filename: ", InFile$
INPUT "Enter output filename: ", OutFile$

OPEN InFile$ FOR BINARY AS #1
OPEN OutFile$ FOR BINARY AS #2
```

```
' DIM a single character string.

DIM char AS STRING * 1

count% = 1
FOR i% = 1 TO LOF(1)

  'Input a single character.

  GET #1, , char

  ' If it's in the correct range, write it to the output file
  ' and update the count.

  IF ASC(char) > 31 AND ASC(char) < 131 THEN
    PUT #2, , char
    LOCATE 10, 1
    PRINT "Transferring character "; count%
    count% = count% + 1
  END IF

NEXT i%

CLOSE
END
```

Text-Mode Screens

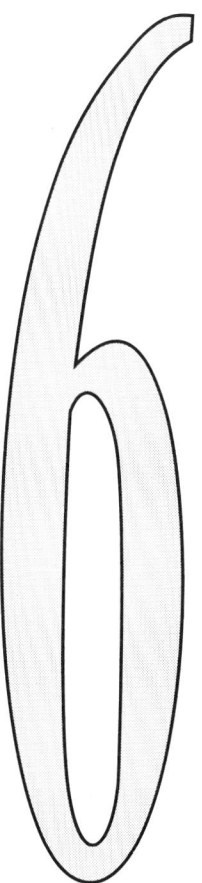

PC video displays can operate in two modes, text and graphics. These modes differ as follows:

- In *text* mode you can display only a predefined set of characters. This set includes letters, numbers, punctuation marks, and other symbols. To see the entire set, select ASCII Character Codes from the QBX Help system's Contents page.

- In *graphics* mode, you have control over every dot on the screen, allowing you complete freedom to control the shape and size of displayed images.

BASIC 7's text-mode programming features are covered in this chapter. The chapter first reviews the basics of text-mode programming (for readers not familiar with text-mode screens), and then presents the various statements and functions that you can use when programming text-mode screens.

Text-Mode Basics

In text mode, the screen is divided up into a grid of *character cells*. Each cell can display one of the predefined characters. The position of each cell is specified by its row and column location. For example, the cell at the intersection of row 5 and column 12 has position 5,12. Columns and rows are numbered starting at 1, so the character cell in the upper-left corner of the screen is located at coordinates 1,1. The default screen has 25 rows and 80 columns. Depending upon the installed video hardware, you can change the number of rows and columns using the **WIDTH** statement.

A text-mode screen always displays a cursor, which is located in one of the character cells. The cursor marks the location where certain screen operations, such as text display, will occur. You can change the location and appearance of the cursor using the **LOCATE** statement. To determine the current position of the cursor, use the **POS()** and **CSRLIN** functions.

A video *page* is a single screen full of information. Only a single page can be displayed at once, but some video adapters can store multiple pages at one time. To determine which of the stored pages is displayed, use the **SCREEN** statement. You also use the **SCREEN** statement to switch video modes; i.e., to switch between text and graphics modes.

If your system has color video hardware installed, you can control the color of the display with the **COLOR** statement. To restrict text output to a screen window, use the **VIEW PRINT** statement.

The SCREEN Statement

The **SCREEN** statement sets the video mode and controls the active and displayed video pages. This satement's syntax is:

```
SCREEN mode% [, [color%] [, [activepage%] [,visiblepage%]] ]
```

mode% is the screen mode. Text mode is mode 0, and is the default mode at program startup. (Other modes are graphics modes, and are discussed in Chapter 9.)

color% switches the monitor display between color and noncolor. This argument is functional only in screen modes 0 and 1, and only if you're using a composite monitor.

activepage% specifies the video page that output is sent to, and *visiblepage%* specifies the video page that is displayed on the screen. *activepage%* and *visiblepage%* can range from 0 to *n-1*, where *n* is the number of pages available. The number of pages ranges from 1-8, and depends upon the installed video hardware and screen mode. (See Adapters and Displays in the QBX Help system for details.)

The use of multiple screen pages can be a handy programming technique. Switching between pages occurs instantly, so the new text simply appears on the screen without delay. You could, for example, display a program screen on one page and a hclp screen on another, and switch between them instantly as needed. To copy information from one screen page to another, use the **PCOPY** statement (described later in this chapter).

The following program demonstrates the use of multiple screen pages. It sends information to screen pages 0 and 1, and then switches the display between them until you press a key.

```
' Demonstrates screen pages.

' Fill screen 0 (the default) with text.

FOR i = 1 TO 220
  PRINT "   Screen 0     ";
NEXT i

' Make screen 1 the active screen.

SCREEN , , 1

' Fill screen 1 with text.

FOR i = 1 TO 220
  PRINT "Screen 1       ";
NEXT i

' Loop until a key is pressed.

WHILE INKEY$ = ""

  ' Make screen 1 the visible screen, then wait a bit.

  SCREEN , , , 1
  SLEEP 1

  ' Make screen 0 the visible screen, then wait a bit.

  SCREEN , , , 0
  SLEEP 1

WEND

' Reset default screen.

SCREEN 0, 0, 0, 0
END
```

The LOCATE Statement

The **LOCATE** statement changes the position and appearance of the screen cursor. The syntax of this statement is the following:

```
LOCATE  [row%] [,[column%] [,[cursor%] [,start% [,stop%]]]]
```

row% and *column%* specify the cursor's new screen location. If you try to position the cursor off the screen, an Illegal function call error occurs. If you omit *row%*, the cursor stays in the same row and moves to the new column. If you omit *column%*, the cursor stays in the same column and moves to the new row. If you omit both *row%* and *column%*, the cursor is not moved.

cursor% is set to 1 for a visible cursor or to 0 for an invisible cursor. Even when the cursor is invisible, it exists, can be moved, and has a definite position.

start% and *stop%* must be in the range of 0 to 31. They specify the screen scan lines that form the cursor. For example, use *start%* = **0** and *stop%* = **1** to display a thin underline cursor, and use *start%* = **0** and *stop%* = **31** to display a full block cursor.

The PRINT Statement

The **PRINT** statement displays data on the screen. The syntax of **PRINT** is:

```
PRINT [expressionlist] [,|;]
```

expressionlist is a list of BASIC expressions, separated by either commas or semicolons. When you use a semicolon, the next item is positioned immediately after the preceding item. When you use a comma, the next item is positioned at the next print zone. If you omit *expressionlist*, a blank line is output.

[;|,] at the end of *expressionlist* determines where the cursor is positioned after the **PRINT** statement executes. A semicolon positions the cursor immediately after the last character output, and a comma positions the cursor at the beginning of the next print zone. If you don't place either a comma or a semicolon at the end of *expressionlist*, the cursor is moved to the beginning of the next line.

The screen is divided into print zones that are 14 characters wide. The positioning of individual items in *expressionlist*, and the positioning of items printed by successive **PRINT** statements, depends upon your use of commas and semicolons in the **PRINT** statement. Here are some examples:

```
PRINT "Apples"; "Oranges"; "Peaches"
PRINT "Grapefruit", "Mangos", "Pears";
PRINT "Grapes", , "Blueberries"
```

These statements produce this output:

```
ApplesOrangesPeaches
Grapefruit    Mangos        PearsGrapes
Blueberries
```

PRINT follows certain rules when it outputs numbers. A number is always followed by a space. Positive numbers are also preceded by a space, and negative numbers are preceded by a minus sign. Fixed-point format is used for single precision numbers if they can be displayed with seven or fewer digits with no loss of accuracy; otherwise, floating-point format is used. The same is true of double-precision numbers, with a limit of 15 or fewer digits. Here are some examples:

```
PRINT -2; -1; 0; 1; 2
x1! = .0000023#
x2! = .0000000023#
PRINT x1!
PRINT x2!
x1# = .00000000023#
x2# = 2.3D-15
PRINT x1#
PRINT x2#
```

These examples produce this output:

```
-2 -1  0  1  2
 .0000023
 2.3E-09
 .00000000023
 2.3D-15
```

The PRINT USING Statement

The **PRINT USING** statement displays data with a user-specified format. The syntax of this statement is:

```
PRINT USING formatstring$; expressionlist [;|,]
```

formatstring$* is a string literal or variable that controls the format of the output. *formatstring$ can contain literal text to be output (e.g., labels), as well as special formatting characters.

expressionlist is a list of one or more BASIC expressions to be displayed. These expressions can be separated by commas, spaces, semicolons, or tabs. The delimiters have no effect on the appearance of the output.

[;|,] determines the cursor position after the **PRINT USING** statement is executed, in the same manner described earlier for the **PRINT** statement.

Printing Strings with PRINT USING

You can use three formatting characters when you print strings with **PRINT USING**. Each formatting character represents a different print instruction:

!   Print the first character of the string.

&   Print the string as is.

\ \   Print n+2 characters of the string, where n is the number of spaces between the backslashes. If the format field is longer than the string, the string is left justified within the field, and padded with spaces.

If you include any literal characters (spaces, letters, etc.) in the format string, they are printed as well. Here are some examples:

```
x1$ = "Apples"
x2$ = "Oranges"
```

```
PRINT USING "!"; x1$; x2$
PRINT USING "!--"; x1$; x2$
PRINT USING "\ \"; x1$; x2$
PRINT USING "\ \   "; x1$; x2$
PRINT USING "&"; x1$; x2$
PRINT USING "& and & "; x1$; x2$
```

These code examples produce this output:

```
AO
A--O--
Appl0ran
Appl    Oran
ApplesOranges
Apples and Oranges
```

Printing Numbers with PRINT USING

You can use several formatting characters to control the format of numbers printed with **PRINT USING**. Each of these characters generates a different number format:

Represents a digit position. If the number has fewer digits than the number of digit positions you specified, it is padded with spaces and right justified in the field. You can specify a maximum of 24 digits. You must include one or more # characters in every numeric format string.

.   Specifies the position of the decimal point relative to the digit positions. For example, ##.# specifies two digits before and one digit after the decimal point.

+   Causes the sign of the number to be printed in the specified position. You can place this formatting character at the beginning or the end of the format string.

-      If placed at the end of a format string, prints a negative number with a trailing minus sign.

**   Fills leading spaces in the field (spaces that would otherwise be blank) with asterisks, and specifies two more digit positions.

$$ Prints the number with a leading dollar sign, and specifies two more digit positions (one of which is occupied by the dollar sign).

**$ Combines the effects of ** and $$.

,   If a comma is included in the format string immediately to the left of the decimal point, this character causes numbers to be printed with thousands separators (e.g., 1,000,000). If a comma is included in the formatting string to the right of the decimal point, this character prints as a literal character.

^^^^   Prints the number in exponential format.

_   (an underscore in a format string) Specifies that the next character is to be treated as a literal, rather than as a formatting character.

If the number being printed is too large to fit in the specified field, a percent sign (%) is printed before the number. The following code demonstrates examples of numeric formatting:

```
x = 1234567.89#
y = 1.00123
PRINT USING "#########.####"; x; y
PRINT USING "$$##########,.##"; x; y
PRINT USING "####.####^^^^"; x
PRINT USING "_###.####"; y
PRINT USING "**$########.### per year."; x
```

These examples produce this output:

```
1234567.8750          1.0012
$1,234,567.88            $1.00
123.4568E+04
```

```
# 1.0012
***$1234567.8750 per year.
```

If *expressionlist* contains multiple expressions and *formatstring$* contains only a single format specifier, that format specifier is applied to all of the expressions being printed. If a string-format specifier is matched with a numeric expression, or *vice versa*, a Type mismatch error occurs.

You can include multiple format specifiers in *formatstring$*, and they will be applied in turn to the expressions in *expressionlist*. If there are more format specifiers than expressions, the extra format specifiers are ignored. If there are fewer format specifiers than expressions, BASIC 7 cycles through the list of format specifiers until all expressions have been printed. Here is a demonstration:

```
profit = 1000000
co$ = "Acme Manufacturing"
PRINT USING "The profit for & was$$#########,.##."; co$;
              profit
rate = .12
payment = 125

PRINT USING "At ##% the payment is$$###.##."; rate * 100;
              payment
```

This results in the following output:

```
The profit for Acme Manufacturing was $1,000,000.00.
At 12% the payment is $125.00.
```

The COLOR Statement

The **COLOR** statement changes the colors used for displaying text on the screen. You can use the **COLOR** statement in graphics modes as well as text modes, to change screen colors. For the sake of our discussion the next section deals with screen mode 0 only. The syntax of the **COLOR** statement is:

```
COLOR foreground&, background&, [border&]
```

foreground& is a value between 0 and 31 that specifies the *foreground* color, i.e., the color used for text characters. The values 0 to 15 specify one of 16 available colors. To obtain blinking text, add 16 to a color number.

background& is a value between 0 to 7 that specifies the background color. Each character cell can have a different background color. The background cannot be made to blink.

border& is a value between 0 and 7 that specifies the color of the screen border, outside of the text display area. All of the colors available for the background are also available for the screen border. The *border&* argument has no effect with EGA, MCGA, or VGA adapters.

Table 6.1 lists the colors associated with the color numbers 0 to 15. The default foreground and background colors are 7 and 0, respectively.

When you execute a **COLOR** statement, it affects only subsequently output text; text already on the screen is not affected. You can, therefore, display a wide variety of foreground and background colors on the screen at the same time. To hide text (such as when a secret password is being entered), set the foreground and the background colors to the same color.

With a monochrome monitor you can't display color but you can control the intensity and underlining of characters. Table 6.2 shows the values of the *foreground&* and *background&* arguments to use for this purpose.

Table 6.1. Color numbers and the associated colors.

0	Black	8	Gray
1	Blue	9	Light blue
2	Green	10	Light green
3	Cyan	11	Light cyan
4	Red	12	Light red
5	Magenta	13	Light magenta
6	Brown	14	Yellow
7	White	15	High-intensity white

Table 6.2. Using color values on a monochrome monitor.

Foreground	Background	Effect
7	0	Normal white-on-black
0	7	Reversed (black on white)
1	0	Underlined text
Add 8	-	Bright white
Add 16	-	Blinking

The following demonstration program shows some of the effects possible in screen mode 0, using the **COLOR** statement. Run this program only if you have a color video system.

```
' Demonstrates the COLOR statement

DEFINT A-Z
CLS

FOR back = 0 TO 7

  COLOR , back

  FOR fore = 0 TO 31
    COLOR fore
    LOCATE back + 8, fore * 2 + 10
    PRINT "X!";
  NEXT fore
NEXT back

LOCATE 24, 1
COLOR 7, 0
PRINT "Press any key...";

SLEEP
CLS
END
```

The WIDTH Statement

You can modify the number of rows and columns on a text-mode screen using the **WIDTH** statement. The number of options available depends on the installed video hardware. The syntax of the **WIDTH** statement is:

```
WIDTH [width%][,height%]
```

width% specifies the number of screen columns. The default is 80, and the possible values are 40 and 80. *height%* specifies the number of screen rows. The possible values for *height%* are 25, 30, 43, 50, and 60.

A screen width of 40 columns is supported by all video adapters except the MDPA and the HGC. When you use a width of 40 columns, the only supported height is 25 rows (except for a 40x43 mode, which is possible with an EGA or VGA). When you use a width of 80 columns, the heights supported by each adapter/monitor combination are listed in Table 6.3.

Executing a **WIDTH** statement clears the screen and resets the cursor to position 1,1 at the top-left corner of the screen. If you try to execute a **WIDTH** statement using a width or height argument not supported by your hardware, an Illegal function call error occurs.

Table 6.3. Screen heights supported by different video adapters.

Adapter	Monitor	Heights
CGA	Color	25
EGA	Color	25
	Enhanced color	25, 43
	Monochrome	25, 43
MCGA	Analog	25, 30, 60
VGA	Analog	25, 43, 50

The CSRLIN and POS() Functions

The **CSRLIN** and **POS()** functions determine the current position of the text-mode cursor. The syntax of each statement (respectively) is as follows:

```
currentline% = CSRLIN
currentcol% = POS(x)
```

x is a dummy argument, and can be any numeric expression. This argument has no effect upon the function but is required for syntax compatibility with earlier versions of BASIC. Use **POS()** and **CSRLIN** when you want to return the cursor to its original position after displaying some information (such as an error message):

```
...
oldrow% = CSRLIN
oldcol% = POS(1)
LOCATE newrow%, newcol%
...
LOCATE oldrow%, oldcol%
...
```

The TAB() and SPC() Functions

The **TAB()** and **SPC()** functions control the horizontal position of output. They can be used only as part of the expression list in a **PRINT**, **LPRINT**, or **PRINT #** statement. The syntax for these functions is:

```
TAB(column%)
SPC(spaces%)
```

column% is an integer expression in the range of 1 to 255. **TAB()** advances the cursor to the specified *column%* position on the same line, or, if the cursor is already past that position, to the specified *column%* position on the next line.

spaces% is an integer expression in the range of 1 to 255. **SPC()** displays the indicated number of blank spaces.

The following program illustrates the use of these functions.

```
' Demonstrates TAB() and SPC() functions.

DEFINT A-Z
CLS

FOR i = 1 TO 20 STEP 2
  PRINT "Microsoft"; SPC(i); "BASIC"
NEXT i

PRINT
PRINT "Abalene"; TAB(25); "Texas"
PRINT "Springfield"; TAB(25); "Massachusetts"
PRINT "Troy"; TAB(25); "New York"
PRINT "Minneapolis-Saint Paul"; TAB(25); "Minnesota"

END
```

This program produces the following output:

```
Microsoft BASIC
Microsoft   BASIC
Microsoft     BASIC
Microsoft       BASIC
Microsoft         BASIC
Microsoft           BASIC
Microsoft             BASIC
Microsoft               BASIC
Microsoft                 BASIC
Microsoft                   BASIC

Abalene                 Texas
Springfield             Massachusetts
Troy                    New York
Minneapolis-Saint Paul  Minnesota
```

The SCREEN() Function

The **SCREEN()** function determines the character displayed at a particular screen location. (Do not confuse it with the **SCREEN** statement, which sets video modes.) The syntax of the **SCREEN()** function is:

```
char% = SCREEN ( row%, col% [,flag%])
```

row% and *col%* are integer expressions specifying the screen location to be read, and must be within the range of rows and columns displayed on the screen. This range is 1 to 25 for rows and from 1 to 80 for columns, unless you've used a **WIDTH** statement to change the screen dimensions.

flag% is an optional argument that determines what is returned by the **SCREEN()** function. If *flag%* is either omitted or set equal to 0, **SCREEN()** returns the ASCII code of the character at the specified screen location. If that location is blank, **SCREEN()** returns 32 (the ASCII code for a space). If *flag%* = **1** then **SCREEN()** returns the character's attribute byte (which controls its foreground and background colors).

The following program demonstrates the uses of the **SCREEN()** function. This program scans the entire 80x25 screen, and counts the number of dollar signs that appear on the screen.

```
' Demonstrates the SCREEN() function.

DEFINT A-Z
CLS

LOCATE 10, 10
PRINT "$ $ $ $"
LOCATE 20, 60
PRINT "$ $ $ $"

count = 0

FOR row = 1 TO 25
  FOR col = 1 TO 80
    IF SCREEN(row, col) = ASC("$") THEN
      count = count + 1
    END IF
  NEXT col
NEXT row

LOCATE 24, 1
PRINT count; "dollar signs found.";
```

```
SLEEP

END
```

The VIEW PRINT Statement

The **VIEW PRINT** statement restricts text output to a range of rows on the screen. This region is called a *text viewport*. This statement's syntax is:

```
VIEW PRINT [top% TO bottom%]
```

top% and *bottom%* are integer expressions specifying the upper and lower rows, respectively, to be included in the text viewport. Both *top%* and *bottom%* must be within the range of the number of screen rows in effect. Executing **VIEW PRINT** without arguments cancels the text viewport, and restores text output to the entire screen.

The text viewport extends for the entire width of the screen. Text output and scrolling are limited to the viewport. The **CLS, LOCATE, PRINT, WRITE**, and **INPUT** statements, and the **SCREEN()** function, respect a text viewport. The following program demonstrates the use of **VIEW PRINT**.

```
' Demonstrates the VIEW PRINT statement.

DEFINT A-Z
CLS

' Fill the screen with dashes.

FOR i = 1 TO 2000
  PRINT "-";
NEXT i

' Set up a text viewport and clear it.

VIEW PRINT 10 TO 18
CLS
```

```
' Display messages in the viewport,
' pausing between each line.
' Terminate when a key is pressed.

WHILE INKEY$ = ""
  PRINT "This is displayed...   "
  SLEEP 1
  PRINT "In the viewport...   "
  SLEEP 1
  PRINT "Press any key to terminate demonstration.   "
  SLEEP 1
WEND

' Reset default text viewport and clear screen.

VIEW PRINT
CLS

END
```

Creating Text Graphics

You can create certain graphics effects on a text-mode screen by using the extended ASCII character set, which includes a number of specialized characters. The characters and their ASCII codes are listed in Table 6.4.

To display these characters, use the **CHR$()** function, which returns the character corresponding to a specific ASCII code. This function is demonstrated in the following program, which includes a procedure that accepts a text argument and then prints the text argument in a double-line box, centered near the bottom of the screen.

```
DECLARE SUB TextInBox (x$)

' Demonstrates using graphics characters in text mode.

CLS

INPUT "Enter some text: ", x$

CALL TextInBox(x$)
```

Table 6.4. The extended ASCII characters.

176	▒	192	L	208	╨
177	▓	193	┴	209	╤
178	█	194	┬	210	╥
179	│	195	├	211	╙
180	┤	196	─	212	╘
181	╡	197	┼	213	╒
182	╢	198	╞	214	╓
183	╖	199	╟	215	╫
184	╕	200	╚	216	╪
185	╣	201	╔	217	┘
186	║	202	╩	218	┌
187	╗	203	╦	219	█
188	╝	204	╠	220	▄
189	╜	205	═	221	▌
190	╛	206	╬	222	▐
191	┐	207	╧	223	▀

```
SLEEP

END

SUB TextInBox (x$)

' Print text argument in a box centered near the bottom
' of the screen.

' Set box position centered on rows 20-22.
```

```
row = 20
col = (80 - LEN(x$)) \ 2

' Print box.

LOCATE row, col - 1
PRINT CHR$(201)
LOCATE row + 1, col - 1
PRINT CHR$(186)
LOCATE row + 2, col - 1
PRINT CHR$(200)
LOCATE row, col + LEN(x$) + 2
PRINT CHR$(187)
LOCATE row + 1, col + LEN(x$) + 2
PRINT CHR$(186)
LOCATE row + 2, col + LEN(x$) + 2
PRINT CHR$(188)
LOCATE row, col
PRINT STRING$(LEN(x$) + 2, CHR$(205))
LOCATE row + 2, col
PRINT STRING$(LEN(x$) + 2, CHR$(205))

' Print text.

LOCATE row + 1, col + 1
PRINT x$

END SUB
```

The program output looks like this:

```
┌─────────────────────────────────────┐
│ BASIC 7: A Programmer's Reference    │
└─────────────────────────────────────┘
```

The PCOPY Statement

To copy information from one video page to another, use the **PCOPY**
statement:

```
PCOPY source%, destination%
```

The integer expressions *source%* and *destination%* specify the video pages that information is copied between. They may range between 0 and n; the value of n depends upon the video hardware installed and the current video mode.

If your video hardware supports multiple pages, use **PCOPY** for temporary screen storage. For example, if you need to display a Help screen, first use **PCOPY** to copy the original program screen to an unused video page. After the user is finished viewing the Help screen, copy the original program screen back to the original page.

Accepting Input from the Keyboard

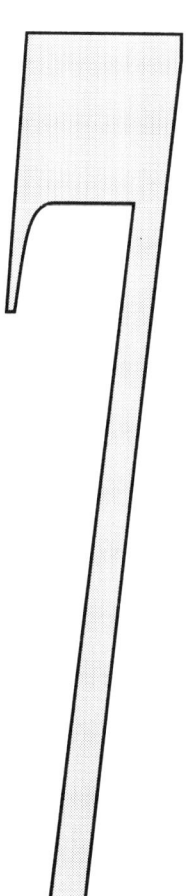

With few exceptions, all computer programs interact with the user via the keyboard. BASIC 7's keyboard-input statements provide full flexibility for your programs.

The INPUT Statement

The **INPUT** statement accepts user input from the keyboard and assigns it to one or more program variables. The syntax for this statement is:

```
INPUT [;] ["prompt"{;|,}] variablelist
```

The optional semicolon following the **INPUT** keyword determines where the cursor is positioned after the **INPUT** statement executes. If you include the semicolon, the cursor is positioned immediately after the user's input. If you exclude the semicolon, the cursor is positioned at the start of the next line.

"prompt" is an optional string expression. If you include it, the **INPUT** statement displays this expression before accepting user input. If *"prompt"* is followed by a semicolon, a question mark is appended to *"prompt"*. If this string expression is followed by a comma, no question mark is added.

variablelist is a list of one or more program variables that will receive user input. Each variable in *variablelist* can be a simple numeric or string variable, a numeric or string array element, or a record element.

When execution reaches an **INPUT** statement, the program pauses and waits for the user to enter as many variables as are the number of variables contained in *variablelist*. The variables entered by the user must be of the same type, and in the same order, as the variables in *variablelist*. When you enter multiple variables, separate them with commas; to enter a string that includes a comma, enclose the string in double quotation marks. If a discrepancy occurs in the type or number of variables entered by the user, BASIC 7 displays the Redo from start message and prompts the user again for input.

The following program demonstrates the **INPUT** statement. When you examine the output, note that an error was intentionally made in the response to the second **INPUT** prompt.

```
INPUT "Enter your name: ", Name$
INPUT "Enter 3 numbers: ", a, b, c
INPUT "What is your age"; age%
INPUT "Enter your city and zip code: ", City$, Zip%
```

This output results in:

```
Enter your name: Peter Aitken
Enter 3 numbers: 1,2

Redo from start
Enter 3 numbers: 1,2,3
What is your age? 43
Enter your city and zip code: Durham, 27705
```

The LINE INPUT Statement

LINE INPUT is similar to **INPUT** in that it displays an (optional) prompt and assigns keyboard input to a variable. Unlike **INPUT**, **LINE INPUT** accepts an entire line of input at once, and assigns it to a single string variable. The syntax for **LINE INPUT** is:

```
LINE INPUT [;] [ "prompt";] var$
```

The optional semicolon following the **LINE INPUT** keyword determines where the cursor is positioned after the **LINE INPUT** statement executes. If you include the semicolon, the cursor is positioned immediately after the user's input. If you omit the semicolon, the cursor is positioned at the beginning of the next line.

"prompt" is an optional string expression. If you include it, the **LINE INPUT** statement displays it before accepting user input. *var$* is a single string variable to which the user's input is assigned.

LINE INPUT accepts an entire line of input (up to 255 characters long) and assigns it to a string variable. The end of input is marked by pressing the Enter key. **LINE INPUT** pays no special attention to commas or quotation marks, treating them as regular characters.

The INPUT$() Function

INPUT$() accepts a predefined number of characters from the keyboard and returns the resulting string. When you use **INPUT$()**, no prompt can be displayed and the input characters are not echoed on the screen. The syntax for **INPUT$()** is:

```
var$ = INPUT$(n)
```

var$ is the string variable to hold the input, and **n** is the number of characters to accept.

As with all functions, **INPUT$()** can be used directly in a statement:

```
...
IF INPUT(1) = "y" THEN
...
```

INPUT$() can accept any keyboard input, including a press of the Enter key. When an **INPUT$()** function is encountered, program execution pauses until the specified number of characters is entered.

The INKEY$ Function

INKEY$ is the most flexible of BASIC 7's keyboard functions. The syntax is simply:

```
INKEY$
```

When **INKEY$** is called, it examines the keyboard buffer to see if a key has been pressed. If no key has been pressed, **INKEY$** returns a Null string. If a keystroke is waiting in the buffer, **INKEY$** removes it from the buffer and returns one of the following strings:

- If the first keystroke in the buffer is a normal ASCII character, **INKEY$** returns a one-character string which is the actual character.

- If the first keystroke in the buffer is an extended code, **INKEY$** returns a two-character string. In this case, the first character is always 0, and the second character identifies the key that was pressed. (See Appendix B for a list of extended ASCII codes.)

INKEY$** does not echo keystrokes. The following short program demonstrates the use of **INKEY$. This program accepts keystrokes, displays them on the screen, and exits when the Enter key is pressed.

```
' Demonstrates INKEY$.
CLS

DO

  ' Loop until a key is pressed.

  DO
    k$ = INKEY$
  LOOP UNTIL k$ <> ""

  ' The ASCII code for ENTER is 13.

  IF ASC(k$) = 13 THEN
    EXIT DO
  ELSE
    PRINT k$;
  END IF

LOOP

END
```

A common use for **INKEY$** is to pause program execution until a key is pressed. One way to do this is shown in the **DO...LOOP** structure in the last sample program. The following code shows a more concise approach:

```
PRINT "Press any key to continue..."
WHILE INKEY$ = "" : WEND
```

The **SLEEP** statement also pauses for a keypress, but doesn't allow you to read the key that was pressed. Because **INKEY$** can accept any keystroke, including the arrow keys and the function keys, it is very flexible and can be used to program almost any sort of customized keyboard-entry routine. The only keys that **INKEY$** cannot accept are Ctrl+Break, Ctrl+NumLock, Shift+PrtSc, and Ctrl+Alt+Del.

The function **GetFKey**, demonstrated in the next program, is an example of **INKEY$**'s flexibility. This function pauses until any function key from F1 to F10 is pressed. It then returns an integer (from 1 to 10) indicating which key was pressed. **GetFKey** can be useful in responding to menus, and can serve as a model for functions that accept other input (e.g., cursor key presses).

```
DECLARE FUNCTION GetFKey% ()

' Demonstrates use of INKEY$ to accept function key input.

DEFINT A-Z
CLS

PRINT "Press any function key F1-F9; press F10 to exit."

DO

k = GetFKey

SELECT CASE k
  CASE 1 TO 9
    PRINT "You pressed F"; k
  CASE 10
    EXIT DO
END SELECT

LOOP

END

FUNCTION GetFKey

' Main loop

DO

' Loop until a key is pressed.
```

```
DO
  k$ = INKEY$
LOOP UNTIL k$ <> ""

' Pressing a function key returns an extended code.
' The ASCII value of the second character is 59-68 for
' keys F1-F10. If an extended key was pressed, assign value
' to code.

IF LEN(k$) = 2 THEN
  code = ASC(RIGHT$(k$, 1))
ELSE
  code = 0
END IF

' Beep if it's not a function key.

IF code < 59 OR code > 68 THEN
  BEEP
END IF

' Continue looping until a function key is pressed.

LOOP UNTIL code > 58 AND code < 69

' Subtract 58 from code so the function returns the number of
' the key pressed.

GetFKey = code - 58

END FUNCTION
```

Manipulating String Data

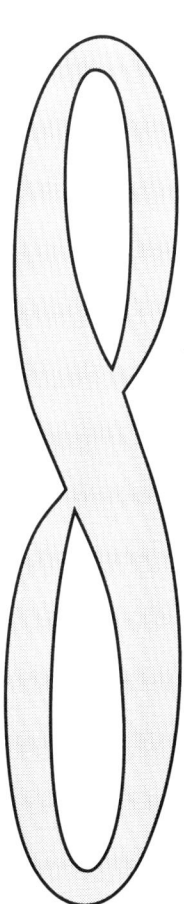

A *string* is any sequence of characters. Strings are one of BASIC 7's two fundamental data types, and play an important role in most applications programs. This chapter covers BASIC 7's functions and statements for manipulating strings. Note that functions that return a string value have the $ character at the end of their name.

Extracting Portions of Strings

The LEFT$() and RIGHT$() Functions

The **LEFT$()** and **RIGHT$()** functions extract a portion of a string starting respectively at the left or the right side of the string. The syntax for these functions is:

```
LEFT$(stringexpression, n%)
RIGHT$(stringexpression, n%)
```

stringexpression is the expression that you want to extract characters from, and *n%* is the number of characters to extract. **LEFT$()** returns the leftmost *n%* characters, and **RIGHT$()** returns the rightmost *n%* characters. If *n%* is greater than the length of *stringexpression*, the entire expression is returned. Neither function modifies *stringexpression*.

The LTRIM$() and RTRIM$() Functions

The **LTRIM$()** and **RTRIM$()** functions remove trailing or leading blanks from a string. Their syntax is:

```
RTRIM$(stringexpression)
LTRIM$(stringexpression)
```

RTRIM$() returns *stringexpression* with trailing blanks (if any) removed. **LTRIM$()** returns *stringexpression* with leading blanks (if any) removed.

The MID$() Function

The **MID$()** function can return characters from anywhere in a string. The syntax for this function is:

```
MID$(stringexpression, start%, n%)
```

start% is the position of the first character to return, and *n%* is the number of characters to return. If *start%* is greater than the length of *stringexpression*, **MID$()** returns the null string. If *start%* is less than the length of *stringexpression*, but *start%* + *n%* is greater than the length of *stringexpression*, **MID$()** returns all of the characters between *start%* and the end of *stringexpression*.

The following short program demonstrates the functions that extract portions of strings.

```
' Demonstrates string extraction functions.

DEFINT A-Z
CLS
x1$ = "     Norway      "
x2$ = "Scandinavia"

PRINT "["; LTRIM$(x1$); "]"

PRINT "["; RTRIM$(x1$); "]"
PRINT

PRINT LEFT$(x2$, 6)
PRINT RIGHT$(x2$, 5)
PRINT

FOR i = 1 TO 12
  PRINT MID$(x2$, i, 4)
NEXT i

PRINT "Done!"

END
```

This program produces the following output:

```
[Norway    ]
[     Norway]

Scandi
navia
Scan
cand
andi
ndin
dina
inav
navi
avia
via
ia
a

Done!
```

Searching for Strings

The INSTR() Function

To search for one string within another, use the **INSTR()** function:

```
INSTR([start%,] stringexpression1$, stringexpression2$)
```

stringexpression1$ is the *target* string, the string being searched. *stringexpression2$* is the *search* string, the string you are looking for. *start%* is the character position in *stringexpression1$* where the search is to begin. If you omit *start%*, the search begins at the first character.

If the search string is found within the target string, **INSTR()** returns the character position where the match was found. If the search string is not found within the target string, **INSTR()** returns 0.

The **INSTR()** function is demonstrated by the following program.

```
CLS
Target$ = "Albuquerque"

PRINT INSTR(Target$, "A")
```

```
PRINT INSTR(2, Target$, "A")
PRINT INSTR(Target$, "que")
END
```

The program produces this output:

```
1
0
5
```

Converting Between Strings and Values

The VAL() and STR$() Functions

Recall that strings and numbers are BASIC 7's two fundamental data types. You cannot assign a string value to a numeric variable, or assign a numeric value to a string variable. You can, however, convert between strings and numbers using the **VAL()** and **STR$()** functions. The syntax for these functions is:

```
stringvariable$ = STR$(numericexpression)
numericvariable = VAL(stringexpression)
```

STR$() returns the string representation of the evaluation of **numericexpression**.

VAL() returns the numeric value represented by a string expression. **VAL()** reads each character in **stringexpression** until it reaches either the end of the string expression, or a nonnumeric character. (The numeric characters are the digits 0 to 9, the decimal point, the plus and minus signs, and the letters E and D used in exponential notation.) If the first character in **stringexpression** is nonnumeric, **VAL()** returns 0.

The following short program demonstrates how to convert between strings and values.

```
CLS
num = 125000
st$ = "45 Oak Street"
```

```
PRINT STR$(.01), STR$(3 / 12), STR$(SQR(88)), STR$(num)
PRINT VAL("3.000"), VAL(st$), VAL("BASIC"), VAL("5E+3")

END
```

This output is the result:

```
.01              .25            9.380832       125000
3                45             0              5000
```

Comparing Strings

You can compare strings by using the same relational operators that you use for comparing numbers. These operators are:

=	Equal to
<>	Not equal to
>	Greater than
<	Less than
<=	Less than or equal to
>=	Greater than or equal to

Recall that the comparison operators are used in Boolean expressions that return either -1 (true) or 0 (false). When you make string comparisons, the meanings of = and <> are clear: two strings are equal if they are identical; otherwise, they are not equal. Thus, "A" = "A" is true, "A" <> "a" is true, and "A" = "AA" is false.

Greater than and less than comparisons are interpreted in terms of the characters' ASCII values (see Appendix C for a table of ASCII values). Thus, char1 < char2 is true if ASC(char1) < ASC(char2) is true. When comparing multiple character strings, the ASCII value of the first nonmatching character is used. For example, "abc" < "abd" is true.

The ASCII codes for the lowercase letters a to z are 97 to 122. The ASCII codes for the uppercase letters A to Z are 65 to 90. This means that uppercase letters are always "less than" lowercase letters. Thus, "Z" < "a" is true, which seems contrary to alphabetical order. To use the comparison operators to alphabetize strings, use **UCASE$()** or **LCASE$()** to convert strings to the same case before you perform the comparison.

If you have loaded the Indexed Sequential Access Method engine, you also have access to the **TEXTCOMP()** function that compares strings differently from the relational operators. When you use **TEXTCOMP()**, take note of the following information:

1. Case is not significant. Thus, "apple" and "APPLE" are considered the same, and "aardvark" is considered to be less than "ZEBRA".

2. International characters, such as accented letters (ä, à, å) are taken into account in string comparisons. The character sort order was selected when you initially installed BASIC 7. (See Appendix E, International Character Sort Order Tables, in your BASIC 7 Language Reference for more information.)

The syntax of **TEXTCOMP()** is:

```
TEXTCOMP(string1$, string2$)
```

string1$* and *string2$ are the strings being compared. **TEXTCOMP()** returns -1 if *string1$* is less than *string2$*, 0 if the strings are equal, and 1 if *string1$* is greater than *string2$*.

See Chapter 14, Database Programming Using Isam, for more information on the ISAM engine.

Miscellaneous String Functions

Changing Case

To change the case of letters in a string, use the **UCASE$()** and **LCASE$()** functions:

```
UCASE$(stringexpression)
LCASE$(stringexpression)
```

UCASE$() returns *stringexpression* with all lowercase letters converted to uppercase; **LCASE$()** returns *stringexpression* with all uppercase letters converted to lowercase. Nonletter characters are not affected.

Using ASCII Values

Each ASCII character is associated with a specific numeric value between 0 and 255, called the character's *ASCII value*. BASIC 7 provides functions that convert between ASCII characters and ASCII values. The syntax for these functions is:

```
ASC(stringexpression)
CHR$(val%)
```

ASC() returns the ASCII value of the first character in *stringexpression*. **CHR$()** returns the character with ASCII value *val%*. *val%* must be in the range of 0 to 255 or an Illegal function call error results.

Finding String Length

Use the **LEN()** function to determine the length of a string:

```
LEN(stringexpression)
```

LEN() returns the length of *stringexpression*, i.e., the number of characters. Remember that spaces are counted as characters: **LEN("Big top")** = 7.

Fundamentals of Graphics

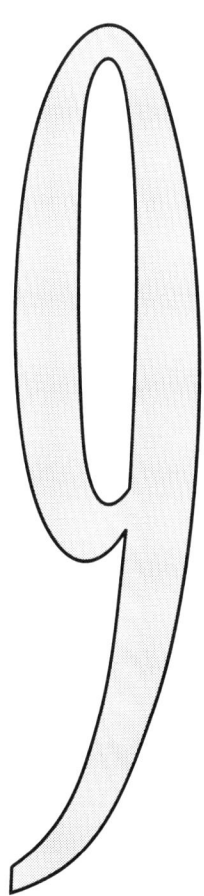

Most of today's PCs have video systems that can operate in graphics mode. In graphics mode, your program has complete control over every dot of the display screen. With this control, you can display not only text, but just about any shape or structure you can imagine. This chapter covers BASIC 7's graphics capabilities.

Graphics Basics

Every PC video display is composed of a matrix of small dots, or *pixels* (short for *picture element*). Each pixel can be turned on (illuminated) and turned off; with color displays, the pixel color can be controlled as well. Any text or other pattern that is displayed on the screen is created by these pixels.

The *resolution* is the number of pixels available on the screen. A screen that displays 640 pixels horizontally and 200 pixels vertically has a resolution of 640x200. The total number of pixels on the screen equals the product of the horizontal and vertical resolutions. Different PC video systems offer different resolutions. Higher resolution provides a clearer, easier-to-use screen image.

Each screen pixel has *coordinates* that specify its horizontal and vertical position. Coordinates are written as *x, y* where *x* is the horizontal position and *y* is the vertical position. By convention, the row at the top of the screen is row 0, and the column at the left of the screen is column 0. Therefore, the pixel at the upper-left corner of the screen has coordinates 0, 0. For a screen with horizontal resolution *xres* and vertical resolution *yres*, the pixel in the lower-right corner of the screen has coordinates xres - 1, yres - 1.

The graphics screen contains a *graphics cursor*. The graphics cursor is never visible, but has a position that marks the screen location where certain graphics output occur. When you first set a graphics mode using the **SCREEN** statement, the cursor is located in the center of the screen. Some graphics operations move the graphics cursor.

Setting Graphics Modes

Before executing any graphics statements, you must set your video system to a graphics mode. This is done using the **SCREEN** statement:

```
SCREEN mode% [, [color%] [, [activepage%] [,visiblepage%]] ]
```

mode% is the screen mode. The available graphics modes depend upon your video system. If you try to set a mode that is not supported by your hardware, an Illegal function call error occurs.

color% switches the monitor display between color and noncolor. This argument is functional only in screen modes 0 and 1, and only if a composite monitor is in use.

activepage% specifies the video page that output is sent to, and *visiblepage%* specifies the video page displayed on the screen. *activepage%* and *visiblepage%* can range from 0 to *n-1*, where *n* is the number of pages available. The number of pages available in graphics modes ranges from 1 to 8 and depends upon the installed video hardware and screen mode. (See Adapters and Displays in the QBX Help system for details.)

The graphics modes that you can use with the various IBM compatible video adapters are summarized in Table 9.1. (For complete details, see the QBX Help system.)

The "higher" video adapters can emulate the lower ones. For example, you can set mode 2 on a VGA system. Emulations are summarized below.

Adapter	Can emulate
EGA	CGA
MCGA	EGA, CGA
VGA	MCGA, EGA, CGA

Working with Pixels

You can control individual screen pixels using the **PSET()** and **PRESET()** functions:

Table 9.1. PC video adapter graphics modes.

Adapter	Monitor	Mode	Resolution	Colors	Pages
CGA	-	1	320x200	4	1
		2	640x200	2	1
Hercules	Monochrome	3	720x348	2	2
Olivetti AT&T	Color	4	640x400	16	1
EGA	Monochrome	10	640x350	9**	2*
EGA	Color	7	320x200	16	8*
		8	640x200	16	4*
		9	640x350	16	2*
MCGA	Analog	11	640x480	2	1
		13	320x200	256	1
VGA	Monochrome	10	640x350	9**	2
VGA	Analog	11	640x480	2	1
		12	640x480	16	1
		13	320x200	256	1

* Assumes full 256K memory installed
** "Colors" are displayed as shades of gray.

```
PSET [STEP] ( x%,y%) [,color&]
PRESET [STEP] ( x%,y%) [,color&]
```

x% and *y%* are integer expressions specifying the screen coordinates of the pixel. **STEP** is an optional keyword. If you include **STEP**, then *x%* and *y%* express a pixel position relative to the graphics cursor. If you omit **STEP**, then *x%* and *y%* express a pixel position relative to the screen origin.

color& is a numeric expression that specifies the pixel color. If you omit the *color&* argument, **PSET()** uses the current foreground color, and **PRESET()** uses the current background color.

Either **PSET()** or **PRESET()** moves the graphics cursor to the specified position. The following code illustrates how to use **PSET()** with and without the **STEP** keyword.

```
' Demonstrates the STEP keyword in PSET() statement. Draws a
' 100 by 100 pixel box in the upper-left screen corner with
' and without using STEP.

SCREEN 2

' Not using STEP; draw top of box.

FOR i = 0 TO 99
  PSET (i, 0)
NEXT i

' Draw right side.

FOR i = 0 TO 99
  PSET (99, i)
NEXT i

' Draw bottom.

FOR i = 99 TO 0 STEP -1
  PSET (i, 99)
NEXT i

' Draw left side.

FOR i = 99 TO 0 STEP -1
  PSET (0, i)
NEXT i

SLEEP
CLS

' Using STEP; first move graphics cursor to (0,0)

PSET (0, 0)

' Draw top.
```

```
FOR i = 0 TO 99
  PSET STEP(1, 0)
NEXT i

' Draw right side.

FOR i = 0 TO 99
  PSET STEP(0, 1)
NEXT i

' Draw bottom.

FOR i = 0 TO 99
  PSET STEP(-1, 0)
NEXT i

' Draw left side.

FOR i = 0 TO 99
  PSET STEP(0, -1)
NEXT i

END
```

Drawing the Basic Shapes

Lines and Rectangles

To draw a straight line or a rectangle, use the **LINE** statement:

```
LINE [[STEP](x1,y1)] - [STEP](x2,y2) [,[color] [,[B[F]]
     [,style]]]
```

x1,y1 and *x2,y2* are the screen coordinates either of the ends of the line, or of diagonally opposite corners of the rectangle. After drawing the line or the rectangle, **LINE** moves the graphics cursor to *x2,y2*.

When you use the **STEP** keyword with either (or both) screen coordinate pair(s), **LINE** interprets the coordinates as relative to the graphics cursor. When you don't use **STEP**, the coordinates are interpreted as absolute coordinates that are relative to the screen origin.

color specifies the color to use for the line or the rectangle. If you omit *color*, the current foreground color is used. The **B** option draws a rectangle. Use **F** in conjunction with **B** to draw a filled (solid) rectangle.

style is an integer expression whose bit pattern specifies the line style used. *style* has no effect for filled rectangles. The default style is a solid line.

If one or both of the coordinate pairs used in a **LINE** statement is off the screen, no error occurs. The line or rectangle is *clipped*; only the portion that falls within the screen coordinates is displayed.

style is an integer expression that controls the pixel pattern used by **LINE** to draw lines and rectangles. An integer is comprised of 16 bits, each of which can have a value of 0 or 1. The 16 bits in *style* control each 16-pixel segment of the line. For each bit set to 1, the corresponding pixel is illuminated; for each bit set to 0, the corresponding pixel is not illuminated. The *style* argument is easiest to specify using hexadecimal constants. Here are some examples:

style argument	Bit pattern	Line style
&HFFFF	1111111111111111	Solid (the default)
&H5555	0101010101010101	Dotted
&H3333	0011001100110011	Short dashes
&H0F0F	0000111100001111	Long dashes
&H4F4F	0100111101001111	Dot-dash

Circles and Arcs

To draw circles and arcs use the **CIRCLE** statement:

```
CIRCLE [STEP] (x!,y!),radius![,[color&] [,[start!] [,[end!]
       [,aspect!]]
```

x!,y! specify the screen coordinates of the center of the circle or ellipse. The **STEP** keyword causes **CIRCLE** to interpret the coordinates as relative to the graphics cursor. When you omit **STEP**, the coordinates are interpreted as absolute coordinates that are relative to the screen origin.

radius! is a numeric expression that specifies the length of the radius along the x-axis, measured in the current coordinate system.

color& is a numeric expression that specifies the color to be used. The default color is the current foreground color. The available colors depend upon the **SCREEN** mode and the installed video hardware.

Use *start!* and *end!* to draw an arc. These arguments specify the start and end points of the arc as angles relative to the horizontal, in radians. If you omit *start!* and *end!*, the default values of 0 and 2PI radians are used, and a full circle is drawn.

aspect! is a numeric expression that specifies the ratio between the y radius and the x radius. The default value for *aspect!* is the value needed to draw a true circle in the current **SCREEN** mode. Use other values of *aspect!* to draw ellipses or elliptical arcs.

If you use a negative value for *start!* and/or *end!*, a straight line is drawn from the center of the arc to the corresponding end of the arc. This technique is useful for drawing wedge shapes, such as sections of pie charts.

The *aspect ratio* controls the shape of the circle or the arc. When *aspect!* < 1, an ellipse is drawn that is wider than its height. When *aspect!* > 1, an ellipse is drawn that is taller than its width.

```
' Demonstrates the CIRCLE statement.

CONST PI = 3.141593
SCREEN 2

FOR i = 1 TO 5

  ' Circles.

  CIRCLE (100, 100), i * 20

  ' Arcs

  CIRCLE (300, 60), i * 20, , 0, PI * i / 5

  ' Pie wedges.

  CIRCLE (300, 160), i * 20, , -.01, -PI * i / 5
```

```
' Ellipses.

CIRCLE (500, 100), 80, , , , i / 3

NEXT i

SLEEP
SCREEN 0

END
```

Filling Screen Regions

Use the **PAINT** statement to fill an enclosed screen region with a solid color or a pattern:

```
PAINT [STEP] (x!,y!)[,[paint] [,[bordercolor&] [,background$]]]
```

x! and *y!* are the screen coordinates of the *seed point*, a point inside the screen region to be painted. When you include the **STEP** keyword, **PAINT** interprets *x!* and *y!* as relative to the graphics cursor, rather than relative to the screen origin.

When you want to fill in a region with a solid color, *paint* is a numeric expression specifying the color to use; the default is the current foreground color. When you want to fill in a region with a pattern, *paint* is a string expression that specifies the tile pattern to use.

bordercolor& specifies the *boundary color*, the color at which painting is to stop. The default *bordercolor&* is the color specified by *paint*. *background&* is a string expression that specifies the tile pattern to skip during boundary checking.

When filling a shape with a solid color, **PAINT** starts at the seed point and fills the shape with the color attribute specified by *paint*. Filling stops when pixels of color *bordercolor&* are reached. If the screen is displaying an enclosed figure (such as a circle) in color *boundarycolor&*, **PAINT** can have one of three effects:

- If *x!,y!* specify a point within the circle, the entire circle is filled, and the region outside the circle is not affected.

- If *x!,y!* specify a point outside of the circle, the region outside of the circle is filled, and the inside of the circle is not affected.

- If *x!,y!* specify a point on the circumference of the circle, no action is taken.

When you use **PAINT** to fill enclosed shapes, there must be no "leaks." Even a small gap in an otherwise enclosed figure allows the fill color to leak out and fill the entire screen.

The use of **PAINT** to fill a screen region with a pattern is known as *tiling*. A particular pattern, the *tile*, is repeated over and over again to fill the region. The procedure for defining and using a tile pattern differs depending upon the video hardware in use. You can find an excellent explanation in the Basic 7 *Programmer's Guide*.

The DRAW Statement

DRAW operates somewhat like a miniature programming language embedded within BASIC 7. After you put one or more commands into a string expression, the string expression is passed to the **DRAW** statement, which executes the commands to produce screen images. What you can accomplish using **DRAW** is limited only by your creativity. The syntax of **DRAW** is:

```
DRAW stringexpression$
```

stringexpression$ contains the commands to be executed.

The use of the **DRAW** statement is conceptually similar to drawing on a piece of paper with a pencil. When drawing with a pencil, you control the direction and distance the pencil moves, whether or not it makes a line (by lifting it from the paper), and the color of the line (by changing pencils). With the **DRAW** statement, you control the same parameters of drawing (color, of course, is available only if you have a color display).

The following are the basic drawing commands; in these commands, *n* specifies the number of pixels. All **DRAW** commands move the graphics cursor and use its position as their starting reference.

Un	Up
Dn	Down
Ln	Left
Rn	Right
En	Diagonally up and right
Fn	Diagonally down and right
Gn	Diagonally down and left
Hn	Diagonally up and left
M{+|-}x,y	Draw to point **x,y**. If you include a + or - sign, the move is made relative to the graphics cursor. Otherwise, the move is made to the absolute screen coordinates x,y.

You can add the following prefixes to modify any of the drawing commands:

B	Move without drawing
N	Draw and return

Use the following commands to modify the color, the scale, and the rotation of the object being drawn:

Cn	Change the drawing (foreground) color to color attribute n.
Pp,b	Fill enclosed shape with color p using color b as the boundary color.
Sn	Set the movement value to n. (The default is 4.)
An	Rotate the direction of the drawing by (n * 90) degrees (n = 0, 1, 2, or 3).
TAn	Rotate the direction of drawing by n degrees ($0 <= n <= 360$).

To include a numeric variable in a **DRAW** command, use the following form, where *X* is the single letter **DRAW** command, and *n* is the numeric variable:

```
"X=" + VARPTR$( n )
```

Here are three ways to draw a line upward 40 pixels:

```
DRAW "U40"

n1$ = "40"
DRAW "U" + n1$

n1% = 40
DRAW "U=" + VARPTR$(n1%)
```

Using Viewports

A *viewport* lets you restrict graphics output to a rectangular region of the screen and, optionally, move the origin of the screen-coordinate system. To define the viewport, use the **VIEW** statement:

```
VIEW [[SCREEN] (x1!,y1!)-(x2!,y2!) [,[color&] [,border&]]]
```

If you include the **SCREEN** keyword, the coordinates of subsequent graphics statements are absolute in relation to the screen, not relative to the viewport. *x1!,y1!* and *x2!,y2!* are numeric expressions specifying the screen coordinates of diagonally opposite corners of the viewport.

color& specifies the color that the viewport is filled with. If you omit the *color&* argument, the viewport is not filled. *border&* specifies the color used to draw a border around the viewport. If you omit *border&*, no border is drawn.

When you execute **VIEW** with no arguments, the effects of any previous **VIEW** statements are cancelled.

After you execute a **VIEW** statement, all subsequent graphics output is limited to the screen rectangle defined by the diagonally opposite corners *x1!,y1!* and *x2!,y2!*. Graphics that would appear outside of this region are clipped. Any graphics images already on the screen when **VIEW** is executed are not affected. If you execute **CLS** only the viewport is cleared.

Text is not affected by a **VIEW** statement, and can be displayed anywhere on the screen. If you include the **SCREEN** keyword in the **VIEW** statement, the screen coordinate system does not change and coordinates remain relative to the screen origin 0,0 in the upper-left corner of the screen. If you omit the **SCREEN** keyword, the origin is shifted to *x1!,y1!* (the upper-left corner of the viewport), and subsequent graphics statements operate relative to the new origin.

An example will help clarify this. In **SCREEN 1** mode, resolution is 320x200, and the pixel in the center of the screen has coordinates 160,100. After you execute the statement

```
VIEW SCREEN (160,100)-(319,199)
```

graphics output is restricted to the lower-right quarter of the screen, but the coordinate system remains unchanged: the pixel in the center of the screen still has the coordinates 160,100. In contrast, after you execute the statement

```
VIEW (160,100)-(319,199)
```

graphics output is restricted in the same manner, but the coordinate system origin is now shifted. The pixel in the center of the screen has coordinates 0,0, and the pixel in the upper-left corner has coordinates -160,-100.

The following program demonstrates viewports. The code first sets up four viewports in different regions of the screen, using the **SCREEN** keyword for each viewport. After each viewport is established, a series of concentric circles is drawn centered on coordinates 320,100.

The code clears the screen next, establishes the same four viewports without using the **SCREEN** keyword, and draws the same circles. The effect of omitting **SCREEN** is clear—the center of the circles shifts relative to each viewport. The program output is shown in Figures 9.1 and 9.2.

```
' Demonstrates viewports.

DECLARE SUB circles ()

SCREEN 2

' Set up four viewports with SCREEN keyword. Draw circles
' in each.

VIEW SCREEN (20, 20)-(300, 80), , 7
CALL circles
VIEW SCREEN (20, 120)-(300, 180), , 7
CALL circles
VIEW SCREEN (340, 20)-(620, 80), , 7
CALL circles
VIEW SCREEN (340, 120)-(620, 180), , 7
CALL circles

LOCATE 13, 20
PRINT "Viewports with SCREEN. Press a key to continue."
```

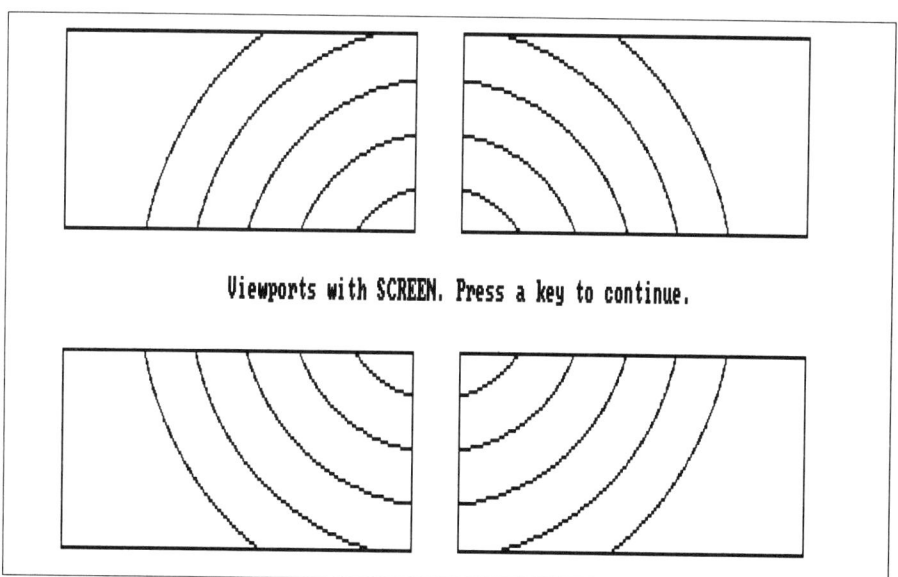

Figure 9.1. The first output screen produced by the viewport demonstration program.

```
SLEEP

VIEW
CLS

' Set up the same 4 viewports without SCREEN keyword, and
' draw circles in each.

VIEW (20, 20)-(300, 80), , 7
CALL circles
VIEW (20, 120)-(300, 180), , 7
CALL circles
VIEW (340, 20)-(620, 80), , 7
CALL circles
VIEW (340, 120)-(620, 180), , 7
CALL circles

LOCATE 13, 18
PRINT "Viewports without SCREEN. Press a key to continue."
```

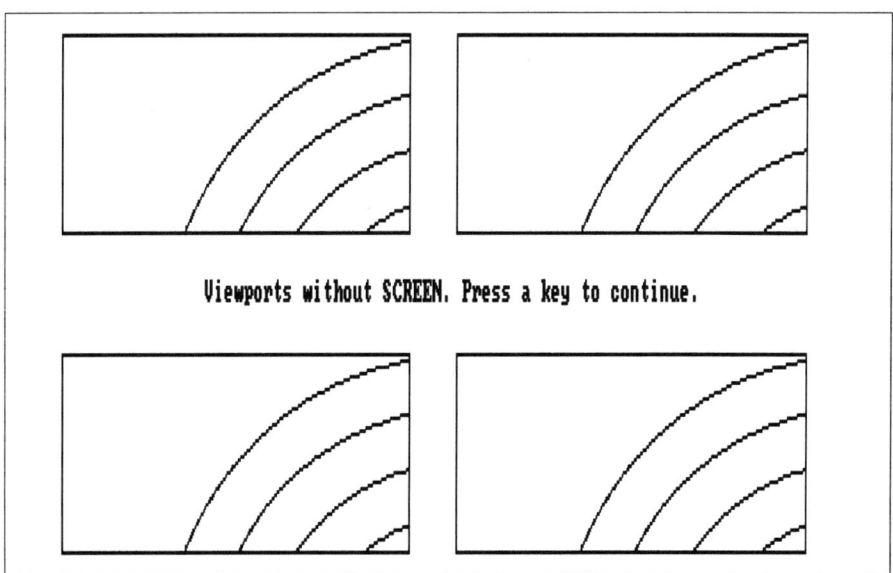

Figure 9.2. The second output screen produced by the viewport demonstration program.

```
SLEEP
SCREEN 0, 0, 0

END

SUB circles

' Draw 6 concentric circles.

FOR i = 1 TO 6
    CIRCLE (320, 100), i * 40
NEXT i

END SUB
```

Using Windows

Use the **WINDOW** statement to modify the screen coordinate system:

```
WINDOW [[SCREEN] (x1!,y1!)-(x2!,y2!)]
```

x1!,y1! and *x2!,y2!* are single-precision values. *x1!* and *x2!* specify the new coordinates that will refer to the left and right edges of the window, respectively. *y1!* and *y2!* specify the new coordinates that will refer to the top and bottom of the window, respectively.

If you include the **SCREEN** keyword in the **WINDOW** statement, the window y coordinate system places lower y values closer to the top of the screen (like the default screen coordinate system). If you omit **SCREEN**, lower y values refer to window locations closer to the bottom of the screen (like traditional Cartesian coordinates).

A **WINDOW** statement with no arguments returns the screen to its default hardware coordinates.

When you execute a **WINDOW** statement, the screen coordinate system changes to the values specified in the arguments; existing screen images are not affected. The coordinate arguments to all subsequent graphics-drawing statements are interpreted in terms of the window-coordinate system. Use **WINDOW** to establish a customized coordinate system that is suited to the graphics task at hand. For example, the statement

```
WINDOW (0,0)-(1,1)
```

establishes a coordinate system in which (0,0) refers to the lower-left corner, (1,1) to the upper-right corner, and (.5,.5) to the center of the screen. Text output is not affected by a **WINDOW** statement.

A **WINDOW** statement does not, of course, actually modify the number of pixels available on your graphics screen, or increase your screen's resolution. When a window is active, the window coordinates used by graphics statements are translated to physical pixel coordinates before the image is displayed in the window.

When a window is established, it's fit into the current viewport. By default, this viewport is the entire screen. If a **VIEW** statement has been executed that sets up a partial screen viewport, the window is established within that viewport. In this case, the coordinates *(x1!,y1!)-(x2!,y2!)* passed to the **WINDOW** statement refer to the corners of the viewport.

The following program demonstrates the **WINDOW** statement. The output is shown in Figure 9.3.

```
' Demonstrates the WINDOW statement.

DECLARE SUB shapes ()

SCREEN 2

' Establish a full screen window and draw some shapes in it.

WINDOW (-1, -1)-(1, 1)

CALL shapes

SLEEP

' Clear the window settings, then establish a viewport.

WINDOW

VIEW (80, 50)-(400, 150), , 7

' Clear the viewport and establish the same window
' settings as before. Redraw the shapes.
```

```
CLS
WINDOW (-1, -1)-(1, 1)

CALL shapes

SLEEP
SCREEN 0

END Z

SUB shapes

' Draw 5 circles.

FOR i = -.5 TO .5 STEP .2
  CIRCLE (i, 0), .3
NEXT i

' Draw 2 filled rectangles.

LINE (-.8, -.8)-(.8, -.6), , BF
LINE (-.8, .8)-(.8, .6), , BF

END SUB
```

Notice in Figure 9.3 that when a window is established within a viewport, the graphics output is scaled to fit within the viewport. This is different from establishing a viewport by itself, which simply clips

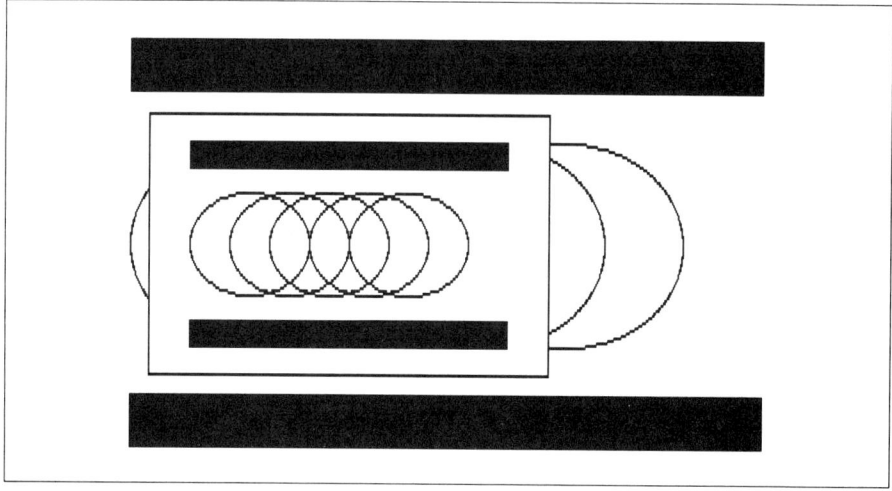

Figure 9.3. The output of the window demonstration program.

graphics output that falls outside of the viewport. The ability to scale graphics output in viewports is a powerful tool that provides great flexibility when you design graphical displays.

Control of Color

Palettes

To understand color control on PC video systems, you need to understand the concept of a *palette*. A video color palette is analogous to a painter's palette (the flat board that holds different colors of paint).

Imagine a painter's palette that has 16 compartments, numbered 0 to 15. The painter squeezes some black paint into compartment 0, blue paint into compartment 1, red paint into compartment 2, and so on. To get a particular color the painter must dip the brush into the proper compartment.

The painter must dip the brush into compartment 2 to get red, but the color red is not permanently associated with compartment 2. The painter could change the palette, placing green into compartment 2 and red into compartment 6.

In color display adapters, each video palette has a certain number of "compartments" or positions. At any particular time, each position contains a specific color, called a *color value*. Palettes have a set of default color values, but these can be changed under program control.

In BASIC 7, specifying a *color attribute* means specifying a palette position. The **PSET**, **PRESET**, **LINE**, **CIRCLE**, and **VIEW** statements each have an optional *color* argument that specifies the color attribute. Thus, the following statement means "Draw a line between (10,10) and (100,200), using the color value in palette position 5."

```
LINE(10,10)-(100,200), 5
```

During the remainder of this discussion, keep in mind the distinction between a color attribute (a palette position), and a color value (a specific color).

CGA Color Control

The Color Graphics Adapter (CGA) has two palettes that each hold four colors. In the CGA 320x200-resolution **SCREEN 1** mode, one of these palettes is active at any given time, and four colors can be displayed on the screen. Three fixed foreground colors and one background color can be modified. The contents of the two CGA palettes are shown in Table 9.2.

In either palette, color attribute 0 always refers to the current background color. The 16 available background colors are listed in Table 9.3.

Table 9.2. Color palettes in **SCREEN 1** mode.

Color attribute	In palette 0	In palette 1
0	Background	Background
1	Green	Cyan
2	Red	Magenta
3	Brown	White

Table 9.3. The sixteen available background colors.

Color number	Color
0	Black
1	Blue
2	Green
3	Cyan
4	Red
5	Magenta

continued

Table 9.3. The sixteen available background colors (*continued*).

Color number	Color
6	Brown (dark yellow on some monitors)
7	White (light gray on some monitors)
8	Gray (black on some monitors)
9	Light blue
10	Light green
11	Light cyan
12	Light red
13	Light magenta
14	Light yellow
15	Bright white

The **COLOR** statement switches between CGA palettes, and sets the current background color:

```
COLOR [background%][,palette%]
```

palette% is a value of 0 or 1 that specifies the palette to use. (The default palette is number 1.) *background%* is a value in the range of 0 to 15 that specifies the background color to use (i.e., the color value in palette position 0).

When you switch palettes and/or background color using the **COLOR** statement, the color of the screen image changes. For example, if you draw a circle in screen mode 1 using color attribute 1 and the default palette (number 1), you have a cyan circle on a black background. If you execute the statement

```
COLOR 5,0
```

you have a green circle on a magenta background (a real treat for the eyes!). The use of palettes in screen mode 1 is demonstrated by the following program, which can be run on a CGA, EGA, or VGA system.

```
' Demonstrates palettes and background colors in screen mode 1.

SCREEN 1

' Draw three boxes, each in a different foreground color.

LINE (60, 20)-(240, 60), 1, BF
LINE (60, 80)-(240, 120), 2, BF
LINE (60, 140)-(240, 180), 3, BF

' Cycle through the 16 background colors and the 2 palettes.

' Exit if a key is pressed.

FOR i = 0 TO 15

  FOR j = 0 TO 1
    COLOR i, j
    LOCATE 24, 5
    PRINT "Palette "; j; " and background "; i;
    SLEEP 1
  NEXT j

  IF INKEY$ <> "" THEN
    EXIT FOR
  END IF

NEXT i

LOCATE 24, 3
PRINT "Press a key to terminate program....";

SLEEP
SCREEN 0

END
```

EGA and VGA Color Control

The EGA and VGA video adapters use palettes for color control, but offer significantly more flexibility than the CGA. In the most frequently used modes (9 for the EGA, 12 for the VGA), these adapters have a palette of 16 available colors, so that 16 graphics colors can be displayed at one time on the screen. As a result, in graphics statements that specify a color attribute, you can specify attributes in the range of 0 to 15. The default palette for both the EGA and VGA is listed in Table 9.4.

Unlike the CGA, the EGA and VGA allow you to change the contents of the palette. The EGA offers a total of 64 colors, and the VGA offers a total of more than 256,000 colors. Any 16 of these colors can be available in the palette at one time. The color in palette position 0 is always the screen-background color.

How are the color values determined? Each color value is created by combining different intensities of the primary colors red, green, and blue. The EGA allows four intensities for each color: off, low, me-

Table 9.4. The default EGA / VGA palette.

Attribute number	Color value	Attribute number	Color value
0	Black	8	Gray
1	Blue	9	Light blue
2	Green	10	Light green
3	Cyan	11	Light cyan
4	Red	12	Light red
5	Magenta	13	Light magenta
6	Brown	14	Light yellow
7	White	15	Bright white

dium, and high. We therefore have available (4 red) x (4 green) x (4 blue) = 64 colors. These 64 colors have been arbitrarily assigned numbers from 0 to 63. The default EGA palette places the color values 0 to 15 in attribute positions 0-15. (Remember the distinction between a color *attribute* and a color *value*.) To see how all 64 colors look, run the EGA palette demonstration program given later in this section.

The VGA allows 64 intensities of each of the three primary colors, giving a total of 64 x 64 x 64 = 262,144 possible colors. To create a specific color, the intensity of each primary is given a value between 0 (off) and 63 (bright). The color value, which is a long integer, is calculated as follows:

```
color value = (65536 * blue) + (256 * green) + red
```

Note that the 262,144 VGA color values do not range from 0 to 262,143.

Now that you see how EGA and VGA color values are determined, use the **PALETTE** statement to change a single palette position. The syntax of this statement is:

```
PALETTE [attribute%,color&]
```

attribute% is an integer expression in the range of 0 to 15 that specifies the color attribute (palette position) to change.

color& is a numeric expression specifying the new color value for palette position *attribute%*. *color&* must be in the appropriate range for an EGA or VGA (as discussed earlier). *color&* can be an integer or a long integer when you change the EGA palette. It must be a long integer when you change a VGA palette.

When you execute **PALETTE** with no arguments, the palette is reset to the default color values.

To change the entire palette at once, use the **PALETTE USING** statement:

```
PALETTE USING array [(index)]
```

array is the name of an array that holds the new color values to be placed in the palette. *array* must be at least 16 elements long. *index* specifies the array element where the process of filling the palette starts. If you omit *index*, the filling process begins with the array's first element.

When **PALETTE USING** is executed, each color attribute (palette position) is assigned the corresponding color value from the array. If an array element contains -1, the palette's original color value is left unchanged. You can use an integer or a long integer array when changing the EGA palette; you must use a long integer array to change a VGA palette.

The following two programs demonstrate how to view EGA and VGA palettes and color values. You can use the first listing to view the 64 different colors available with an EGA video adapter. The program displays eight rectangles, using color attributes 1 to 8. Use the Left Arrow and Right Arrow keys to scroll through the available colors. The EGA color value is displayed below each rectangle.

```
' Demonstrates the EGA palette colors. Requires an EGA or VGA
' adapter to run.

DECLARE SUB ShiftPalette (StartVal%)
SCREEN 9

' Initialize an array with color values 0-63.

DIM colors%(63)

FOR i = 0 TO 63
  colors%(i) = i
NEXT i

' Display 8 rectangles using color attributes 1-8.

clr% = 1
FOR i% = 17 TO 632 STEP 77
  LINE (i%, 20)-(i% + 60, 120), clr%, BF
  clr% = clr% + 1
NEXT i%

' Call ShiftPalette to display color values under rectangles.
' The palette itself is not modified by this call.
```

```
StartVal% = 1
CALL ShiftPalette(StartVal%)

' Display instructions.

LOCATE 20, 5
PRINT "Left and right arrow keys move through EGA colors. ";
PRINT "Press F1 to exit."

' Main loop.

DO

   ' Get a keypress.

  DO
    k$ = INKEY$
  LOOP WHILE k$ = ""

   ' Get extended keycode.

  IF LEN(k$) = 2 THEN
    code% = ASC(RIGHT$(k$, 1))
  ELSE
    code% = 0
  END IF

  SELECT CASE code%
    CASE 59                              ' F1 key, exit
      EXIT DO
    CASE 75                              ' Left arrow
      IF StartVal% > 1 THEN             ' Move down 1
        StartVal% = StartVal% - 1
        CALL ShiftPalette(StartVal%)
      ELSE
        BEEP
      END IF
    CASE 77                              ' Right arrow
      IF StartVal% < 56 THEN            ' Move up 1
        StartVal% = StartVal% + 1
        CALL ShiftPalette(StartVal%)
      ELSE
```

```
              BEEP
            END IF
        CASE ELSE
            BEEP
        END SELECT

LOOP

' Reset palette and screen mode.

PALETTE
SCREEN 0
END


SUB ShiftPalette (StartVal%)

SHARED colors%()

' Print the color numbers under the rectangles.

FOR i% = 1 TO 8
  LOCATE 12, (i% - 1) * 10 + 5
  PRINT StartVal% + i% - 1
NEXT i%

' Change the color values in palette positions 1-8.

FOR i% = 1 TO 8
  PALETTE i%, colors%(StartVal% + i% - 1)
NEXT i%

END SUB
```

The second program demonstrates VGA palettes and color values,
and requires a VGA adapter. The program first changes color attribute
10 so that the three primary colors each have intensity 31. It then
displays a rectangle in that color (which is a medium gray). You can
"tune" the color by incrementing or decrementing the intensity of each
of the primary colors. The new color and the primary intensity values
are displayed on the screen.

```
' Demonstrates changing a VGA palette entry and fine tuning
' a color value.

DECLARE SUB ChangePalette (r%, b%, g%)

' The increment value.

CONST incr = 2

' Set VGA high-resolution mode.

SCREEN 12

' Starting primary-color intensities.

blue% = 31
red% = 31
green% = 31

' Change palette position 10 and draw rectangle.
CALL ChangePalette(red%, blue%, green%)

LINE (40, 40)-(600, 200), 10, BF

'Display instructions.

LOCATE 16, 1
PRINT "        Press F1/F2 to +/- red."
PRINT "        Press F3/F4 to +/- blue."
PRINT "        Press F5/F6 to +/- green."
PRINT
PRINT "        Press F10 to exit."

' Main program loop.

DO

  DO
    k$ = INKEY$
  LOOP WHILE k$ = ""

  IF LEN(k$) = 2 THEN
```

```
        code% = ASC(RIGHT$(k$, 1))
      ELSE
        code% = 0
      END IF
      SELECT CASE code%
        CASE 59                                    ' F1 key
          red% = red% + incr
          IF red% > 63 THEN red% = 63
          CALL ChangePalette(red%, blue%, green%)
        CASE 60                                    ' F2 key
          red% = red% - incr
          IF red% < 0 THEN red% = 0
          CALL ChangePalette(red%, blue%, green%)
        CASE 61                                    ' F3 key
          blue% = blue% + incr
          IF blue% > 63 THEN blue% = 63
          CALL ChangePalette(red%, blue%, green%)
        CASE 62                                    ' F4 key
          blue% = blue% - incr
          IF blue% < 0 THEN blue% = 0
          CALL ChangePalette(red%, blue%, green%)
        CASE 63                                    ' F5 key
          green% = green% + incr
          IF green% > 63 THEN green% = 63
          CALL ChangePalette(red%, blue%, green%)
        CASE 64                                    ' F6 key
          green% = green% - incr
          IF green% < 0 THEN green% = 0
          CALL ChangePalette(red%, blue%, green%)
        CASE 68                                    ' F10 key
          EXIT DO
        CASE ELSE
          BEEP
      END SELECT

LOOP

' reset palette and screen mode.

PALETTE
SCREEN 0

END
```

```
SUB ChangePalette (r%, b%, g%)

NewColor& = 65536 * b% + 256 * g% + r%

PALETTE 10, NewColor&

LOCATE 16, 50
PRINT "  Red ="; r%
LOCATE 17, 50
PRINT " Blue ="; b%
LOCATE 18, 50
PRINT "Green ="; g%
END SUB
```

Saving and Restoring Screen Images

Use the **GET** and **PUT** statements to save screen images and restore them later to the screen. **GET** allows you to save all or part of a screen, and doesn't modify the screen image. The syntax for **GET** is:

```
GET [STEP](x1!,y1!)-[STEP](x2!,y2!),array[(index%)]
```

x1!,y1! and *x2!,y2!* are the coordinates of diagonally opposite corners of the screen region to be saved. The **STEP** keyword makes a coordinate pair relative to the graphics cursor, rather than absolute.

array is the name of a numeric array where the image is stored. It should be an integer array. The method for determining the needed array size is discussed shortly. *index%* is an integer expression specifying the first array element to be used for storage; the default is the first array element.

The array must be large enough to hold the image. The size required for the array depends on three factors:

1. The number of pixels in the screen region being saved. This is calculated as *height* x *width*.

2. The number of bits required for each pixel. This depends upon the number of color attributes available in the active screen

mode. The formula for calculating bits per pixel is:

```
bits per pixel = log₂(attributes)
```

This formula generates the bits per pixel values for different PC video modes, as shown in Table 9.5.

3. The number of bit planes used in the active screen mode, shown in Table 9.6.

Table 9.5. Bits per pixel values for PC video modes.

Attributes	Modes	Bits per pixel
2	2,3,11	1
4	1,9*,10	2
16	4,7,8,9**,12	4
256	13	8

* With 64K video memory.
** With more than 64K video memory.

Table 9.6. Bit planes used in PC video modes.

Screen mode	Bit planes
1,2,11,13	1
9*, 10	2
7,8,9**,12	4

* With 64K video memory.
** With more than 64K video memory.

Once you know these three values, use them in the following formula to calculate the number of bytes needed when you save a screen image using **GET**:

```
bytes = 4 + height * planes * INT((width * bits / planes
        + 7) / 8)
```

Each element of an integer array contains two bytes, so dimension the array with size **bytes/2**. Here's an example. To save a 100x200-pixel region in screen mode 12, use the formula

```
4 + 100 * 4 *INT(200 * 4 / 4 + 7) / 8)
```

which evaluates to 10004 bytes. We could therefore use an array dimensioned **DIM Image(1 TO 5002) AS INTEGER** to hold the image.

To restore an image that was saved with **GET**, use the **PUT** statement:

```
PUT [STEP] (x!,y!),array [(index%)] [,action]
```

x!,y! are the coordinates for the upper-left corner of the restored image. The dimensions of the image were saved with the image, so there is no need to specify the other corner.

array **[(index%)]** specify the array to restore from, and (optionally) the starting array index. *action* specifies the manner in which the restored image interacts with any image already on the screen.

If you attempt to **PUT** an image that will lie totally or partially outside of the active viewport, an Illegal function call error occurs.

The *action* argument has five options: **PSET** completely overwrites the existing screen image with the saved image. **PRESET** also completely overwrites the existing screen image with the saved image, but reverses pixels (ON becomes OFF and vice versa). **AND, OR,** and **XOR** perform the indicated logical operation between saved pixels and the screen pixels. The *action* options are summarized in Table 9.7 for a monochrome screen, where a pixel is either on (1) or off (0).

The effects of the *action* options are more complex with color images, because each screen pixel is controlled by two or more bits. Table 9.7 still holds true, and the indicated combination of stored bits and screen bits occurs for each bit that controls an individual pixel. If you have a color video system, experiment to get a feel for using **PUT** to restore screen images.

Table 9.7. **PSET** action options.

Action Option	PUT pixel	Original screen pixel	Final screen pixel
PSET	0	0	0
	0	1	0
	1	0	1
	1	1	1
PRESET	0	0	1
	0	1	1
	1	0	0
	1	1	0
AND	0	0	0
	0	1	0
	1	0	0
	1	1	1
OR	0	0	0
	0	1	1
	1	0	1
	1	1	1
XOR	0	0	0
	0	1	1
	1	0	1
	1	1	0

Presentation Graphics: The Fundamentals

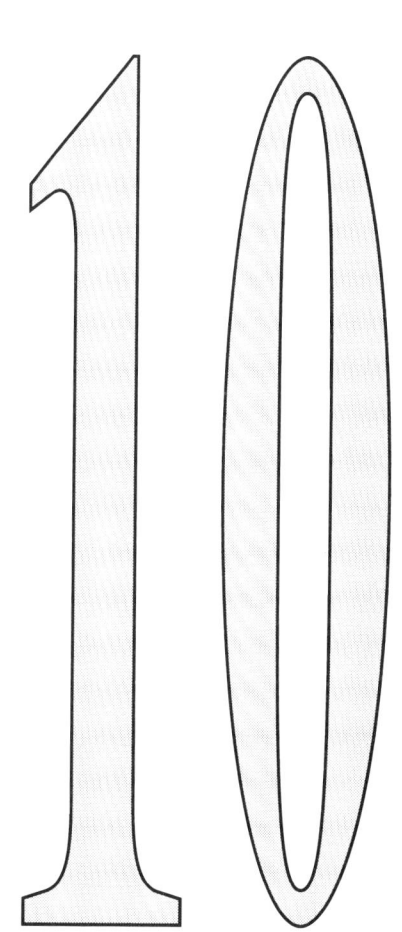

BASIC 7 includes a library of presentation-graphics routines that allow you to easily include high-quality charts in your programs. These charts are ideal for graphical presentations of business data. This chapter covers the fundamentals of BASIC 7 presentation graphics.

Data Types and Data Series

You can use BASIC 7's presentation graphics charts with two types of data: values and categories. *Values* consists of numerical data, such as weight, profit, and distance. Values can be plotted on a chart against other values, or against categories. In BASIC 7, values are represented by single-precision arrays.

A *category* is a nonnumerical classification. When referring to data about people, for example, "city of residence" and "color of hair" are two examples of category data. In BASIC 7, categories are represented by string arrays.

A *data series* is a collection of related data items. For example, if you measure the total rainfall for each month of the year, the resulting 12 values constitute a data series, which in this case is a value series. By placing those 12 values in a single-precision array, you can plot them using the BASIC 7 presentation-graphics routines. The names of the 12 months constitute another data series, which this time is a category series. If you place the names in a string array, you can use them in a chart.

Chart Types

BASIC 7 offers five types of presentation-graphics charts: pie, bar, column, line, and scatter. Except for scatter charts, all types plot values versus categories; a scatter chart plots values versus values. Most readers are probably familiar with these chart types, so the descriptions are brief. With each description is an example chart created using the default settings. Later in the chapter, the code used for creating the example figures is listed.

Pie Charts

A *pie chart* plots the values in a single data series, showing each value as a part of the total. This is the only chart type not plotted on X and Y axes. A pie chart consists of a circle divided into wedges, with one wedge for each category. The size of each wedge is proportional to the corresponding value for that category, and the total value for the entire data series corresponds to the full circle.

Pie charts are typically used for showing the contribution of each category to the whole. For example, Acme Hardware has sales figures for each of six products, as follows:

Product	Sales
Bolts	$1,500
Nuts	865
Nails	2,100
Wire	1,650
Washers	380
Screws	700

Displayed in a pie chart, this data appears as shown in Figure 10.1. Notice that the pie wedge representing the sales of nails is "exploded" from the pie for emphasis. I'll show you how to do this later when we examine the code that produced the figures.

Among all of BASIC 7's chart types, only the pie chart is limited to plotting a single data series.

Line Charts

Line charts (as well as all chart types except pie charts) plot data on a set of X and Y axes. As the name implies, the data points are usually connected by a line. Line charts are well suited for displaying trends over time. For example, Acme Hardware has compiled monthly sales figures for the year 1989, as shown in this table:

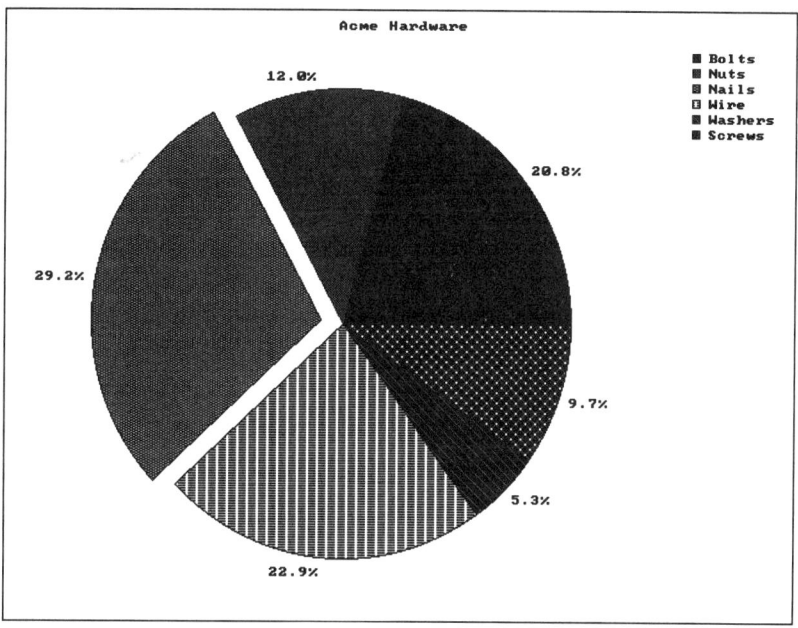

Figure 10.1. Sales data displayed in a pie chart.

Month	Gross sales
Jan	$11,500
Feb	10,650
Mar	11,250
Apr	12,680
May	13,900
Jun	15,430
Jul	17,060
Aug	17,945
Sep	16,465
Oct	15,985
Nov	13,250
Dec	9,500

A line chart that displays Acme's sales totals is shown in Figure 10.2. You can see how the seasonal sales trends are clearly shown in this type of chart.

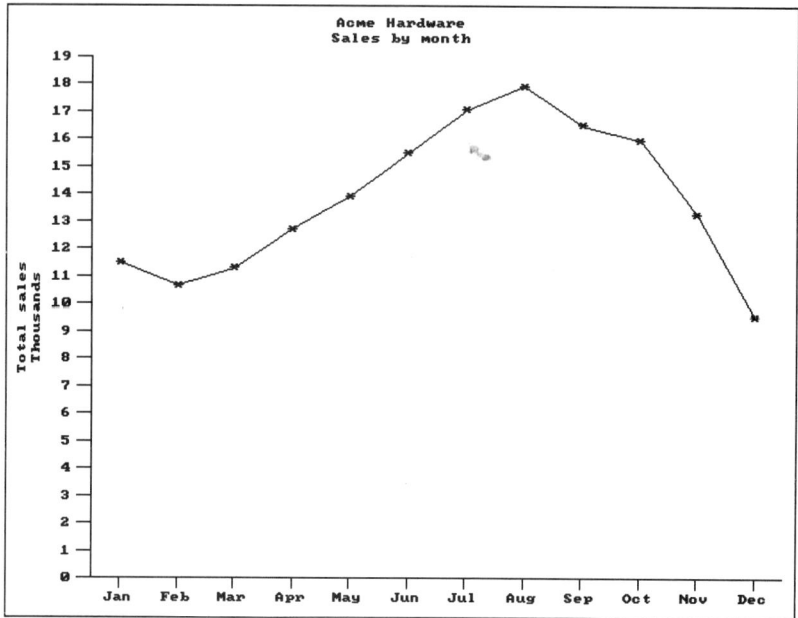

Figure 10.2. Sales data displayed as a line chart.

Column Charts

Another type of chart that illustrates trends over time is the *column chart*. BASIC 7 uses this term to refer to the type of chart usually called a bar chart and uses the term to refer to what is usually called a horizontal bar chart. Figure 10.3 shows Acme Hardware's sales data displayed in a column chart.

Bar Charts

A *bar chart* in BASIC 7 is a column chart turned on its side. The Y axis and data bars run horizontally, and the X axis runs vertically. A bar chart is often used for displaying differences between categories; it's less suited than a column chart for showing trends over time. Figure 10.4 shows Acme Hardware's sales data per product (displayed earlier in a pie chart) in bar-chart form.

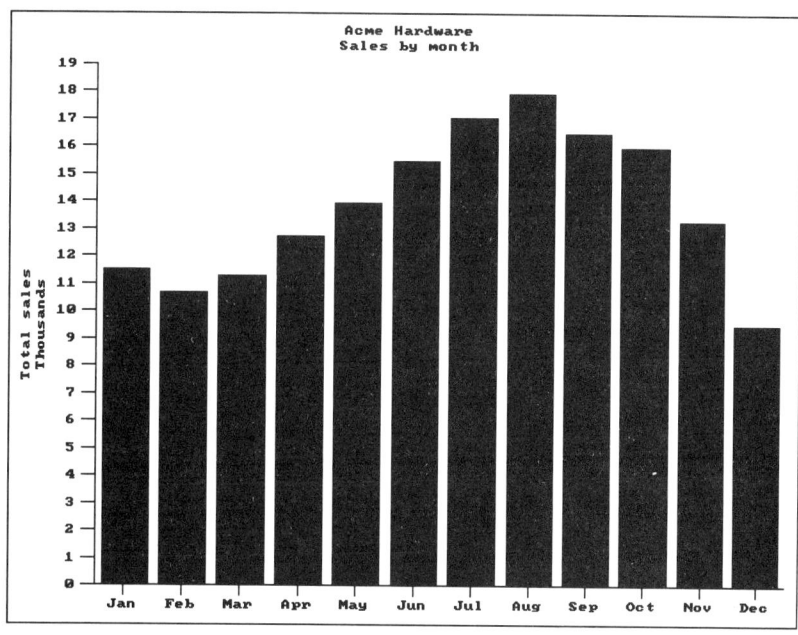

Figure 10.3. Sales data displayed in a column chart.

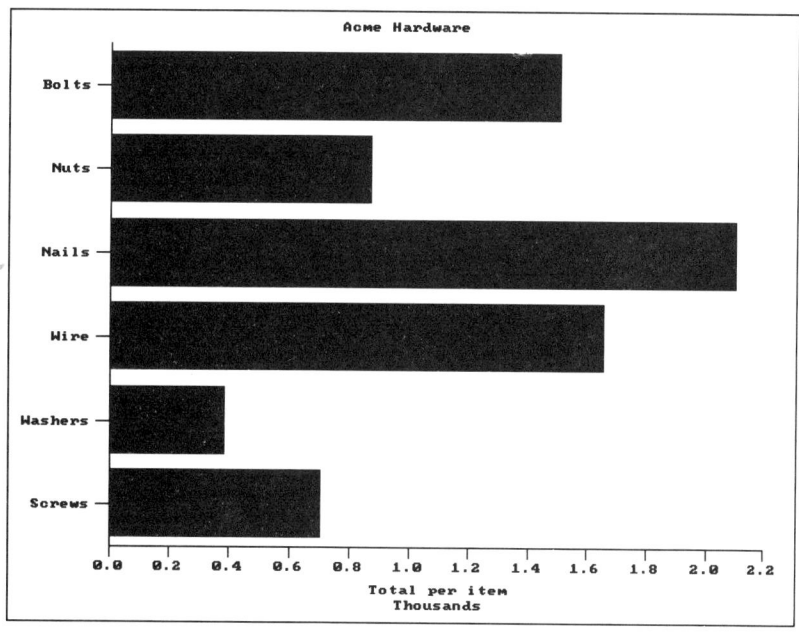

Figure 10.4. Sales data displayed in a bar chart.

Scatter Charts

A *scatter chart* is the only BASIC 7 chart type that plots values against values, rather than values against categories. Scatter charts illustrate the relationship between two sets of numeric data. Each point on a scatter chart corresponds to an (X,Y) number pair. As in the case of screen coordinates, the (X,Y) values determine the position of the point with respect to the X and Y axes. X increases toward the right, and Y increases upward.

For example, a high school principal wants to determine if there's a relationship between time spent doing homework and academic performance. The principal asks each student the number of average hours per week spent on homework. These values are plotted versus grade average on a scatter chart. The data is shown here, and the resulting chart appears in Figure 10.5.

Homework, Hours per week	Grade average
1.0	81
5.0	88
3.0	91
3.5	76
7.0	93
.5	79
12.0	92
9.0	90
5.5	85
8.0	81
2.0	86
11.0	95
7.0	91
5.0	82
2.0	72
7.5	87

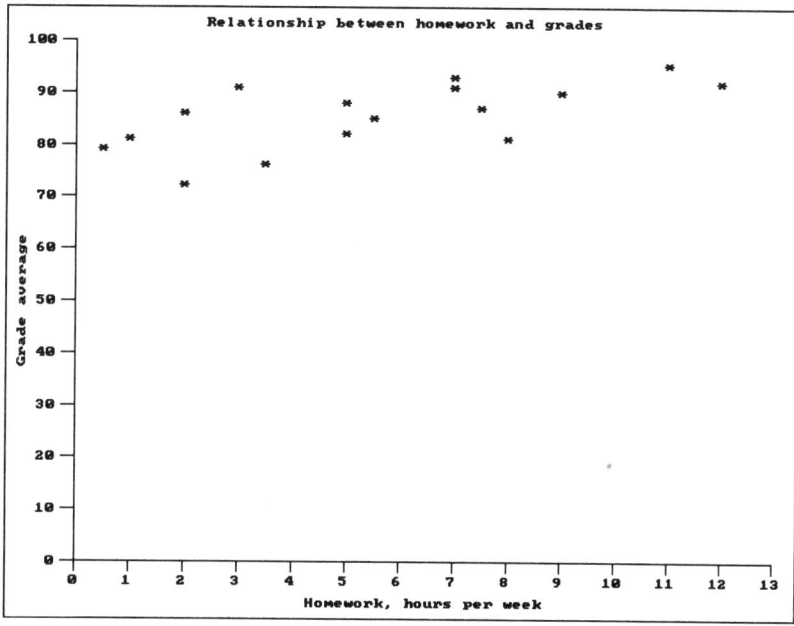

Figure 10.5. The relationship between time spent on homework and grade average, displayed as a scatter chart.

Creating Presentation Charts

The steps required to display a presentation-graphics chart are listed here, and then followed by more detailed explanations.

1. Load the Quick Library CHRTBEFR.QLB when you start QBX.

2. Include the file CHRTB.BI in your program.

3. Assemble the data to be plotted in arrays.

4. Declare a variable of type **ChartEnvironment**.

5. Set the desired graphics screen mode with the **ChartScreen** procedure.

6. Initialize the chart environment with a call to **DefaultChart**.

7. If desired, modify the chart environment to customize the chart. Otherwise, the default settings will be used.

8. Display the chart with a call to one of the chart routines.

9. Pause program execution while the chart is displayed.

Let's look now at the details involved in each of these nine steps.

Step 1

Load the Quick Library CHRTBEFR.QLB when you start QBX.

The presentation-graphics routines are contained in the Quick Library called CHRTBEFR.QLB. You load the library when you start QBX from the DOS prompt by using the /L switch, as shown here:

```
QBX /L CHRTBEFR.QLB
```

You cannot load a Quick Library from within QBX. If you are using stand alone program development, your program must be linked with the library CHRTB???.LIB. (The question marks represent characters that specify the choices of math emulation, string storage, and operating environment that you made when you installed BASIC 7.)

Step 2

Include the file CHRTB.BI in your program.

The include file CHRTB.BI contains the definitions of constants and data structures required by the presentation-graphics routines. Include this file in your program with the statement:

```
' $INCLUDE: 'CHRTB.BI'
```

Step 3

Assemble the data to be plotted in arrays.

Value data must be placed in a single-precision array; category labels must be placed in a string array. Each array must be dimensioned starting at 1, not at 0. When you plot one data series against another, corresponding array elements are paired. For example,

```
DIM Values(1 TO 4) AS SINGLE, Labels(1 TO 4) AS STRING

Values(1) = 12 : Values(2) = 8 : Values(3) = 10 : Values(4) = 5
Labels(1) = "Spring" : Labels(2) = "Summer"
Labels(3) = "Autumn" : Labels(4) = "Winter"
```

When these two data series are plotted, **Values(1)** is paired with **Labels(1), Values(2)** with **Labels(2)**, and so on.

Data can be placed into the arrays from any source: the keyboard, a disk file, a modem, and so on. In the examples given later, **DATA** and **READ** statements are used for placing data into the arrays.

Step 4

Declare a variable of type **ChartEnvironment**.

A variable of the user-defined type **ChartEnvironment** contains all of the information that defines the chart (except for the data). You must declare at least one such variable in your program in this way:

```
DIM Env AS ChartEnvironment
```

ChartEnvironment is defined in the include file CHRTB.BI. (We'll look at the components of this data type in detail in the next chapter.) The presentation-graphics routines automatically initialize the **ChartEnvironment** structure with default values. You can use these defaults, or modify them as shown in the next chapter.

Step 5

Set the desired graphics screen mode using the **ChartScreen** procedure.

You must use **ChartScreen** instead of **SCREEN**. The syntax for **ChartScreen** is:

```
ChartScreen mode%
```

where **mode%** is one of the standard graphics screen modes. Even if you previously set a graphics mode using **SCREEN**, you still must call **ChartScreen**.

Step 6

Initialize the chart environment with a call to **DefaultChart**.

The **DefaultChart** procedure initializes the presentation-graphics system, and then loads the **ChartEnvironment** structure with defaults. The syntax for **DefaultChart** is:

```
DefaultChart( Env, ChartType, ChartOption)
```

Env is a variable of the type **ChartEnvironment**. *ChartType* is a value between 1 and 5 that specifies the type of chart. The include file CHRTB.BI defines constants you can use to specify the chart type:

Constant	Value
cBar	1
cColumn	2
cLine	3
cScatter	4
cPie	5

ChartOption is a value of 1 or 2 that specifies chart style. Two style options are available for each chart type. Table 10.1 lists the options for each chart type, along with the constant defined in CHRTB.BI that you can use in the **DefaultChart** call.

Step 7

If desired, modify the chart environment to customize the chart. Otherwise, the default settings will be used.

You can, for example, add titles to a chart and change its colors. Customizing the chart is covered in detail in Chapter 11.

Step 8

Display the chart with a call to one of the chart routines.

Table 10.1. Chart type options.

Chart type	*ChartOption* = 1	*ChartOption* = 2
Pie	With percentages (**cPercent**)	Without percentages (**cNoPercent**)
Bar	Side by side (**cPlain**)	Stacked (**cStacked**)
Column	Side by side (**cPlain**)	Stacked (**cStacked**)
Scatter	Lines between points (**cLines**)	No lines between points (**cNoLines**)
Line	Lines between points (**cLines**)	No lines between points (**cNoLines**)

Three separate routines are available for displaying charts. To display a bar, column, or line chart, use **Chart**:

```
Chart (Env, Categories(), Values(), n%)
```

Env is the **ChartEnvironment** variable that was initialized with the call to **DefaultChart**. *Categories()* is the string array containing the category labels to be plotted. *Values()* is the single-precision array containing the values to be plotted. *n%* is the number of data points to plot.

To display a pie chart, use **ChartPie**:

```
ChartPie (Env, Categories(), Values(), Explode(), n%)
```

Env is the **ChartEnvironment** variable that was initialized with the call to **DefaultChart**. *Categories()* is the string array containing the category labels to be plotted, and *Values()* is the single-precision array containing the values to be plotted. *explode()* is an integer array controlling the "exploding" of pie wedges. A value of 1 in this array causes the corresponding wedge to be exploded; a value of 0 results in a normal nonexploded wedge. *n%* is the number of data points to plot.

To display a scatter chart, use **ChartScatter**:

```
ChartScatter ( Env, Values1(), Values2(), n%)
```

Env is the **ChartEnvironment** variable that was initialized with the call to **DefaultChart**. *Values1()* is the single-precision array containing the values to be plotted on the X axis. *Values2()* is the single-precision array containing the values to be plotted on the Y axis, and *n%* is the number of data points to plot.

Step 9

Pause program execution while the chart is displayed.

This step is usually performed by using **SLEEP** to wait for a keypress.

The following demonstration program creates the five sample charts displayed earlier in the chapter. Except for adding some titles, the default chart environment is used for these charts.

```
' Demonstrates basic presentation-graphics charts.

' $INCLUDE: 'chrtb.bi'

' Constant for desired video mode. Change this if needed for
' your video system.

CONST VIDEOMODE = 11

' Dimension a ChartEnvironment structure and set the video '
' mode.

DIM Env AS ChartEnvironment

CALL ChartScreen(VIDEOMODE)

' ******************* Pie chart*******************

' Set up arrays for pie chart data, then read data values.
```

```
DIM PieData(6) AS SINGLE
DIM PieLabels(6) AS STRING
DIM Exploded(6) AS INTEGER

FOR i% = 1 TO 6
  READ PieData(i%), PieLabels(i%), Exploded(i%)
NEXT i%

' Initialize chart environment.

CALL DefaultChart(Env, cPie, cPercent)

' Define chart title and options.

Env.ChartWindow.Border = cYes
Env.MainTitle.Title = "Acme Hardware"

' Display the chart.

CALL ChartPie(Env, PieLabels(), PieData(), Exploded(), 6)

' Wait for a keypress.

SLEEP

'*******************Line chart********************

' Set up arrays for line chart data, then read data values.

DIM LineData(12) AS SINGLE
DIM LineLabels(12) AS STRING

FOR i% = 1 TO 12
  READ LineData(i%), LineLabels(i%)
NEXT i%

' Initialize chart environment.

CALL DefaultChart(Env, cLine, cLines)

' Define chart titles and options.

Env.MainTitle.Title = "Acme Hardware"
```

```
Env.SubTitle.Title = "Sales by month"
Env.YAxis.AxisTitle.Title = "Total sales"
Env.ChartWindow.Border = cYes

' Display the chart.

CALL Chart(Env, LineLabels(), LineData(), 12)

SLEEP

'*******************Column chart**************

' Uses same data that was used for the line chart.

CALL DefaultChart(Env, cColumn, cPlain)
' Define chart titles and options.

Env.MainTitle.Title = "Acme Hardware"
Env.SubTitle.Title = "Sales by month"
Env.YAxis.AxisTitle.Title = "Total sales"
Env.ChartWindow.Border = cYes

CALL Chart(Env, LineLabels(), LineData(), 12)

SLEEP

'*******************Bar chart*****************

' Uses same data that was used for the pie chart.

CALL DefaultChart(Env, cBar, cPlain)

Env.ChartWindow.Border = cYes
Env.MainTitle.Title = "Acme Hardware"
Env.XAxis.AxisTitle.Title = "Total per item"

CALL Chart(Env, PieLabels(), PieData(), 6)

SLEEP

'****************Scatter chart****************
```

```
' Set up arrays for scatter-chart data, then read the data.

DIM Homework(16) AS SINGLE, Grade(16) AS SINGLE

FOR i% = 1 TO 16
  READ Homework(i%)
NEXT i%

FOR i% = 1 TO 16
  READ Grade(i%)
NEXT i%


' Initialize chart environment.

CALL DefaultChart(Env, cScatter, cNoLines)

' Define chart titles and options.

Env.ChartWindow.Border = cYes
Env.MainTitle.Title = "Relationship between homework and grades"
Env.XAxis.AxisTitle.Title = "Homework, hours per week"
Env.YAxis.AxisTitle.Title = "Grade average"

' Display chart.

CALL ChartScatter(Env, Homework(), Grade(), 16)
SLEEP
SCREEN 0

END

'************************************************
' Pie chart data.

DATA 1500, "Bolts", 0, 865, "Nuts", 0, 2100, "Nails", 1
DATA 1650, "Wire", 0, 380, "Washers", 0, 700, "Screws",0

' Line chart data.

DATA 11500, "Jan", 10650, "Feb", 11250, "Mar", 12680, "Apr"
DATA 13900, "May", 15430, "Jun", 17060, "Jul", 17945, "Aug"
DATA 16465, "Sep", 15985, "Oct", 13250, "Nov", 9500, "Dec"
```

```
' Scatter chart data.

DATA 1, 5, 3, 3.5, 7, .5, 12, 9, 5.5, 8, 2, 11, 7, 5, 2, 7.5
DATA 81, 88, 91, 76, 93, 79, 92, 90, 85, 81, 86, 95, 91, 82
DATA 72, 87
```

Multiple Series Charts

The BASIC 7 presentation-graphics routines also allow you to create multiple-series charts. A *multiple-series* chart plots two or more data series on a single chart. (The examples given earlier in this chapter are single-series charts.) An example of a multiple-series chart is a chart that plots both total monthly rainfall and average temperature. All chart types (except pie charts) can display multiple series. Figures 10.6 and 10.7 illustrate a multiple-series column chart and a multiple-series scatter chart, respectively.

The steps for creating a multiple-series chart are essentially the same as those just listed for creating single-series charts, except for

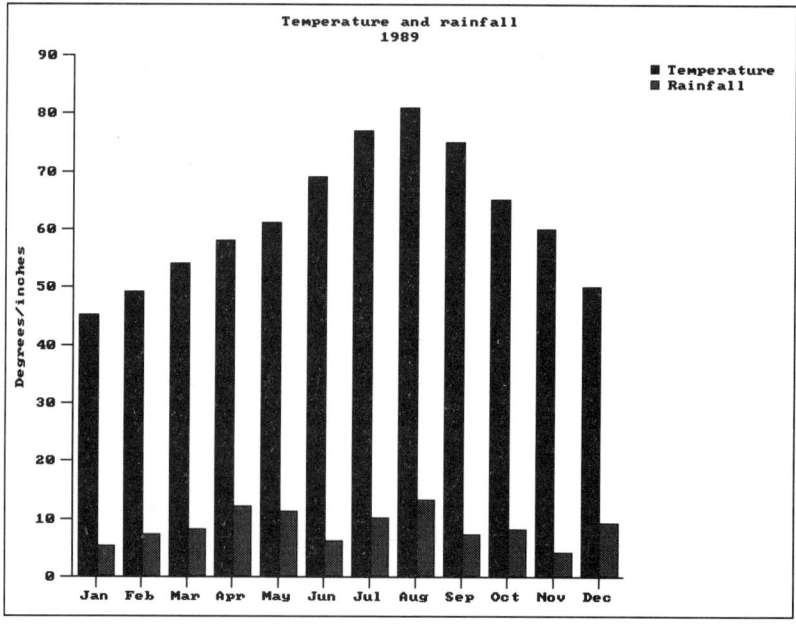

Figure 10.6. A multiple-series column chart.

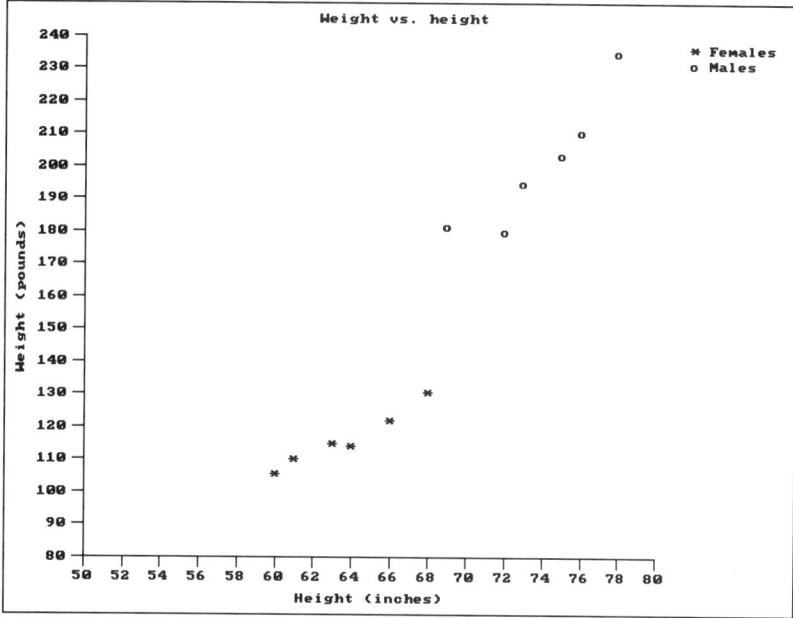

Figure 10.7. A multiple-series scatter chart.

step 8. The procedures that you call for multiple-series charts are different than those for single-series charts. Data for a multiple-series chart must be stored in a two-dimensional single-precision array. The first dimension of the array corresponds to the number of data points per series, and the second dimension corresponds to the number of series. For example, let's say you want to plot monthly sales for two stores over the past year. There are two data series, one for each store. Each series contains 12 data points that each correspond to one month. Your array needs to be the following:

```
DIM SalesData (1 TO 12, 1 to 2) AS SINGLE
```

The January sales figure for store 1 goes in **SalesData(1,1)**, the February figure for store 1 in **SalesData(2,1)**, the January figure for store 2 in **SalesData(1,2)**, and so on.

Multiple-series bar, column, and line charts plot multiple-value series against a single-category series (e.g., "Months" in the example in the previous paragraph). The category labels are treated in the same way as the category labels for a single series chart, and are placed into a string array.

A multiple-series scatter chart plots multiple series of Y values against multiple series of X values. Let's say you want to create a plot of height versus weight for men and women. The height values for men comprise one Y series, and the height values for women comprise another Y series. These values are stored in a two-dimensional array, in the same manner as the values for the multiple-series bar, column, and line charts just described.

The weight values for men and women each comprise one X series. These values are stored in the same way that the Y series are stored, in a two-dimensional array. Array elements are paired on a 1:1 basis: **Yarray(1,1)** is plotted against **Xarray(1,1)**, **Yarray(2,1)** is plotted against **Xarray(2,1)**, and so on.

A multiple-series chart needs some way to identify the series. To meet this need, labels to identify the series are placed in a one-dimensional string array, which is then passed as an argument to the chart procedure. Each label in this array identifies one series. The labels are displayed on the chart, along with a key that relates each label to the proper plot.

The methods for creating multiple-series plots will seem clearer after you examine the next example. First, however, we need to look at the procedures that display multiple-series plots.

To display a multiple-series bar, column, or line chart, call **ChartMS**. (The type displayed is determined by the *ChartType* argument that was passed to **DefaultChart**.) The syntax for **ChartMS** is:

```
ChartMS (Env, Categories(), Values(), n%, first%, last%,
labels())
```

Env is the **ChartEnvironment** variable initialized with the call to **DefaultChart**. *Categories()* is the string array containing the category labels to be plotted, and *Values()* is the two-dimensional, single-precision array containing two or more data series to be plotted. *n%* is the number of data points to plot (the number of values in each series).

first% and *last%* are integer expressions specifying the first and last data series in *values()* to be plotted. With a data array that contains *n* series, set *first%* = 1 and *last%* = *n* to plot all data series. Set *first%*

and *last%* to intermediate values to plot a contiguous subset of the data series.

labels() is the string array containing the series identification labels.

To create a multiple-series scatter chart, use the **ChartScatterMS** procedure:

```
ChartScatterMS ( Env, XValues(), YValues(), n%, first%, last%,
                 labels() )
```

Env is the **ChartEnvironment** variable initialized with the call to **DefaultChart**. *XValues()* is the two-dimensional, single-precision array containing two or more data series to be plotted on the X axis. *YValues()* is the two-dimensional, single-precision array containing two or more data series to be plotted on the Y axis. *n%* is the number of data points to plot (the number of values in each series).

first% and *last%* are integer expressions specifying the first and last data series in *values()* to be plotted. *labels()* is the string array containing the series identification labels.

The process of creating multiple-series charts is demonstrated by the following program, which produces the charts shown in Figures 10.6 and 10.7.

```
' Demonstrates multiple-series, presentation-graphics charts.

' $INCLUDE: 'chrtb.bi'

' Constant for desired video mode. Change this if needed for
' your video system.

CONST VIDEOMODE = 11

' Dimension a ChartEnvironment structure and set the video
' mode.

DIM Env AS ChartEnvironment

CALL ChartScreen(VIDEOMODE)

' ***************Multiple-series column chart***************

' Dimension the arrays needed for data and labels.
```

```
DIM Months(1 TO 12) AS STRING
DIM Weather(1 TO 12, 1 TO 2) AS SINGLE
DIM Labels(1 TO 2) AS STRING

' Read data into arrays.

FOR i% = 1 TO 12
    READ Months(i%)
NEXT i%

FOR i% = 1 TO 2
  FOR j% = 1 TO 12
    READ Weather(j%, i%)
  NEXT j%
NEXT i%

' Series labels.

Labels(1) = "Temperature"
Labels(2) = "Rainfall"

CALL DefaultChart(Env, cColumn, cPlain)

' Define chart titles and options.

Env.MainTitle.Title = "Temperature and rainfall"
Env.SubTitle.Title = "1989"
Env.YAxis.AxisTitle.Title = "Degrees/inches"
Env.ChartWindow.Border = cYes

CALL ChartMS(Env, Months(), Weather(), 12, 1, 2, Labels())

SLEEP

'***************Multiple-series scatter chart****************

' Set up arrays for scatter-chart data, then read the data.

DIM Height(1 TO 6, 1 TO 2) AS SINGLE
DIM Weight(1 TO 6, 1 TO 2) AS SINGLE

FOR j% = 1 TO 2
  FOR i% = 1 TO 6
    READ Height(i%, j%)
```

```
    NEXT i%
  NEXT j%

  FOR j% = 1 TO 2
    FOR i% = 1 TO 6
      READ Weight(i%, j%)
    NEXT i%
  NEXT j%

  ' Reuse Labels() string array.

  Labels(1) = "Females"
  Labels(2) = "Males"

  ' Initialize chart environment.

  CALL DefaultChart(Env, cScatter, cNoLines)

  ' Define chart titles and options.

  Env.ChartWindow.Border = cYes
  Env.MainTitle.Title = "Weight vs. height"
  Env.XAxis.AxisTitle.Title = "Comparing males and females"
  Env.YAxis.AxisTitle.Title = "Weight (pounds)"
  Env.XAxis.AxisTitle.Title = "Height (inches)"
  Env.XAxis.ScaleMin = 50
  Env.YAxis.ScaleMin = 80

  ' Display chart.

  CALL ChartScatterMS(Env, Height(), Weight(), 6, 1, 2, Labels())

  SLEEP
  SCREEN 0

  END

  '**********************************************

  ' Multiple-series, column-chart data.

  DATA "Jan", "Feb", "Mar", "Apr", "May", "Jun"
  DATA "Jul", "Aug", "Sep", "Oct", "Nov", "Dec"
```

```
DATA 45, 49, 54, 58, 61, 69, 77, 81, 75, 65, 60, 50
DATA 5, 7, 8, 12, 11, 6, 10, 13, 7, 8, 4, 9

' Multiple-series, scatter-chart data.

DATA 61, 63, 64, 60, 66, 68
DATA 72, 69, 76, 75, 73, 78
DATA 110, 115, 114, 105, 122, 130
DATA 180, 181, 210, 203, 195, 235
```

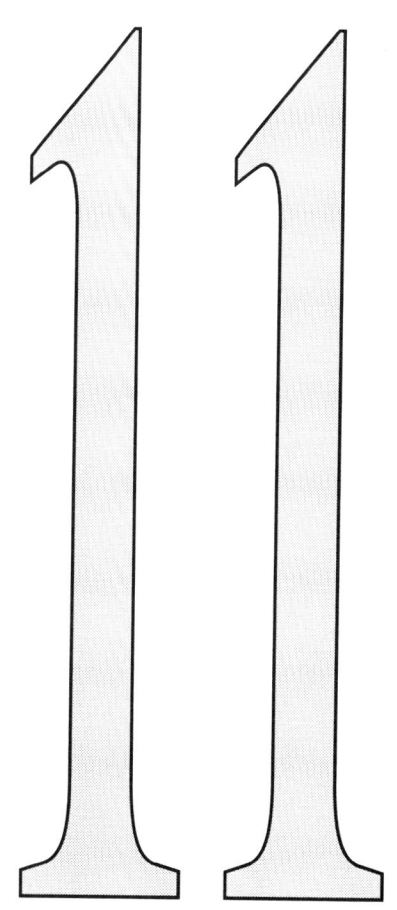

Presentation Graphics: Advanced Topics

Chapter 10 showed you how to quickly and easily create charts using the presentation-graphics system's defaults. This chapter covers the methods for customizing your charts to meet special needs.

Constants

The include file CHRTB.BI defines a variety of constants that you can use when passing option arguments to many of the presentation-graphics routines. Note that all of the presentation graphics constants start with a lowercase "c" and are *mnemonic* (their names remind you of their function). The constants are listed here as they appear in CHRTB.BI.

```
CONST cPalLen = 15              ' Length of charting palette

CONST cMissingValue = -3.4E+38 ' Denotes "missing" data value

CONST cNo = 0
CONST cYes = NOT cNo

CONST cLeft = 1                 ' title placement
CONST cCenter = 2
CONST cRight = 3

CONST cCategory = 1             ' category axis
CONST cValue = 2                ' value axis

CONST cNormFormat = 1           ' tic labels in decimal format
CONST cExpFormat = 2            ' tic labels in exp format

CONST cLinear = 1               ' linear axis
CONST cLog = 2                  ' log axis

CONST cOverlay = 1              ' Legend.Place
CONST cBottom = 2

CONST cBar = 1                  ' bar chart
CONST cPlain = 1                ' unstacked data
CONST cStacked = 2              ' stacked data
```

```
CONST cColumn = 2                  ' column chart

CONST cLine = 3                    ' line chart
CONST cLines = 1                   ' Lines connecting points
CONST cNoLines = 2                 ' No lines connecting points

CONST cScatter = 4                 ' scatter chart

CONST cPie = 5                     ' pie chart
CONST cPercent = 1                 ' Displays slice percent
CONST cNoPercent = 2               ' Doesn't display slice percent

' Constant definitions for error messages (numbers greater
' than 100 are "fatal" errors and will cause charting
' routines to exit):
CONST cBadDataWindow = 105     ' DataWindow calculated too small
CONST cBadLegendWindow = 110   ' LegendWindow coordinates invalid
CONST cBadLogBase = 15         ' LogBase <= 0
CONST cBadScaleFactor = 20     ' ScaleFactor = 0
CONST cBadScreen = 25          ' Invalid screen mode
CONST cBadStyle = 30           ' Invalid chart style
CONST cBadType = 135           ' Invalid chart type
CONST cTooFewSeries = 155      ' Too few series (First > Last)
CONST cTooSmallN = 160         ' No data in series (N=0)
CONST cBadPalette = 165        ' Palette not dimensioned
                               ' correctly
CONST cPalettesNotSet = 170    ' Palette not init'd
                               ' (GetPaletteDef)
CONST cNoFontSpace = 175       ' No room to load default font
CONST cCLUnexpectedOff = 200   ' Added to ERR for unexpected
                               ' error
```

The Chart Environment

All presentation-graphics charts depend on information stored in a user-defined structure of type **ChartEnvironment**. This type is defined in the include file CHRTB.BI as follows:

```
TYPE ChartEnvironment
    ChartType    AS INTEGER
    ChartStyle   AS INTEGER
```

```
DataFont    AS INTEGER
ChartWindow AS RegionType
DataWindow  AS RegionType
MainTitle   AS TitleType
SubTitle    AS TitleType
XAxis       AS AxisType
YAxis       AS AxisType
Legend      AS LegendType
END TYPE
```

The members of the type **ChartEnvironment** are primarily other user-defined types (which are discussed later in this chapter). The three **INTEGER** members are:

1. **ChartType** determines the type of chart to be plotted: 1 = Bar, 2 = Column, 3 = Line, 4 = Scatter, 5 = Pie. **ChartType** is loaded with the value passed as the second argument to **DefaultChart**.

2. **ChartStyle** is an **INTEGER** value of 1 or 2 specifying one of two available chart styles. This member is loaded with the value passed as the third argument to **DefaultChart**. (See Chapter 10 for information on chart styles.)

3. **DataFont** is an **INTEGER** value that specifies the font to use for the data-point characters in line and scatter charts. The number of fonts available depends upon which optional fonts (if any) you have loaded. The default value is 1. (See the section on Using Fonts later in this chapter.)

Chart Titles

Each chart title is controlled by a structure of type **TitleType**, defined in CHRTB.BI as follows:

```
TYPE TitleType
    Title      AS STRING * 70
    TitleFont  AS INTEGER
    TitleColor AS INTEGER
```

```
    Justify      AS INTEGER
END TYPE
```

Title is a fixed-length string that holds the text of the title, with a maximum length of 70. **TitleFont** is an integer value that specifies the font to use for the data-point characters in line and scatter charts. The number of fonts available depends upon which optional fonts (if any) you have loaded. The default value is 1. (See the section on Using Fonts later in this chapter.)

TitleColor is an integer between 0 and the value of the constant **cPalLen** (15 by default) that specifies the title color. Colors are defined as entries in the color palette (described later in this chapter). The default value is 1.

Justify is an integer that specifies how the title is positioned on the chart. Possible values are 1 (**cLeft**) for left justified, 2 (**cCenter**) for centered, and 3 (**cRight**) for right justified.

Chart Axes

All chart types, except pie, have both X and Y axes. The characteristics of each axis are controlled by information in a variable of user-defined type **AxisType**, defined in CHRTB.BI as follows:

```
TYPE AxisType
    Grid         AS INTEGER
    GridStyle    AS INTEGER
    AxisTitle    AS TitleType
    AxisColor    AS INTEGER
    Labeled      AS INTEGER
    RangeType    AS INTEGER
    LogBase      AS SINGLE
    AutoScale    AS INTEGER
    ScaleMin     AS SINGLE
    ScaleMax     AS SINGLE
    ScaleFactor  AS SINGLE
    ScaleTitle   AS TitleType
    TicFont      AS INTEGER
    TicInterval  AS SINGLE
    TicFormat    AS INTEGER
```

```
      TicDecimals  AS INTEGER
   END TYPE
```

Grid is a true/false (cYes/cNo) value that determines whether the axis is displayed with grid lines. Grid lines are drawn perpendicular to the axis, one line per tick mark, and span the entire data window. Grid lines are drawn in the color of the other axis (i.e., the axis they are parallel to).

GridStyle is an integer between 0 and **cPalLen** (15 by default) that specifies the line style (dotted, dashed, etc.) to use in drawing the grid lines. Line styles are defined as entries in the border-style palette (described later in this chapter).

AxisTitle is a structure of type **TitleType** that defines the axis title. **AxisColor** is an integer between 0 and the value of **cPalLen** (15 by default) that specifies the axis color. Colors are defined as entries in the color palette. The default value is 1. This entry specifies only axis color, not axis-title color.

Labeled is a true/false (**cYes/cNo**) value that determines whether tick marks and tick-mark labels are drawn on the axis.

RangeType affects only an axis that is plotting value data. A value of 1 (**cLinear**) creates a linear axis; a value of 2 (**cLog**) creates a logarithmic axis. The default is 1. **LogBase** determines the logarithm base used if **RangeType** is set to **cLog**. The default value is 10.

AutoScale is a true/false (**cYes/cNo**) value that determines whether the presentation-graphics routines automatically determine the proper scale for the axis. If **AutoScale** is set to **cYes**, the routines automatically determine values for **ScaleMax**, **ScaleFactor**, **ScaleTitle**, **TicInterval**, **TicFormat**, and **TicDecimals**, based on the data being plotted. If **AutoScale** is set to **cNo**, the program must provide values for these structure members.

ScaleMin is a single-precision value that specifies the lowest data value represented on the axis. **ScaleMax** is a single-precision value that specifies the highest data value represented on the axis.

ScaleFactor is a value used for dividing all data values before they are plotted; the default is 1. Use **ScaleFactor** to plot extremely large or small values more clearly. For example, to plot the Federal deficit (which ranges between 100 and 200 billion these days) set **ScaleFactor**

to 1,000,000,000 (one billion), **ScaleMin** to 50, **ScaleMax** to 200, and **ScaleTitle.Title** to "billions".

ScaleTitle is a **TitleType** structure that defines the plotting scale used. If **AutoScale** = **cYes** and **ScaleFactor** <> 1, the presentation-graphics routines automatically provide a scale description.

TicFont is an integer value that specifies the font to use for the axis tick marks. The number of fonts available depends on which optional fonts (if any) you have loaded. The default value is 1. (See the section on Using Fonts later in this chapter.) **TicInterval** determines the interval between tick marks. This value is specified in data units.

TicFormat is an integer value that specifies the format used for numerical tick labels. Use 1 (**cDecFormat**) for normal decimal format, 2 (**cExpFormat**) for exponential format. The default is 1. (Note: My copy of CHRTB.BI does not define these two constants, even though they are mentioned in the documentation. You can add them to CHRTB.BI yourself, if you like.)

TicDecimals is an integer value between 0 and 9 specifying the number of digits to display to the right of the decimal point in tick-mark labels.

Chart Regions

Each presentation-graphics chart consists of three regions: the chart region, the data region, and the legend region. The *chart region* encompasses the entire chart. Within the chart region are the *data region* (the area bounded by the two axes) and the *legend region* (the region where the legend is displayed). Each region is associated with a **RegionType** structure, which controls the region's size, screen placement, colors, and so on. Modify the member variables of these structures to change the way the regions are displayed. For example, charts are normally displayed full screen. By changing the dimensions of the chart region, you can display a chart that occupies only a portion of the screen.

The **RegionType** structure is defined in CHRTB.BI as follows:

```
TYPE RegionType
   X1              AS INTEGER
```

```
    Y1          AS INTEGER
    X2          AS INTEGER
    Y2          AS INTEGER
    Background  AS INTEGER
    Border      AS INTEGER
    BorderStyle AS INTEGER
    BorderColor AS INTEGER
END TYPE
```

X1, **Y1**, **X2**, and **Y2** are integers that specify (in pixels) the screen location of the top-left corner (X1, Y1) and bottom-right corner (X2, Y2) of the region. The chart region is positioned relative to the upper-left screen corner. The data and legend regions are positioned relative to the upper-left corner of the chart region.

Background is an integer between 0 and the value of the constant **cPalLen** (15 by default) that specifies the region's background color. Colors are defined as entries in the color palette. The default value is 0.

Border is a true/false (**cYes/cNo**) value that determines whether a border is drawn around the region. **BorderStyle** is an integer between 0 and **cPalLen** that specifies a line style to use for the border (if one is drawn). Line styles are defined as entries in the border style palette. The default value of **BorderStyle** is 1.

BorderColor is an integer between 0 and **cPalLen** that specifies the border color. Colors are defined as entries in the color palette. The default value is 1.

Chart Legend

The characteristics of the chart's legend are controlled by a structure of type **LegendType**, defined in CHRTB.BI as follows:

```
TYPE LegendType
    Legend      AS INTEGER
    Place       AS INTEGER
    TextColor   AS INTEGER
    TextFont    AS INTEGER
    AutoSize    AS INTEGER
    LegendWindow AS RegionType
END TYPE
```

Legend is a true/false (**cYes/cNo**) variable that determines whether a legend is displayed on the chart. **Place** is an integer variable that specifies the position of the legend. Use 1 (**cOverLay**) to position the legend within the data window, 2 (**cBottom**) to position the legend below the data window, and 3 (**cRight**) to position the legend to the right of the data window. If you use **cBottom** or **cRight**, the data window is automatically sized to accommodate the legend.

TextColor is an integer between 0 and **cPalLen** that specifies the legend text color. Colors are defined as entries in the color palette. The default value is 1.

TextFont is an integer value that specifies the font to use for the legend text. The number of fonts available depends on which optional fonts (if any) you have loaded. The default value is 1. (See the section on Using Fonts later in this chapter.)

AutoSize is a true/false (**cYes/cNo**) variable that specifies whether the size of the legend window is automatically determined by the presentation-graphics routines. If **AutoSize** is set to **cNo**, the program must specify the size.

LegendWindow is a **RegionType** structure whose members specify the color, size, and other characteristics of the legend window.

Modifying the Chart Environment

There is no secret to customizing your presentation-graphics charts by modifying the chart environment: simply modify the appropriate structure member(s) after calling **DefaultChart**, but before calling the actual display procedure. Customization is made easier by the analysis routines, which are discussed later in this chapter.

Presentation-Graphics Palettes

The presentation-graphics system uses a series of *palettes* to control the way that various chart elements are displayed. Do not confuse the presentation-graphics palettes with the color palettes used by certain video adapters—the concept is similar, but the two types of palettes are distinct.

Five palettes are available in presentation-graphics, and each contains entries numbered from 0 to **cPalLen**. In the current version of BASIC 7, **cPalLen** is defined as 15 in CHRTB.BI, so each palette has 16 members. The five palettes are:

- The *color* palette, which contains different colors used for plot symbols, titles, and other chart elements. Entries in this palette are color attributes.

- The *line style* palette, which contains different line styles (solid, dotted, etc.) used for the lines in line and scatter charts. Entries in this palette are integers that specify line style in the same manner that the **LINE** statement specifies line style.

- The *fill-pattern* palette contains fill patterns that are used on monochrome displays for different data series in column and bar charts, and for different wedges in pie charts. Entries in this palette are strings that determine the bit pattern of the fill in the same manner that bit patterns are determined for tiling.

- The *plot-character* palette contains different characters (* o x, etc.) used for the data points in line and scatter charts. Each entry in this palette is an integer specifying the ASCII value of the character to use.

- The *border-style* palette contains different line styles used for grid lines and the borders of screen regions. Entries in this palette are integers specifying line style in the same manner that integers specify line style for the line-style palette.

Except for the border styles, all palettes serve one primary purpose: to help distinguish different data series from each other on a multiple-series chart. Thus, data series 1 would be plotted using entry number 1 from whatever palette is appropriate: plot symbol #1 in the case of a line chart, fill pattern #1 in the case of a monochrome column chart, or color #1 in the case of a color bar chart. Data series number 2 would be plotted using palette entry #2, and so on.

The exact contents of the palettes depend upon the video hardware installed and the screen mode set using the **ChartScreen** procedure. For most situations, the default palettes are all you will need. To modify palettes, follow this procedure:

1. Retrieve the current palettes with a call to **GetPaletteDef**.

2. Modify individual palette entries as desired.

3. Make the modified palettes current with a call to **SetPaletteDef**.

4. When finished, restore the default palette entries with a call to **ResetPaletteDef**.

The respective syntax of these procedures is as follows:

```
GetPaletteDef( Colors%(), Lines%(), Fills$(), Chars%(),
              Borders%())

SetPaletteDef( Colors%(), Lines%(), Fills$(), Chars%(),
              Borders%())

ResetPaletteDef
```

Each of the five arrays passed as arguments must be dimensioned 0 to 15. The individual arrays are:

- *Colors%()*, which is an integer array containing color attributes.

- *Lines%()*, which is an integer array containing line styles.

- *Fills$()*, which is a string array containing fill styles. Creating new fill styles is simplified by the procedures **MakeChartPattern$** and **GetPattern$**, which are described in the BASIC 7 documentation.

- *Chars%()*, which is an integer array containing ASCII codes.

- *Borders%()*, which is an integer array containing line styles.

GetPaletteDef copies the current palettes into the arrays passed as arguments. **SetPaletteDef** reverses the process, copying the arrays into the presentation-graphics palettes. As an example, the following code shows how to change the characters used for data series 1 and 2. The default characters are * and o, and this code changes them to @ and $.

```
...
DIM Colors%(15), Lines%(15), Fills$(15), Chars%(15),
    Borders%(15)
...
GetPaletteDef(Colors%(), Lines%(), Fills$(),Chars%(),Borders%())
Chars%(1) = ASC("@")
Chars%(2) = ASC("$")
SetPaletteDef(Colors%(), Lines%(), Fills$(), Chars%(),Borders%())
...
```

Note that it's necessary to retrieve all palettes, even if you want to change only one. You cannot selectively retrieve a single palette.

Chart Analysis Routines

The presentation-graphics analysis routines can be very useful when you want to customize a chart's environment. Five analysis routines that each correspond to one of the chart display routines are available:

```
AnalyzeChart
AnalyzeChartMS
AnalyzePie
AnalyzeScatter
AnalyzeScatterMS
```

Each analysis routine takes exactly the same arguments as the corresponding display routine. It does everything the display routine does, except display the chart. The analysis routine analyzes the data and fills in the chart environment accordingly. You can then modify selected environment variables to customize the chart, and finally call the display routine.

Here's an example. Perhaps you feel that the scatter chart's automatic Y axis scaling provides too small a scale. Using an analysis routine, you could enlarge the scale as shown in this code fragment:

```
CALL DefaultChart(Env, cScatter, cNoLines)
CALL AnalyzeScatter(Env, Data1(), Data2(), num%)

' Enlarge the Y axis scale.

Env.YAxis.ScaleMin = Env.YAxis.ScaleMin * 0.9
Env.YAxis.ScaleMax = Env.YAxis.ScaleMax * 1.1
Env.YAxis.AutoScale = cNo

' Display chart.

CALL ChartScatter(Env, Data1(), Data2(), num%)
```

Labeling Charts

Two routines let you place explanatory labels anywhere on the chart. **LabelChartH** displays a horizontal label, and **LabelChartV** displays a vertical label. The two procedures have the same syntax:

```
LabelChartH( Env, x%, y%, font%, color%, Label$)
LabelChartV( Env, x%, y%, font%, color%, Label$)
```

Env is the **ChartEnvironment** structure associated with the chart being labeled. ***x%*** and ***y%*** specify the position of the left edge (***x%***) and the bottom (***y%***) of the first character in the label. The position is measured in pixels relative to the chart window.

font% is an integer specifying the font to use for the label. The number of fonts available depends on the fonts that have been registered and loaded. If an invalid font number is specified, the first registered font is used. If no font numbers are registered, the default font is used.

color% is an integer specifying the color to use; it's an index into the presentation-graphics color palette. ***Label$*** is the text to display.

The process of displaying a chart label is demonstrated in the next section.

Using Fonts

You can use BASIC 7's graphical fonts in presentation-graphics charts. This section provides a brief summary and demonstration of how to use fonts in charts. The use of fonts is covered in detail in Chapter 12.

Fonts are provided in disk files with a .FON extension. Before using a font, you must register it and then load it. Loaded fonts are available by number, and the number corresponds to the order in which the fonts were loaded. A font specification of 3, for example, specifies the font that was loaded third.

The following program demonstrates how to use graphical fonts in a chart. The program output is shown in Figure 11.1.

```
' Demonstrates using fonts in presentation-graphics charts.

' $INCLUDE: 'chrtb.bi'
' $INCLUDE: 'fontb.bi'

' Constant for desired video mode. Change this if needed for
' your video system.

CONST VIDEOMODE = 11

' Dimension a ChartEnvironment structure and set the video mode.

DIM Env AS ChartEnvironment

CALL ChartScreen(VIDEOMODE)

'***************Scatter chart*****************

' Set up arrays for scatter chart data, then read the data.

DIM Homework(16) AS SINGLE, Grade(16) AS SINGLE

FOR i% = 1 TO 16
  READ Homework(i%)
NEXT i%

FOR i% = 1 TO 16
```

```
    READ Grade(i%)
NEXT i%

' Register and load fonts.

a% = RegisterFonts("HELVB.FON")
b% = LoadFont("N1/N3/N4/N6")

' Initialize chart environment.

CALL DefaultChart(Env, cScatter, cNoLines)

' Define chart titles and options.

Env.ChartWindow.Border = cYes

'Set Y axis scaling and tic mark options.

Env.YAxis.AutoScale = cNo
Env.YAxis.ScaleMin = 70
Env.YAxis.ScaleMax = 100
Env.YAxis.TicInterval = 5
Env.YAxis.TicFormat = 1
Env.XAxis.TicFont = 3
Env.YAxis.TicFont = 3

'Define a main title and title font.

Env.MainTitle.Title = "Relationship between homework and grades"
Env.MainTitle.TitleFont = 4

' Set fonts for axis titles.

Env.XAxis.AxisTitle.TitleFont = 3
Env.YAxis.AxisTitle.TitleFont = 3
Env.XAxis.AxisTitle.Title = "Homework, hours per week"
Env.YAxis.AxisTitle.Title = "Grade average"

' Display chart.

CALL ChartScatter(Env, Homework(), Grade(), 16)

' Add a label.
```

```
Message$ - "High grades take work!"

CALL LabelChartH(Env, 450, 300, 2, 1, Message$)

SLEEP
SCREEN 0

END

'*********************************************
' Chart data

DATA 1, 5, 3, 3. 5, 7, .5, 12, 9, 5.5, 8, 2, 11, 7, 5, 2, 7.5
DATA 81, 88, 87, 76, 93, 79, 92, 90, 85, 81, 86, 95, 91, 82
```

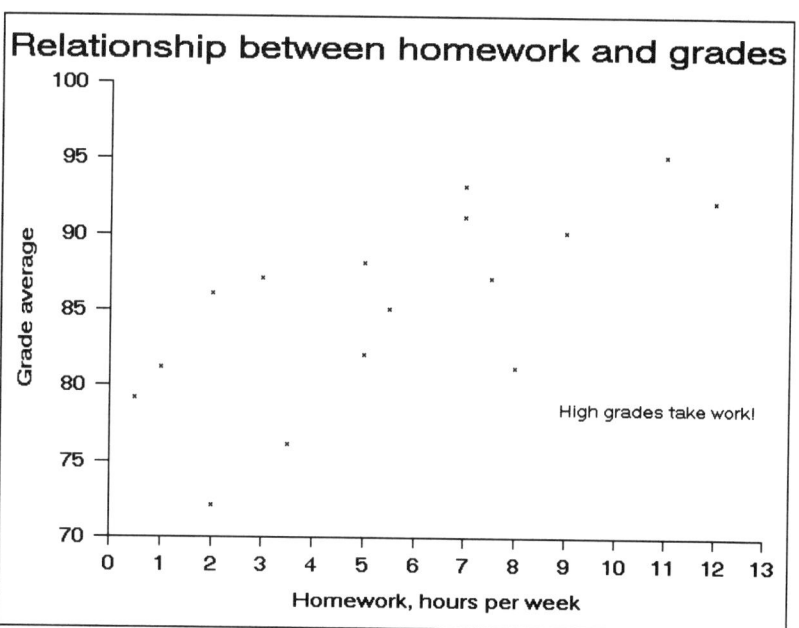

Figure 11.1. The output of the fonts-demonstration program.

Graphical Fonts

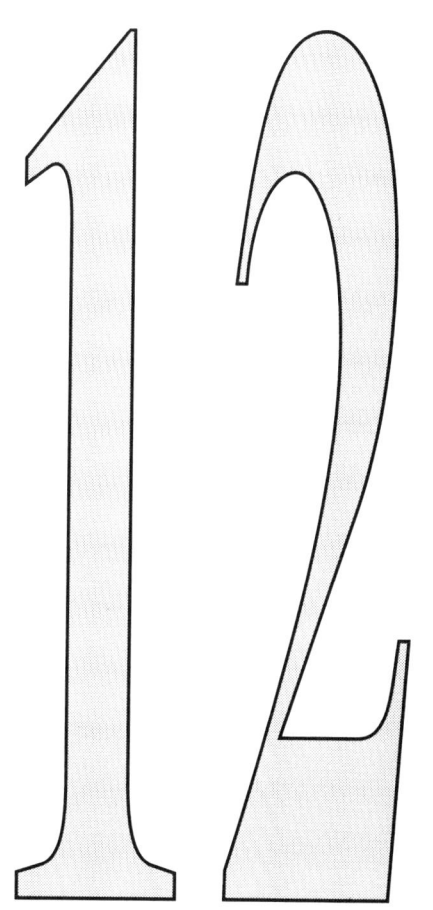

BASIC 7 includes procedures for using graphical fonts in your program. The fonts can be used in presentation-graphics charts (as described in Chapter 11) or to enhance your program's graphics screens. Unlike the default screen text, graphical fonts can be displayed with different typefaces, sizes, and orientations.

Preparing to Use Fonts

The font procedures are located in the fonts toolbox FONTB.BAS, and the object file FONTASM.OBJ. Both of these files are supplied with your BASIC 7 package. No font library is supplied, however—you must create it yourself from the font toolbox files. The first step in creating a library is to compile FONTB.BAS using the BASIC 7 command-line compiler. From the DOS prompt, issue this command:

```
bc fontb.bas /o/x/e/Fs;
```

This step creates a file named FONTB.OBJ. After the file is created, you can create either a Quick Library or a regular library. To create a Quick Library named FONTB.QLB for use in the QBX environment, issue this command:

```
link /Q fontb.obj+fontasm.obj,fontb.qlb,,qbx.lib qbxqlb.lib;
```

To create a regular library named FONTB.LIB for use with standalone linking, issue this command:

```
lib fontb.lib +fontb.obj+fontasm.obj;
```

Any program that uses fonts must include the file FONTB.BI with the **$INCLUDE:** metacommand:

```
' $INCLUDE: 'FONTB.BI'
```

This file contains needed constant and structure definitions and procedure declarations.

Font Basics

Before we explore the basics of using graphical fonts on your programs, let's briefly review some font basics and terminology. A *typeface* is a particular style, or design, of letters, numbers, and symbols. (Typefaces usually have names such as "Times Roman" and "Helvetica".) A *font* is a specific typeface in a specific size. "Times Roman 12 point" is a font, as is "Times Roman 20 point."

BASIC 7 uses bit-mapped fonts that are stored in files with the extension .FON. The name of the file indicates the typeface. Each file contains several fonts; i.e., several sizes of the indicated typeface. For example, the file TMSRB.FON contains six sizes of the Times Roman typeface.

The fonts used by BASIC 7 are the same as those used by the Microsoft Windows environment. More varieties of typestyles are supplied with Microsoft Windows than with BASIC 7. If you have a copy of Windows, you can use its bit-mapped fonts in your BASIC 7 programs (but not its vector fonts).

Registering and Loading Fonts

Your program must take two steps before it can use any graphical fonts:

1. Register one or more font files using the **RegisterFonts%** function. When a font file is registered, header information in the file about the fonts is read into memory, where it is available for use by other font procedures.

2. Load one or more registered fonts with the **LoadFont%** function. When a font is loaded, the actual font bit maps are read into memory and made available for display.

The syntax of the **RegisterFonts%** and **LoadFont%** functions is:

```
RegisterFonts%( FontFileName$ )
LoadFont( FontSpec$ )
```

FontFileName$ is a string expression that specifies the name of the file containing the fonts to be registered. The filename can contain disk and/or path information. **RegisterFonts%** returns the number of fonts registered (i.e., the number of fonts contained in the specified font file).

FontSpec$* is a string expression that specifies which of the registered font(s) to load. *FontSpec$ can contain one or more of the following:

n#   Loads the #th font in the list of registered fonts.

t name   Specifies the font name. *name* is the same as the file name for a font; i.e., fonts loaded from TMSRB.FON would be specified with *t tmsrb*. Use a font name to specify a font to load when more than one font file is registered.

s#,h#   Specifies the size of the font to be loaded. **s** specifies to load a font with point size #. **h** specifies to load a font with the height (measured in pixels) of #.

m#   Specifies that screen mode # is to be used in calculating font sizes that were specified with **s**. The default is the current screen mode. The **m** option does not actually change the screen mode, but specifies that a mode other than the current one is to be used as the basis for calculating how many pixels of font height are needed to obtain a particular point size.

b   Specifies that the "best fit" font is to be loaded if no available font exactly matches the size specified by **s** or **h**.

f   Loads a fixed space font.

p   Loads a proportionally spaced font.

When you execute **LoadFont%**, all previously loaded fonts are removed from memory (but remain registered). To load multiple fonts at one time, you must pass multiple font specifications in the argument to **LoadFont%**, separating font specifications by slashes. For example, pass the following specifications to load three fonts with the point sizes of 8, 12, and 16:

```
numloaded% - LoadFont%("s8/s12/s16")
```

When your program is finished using fonts, the fonts should be unregistered to free up memory for other purposes. This is done with a call to **UnRegisterFonts()**, which takes no arguments. After calling **UnRegisterFonts**, you can't register additional fonts without first calling **SetMaxFonts** (discussed later in this chapter).

Selecting and Displaying Fonts

Once you have loaded one or more fonts, you must select from among them to make one font active. To do so, use the **SelectFont** procedure:

```
SelectFont( n )
```

n is the number of the loaded font to be made active. Loaded fonts are assigned numbers according to the order in which they were loaded. This is demonstrated by the following sample procedure:

```
LoadFont%("s8/s12/s16")

SelectFont(3)       ' Selects 16 point
SelectFont(1)       ' Selects 8 point
```

To display text in the selected font, use the **OutGText%** function:

```
num% - OutGText%( x, y, Message$)
```

x and **y** are single-precision numbers specifying the screen coordinates of the upper-left boundary of the first character. **Message$** is a string expression that provides the text to be displayed.

OutGText% returns an integer value that represents the width, measured in pixels, of the displayed text. Text displayed with

OutGText% obeys viewports established with the **VIEW** statement. It does not, however, obey any **WINDOW** statement in effect.

The next program demonstrates the font procedures jsut discussed. The program output is shown in Figure 12.1.

```
' Demonstrates registering, loading, selecting, and
' displaying graphical fonts.

' $INCLUDE: 'fontb.bi'

CLS
SCREEN 12    ' Use a mode appropriate for your hardware

' Register the TMSRB font.

num% = RegisterFonts%("c:\bc7\bin\tmsrb.fon")
PRINT num%; " fonts registered."

' Load fonts 3 thru 6.

num% = LoadFont%("n3/n4/n5/n6")
PRINT num%; " fonts loaded."
```

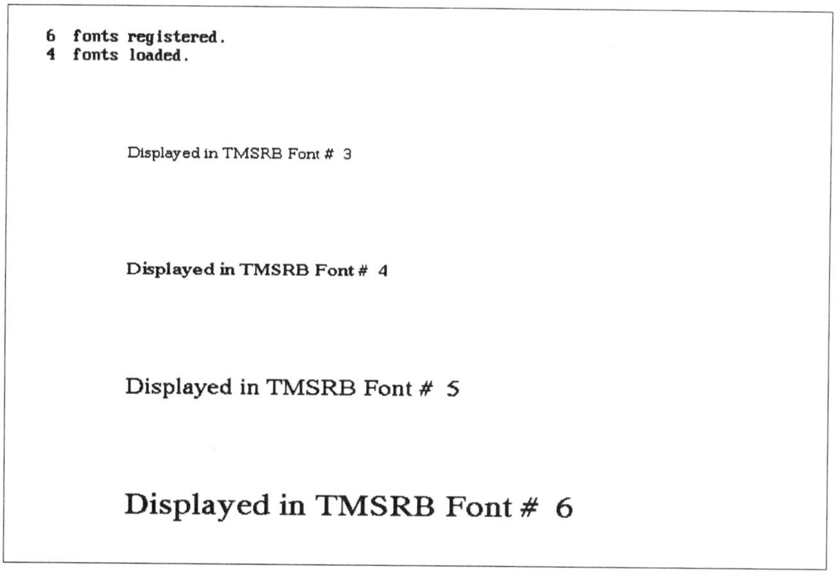

Figure 12.1. The font display created by the demonstration program.

```
' Display a message in each loaded font.

FOR i% = 1 TO 4
  Message$ = "Displayed in TMSRB Font # " + STR$(i% + 2)
  SelectFont (i%)
  num% = OutGText(80, i% * 100, Message$)
NEXT i%

SLEEP

' Free up font memory.

UnRegisterFonts

SCREEN 0
END
```

Other Font Procedures

Obtaining Font Information

You can obtain information about the current font by calling the procedure **GetFontInfo**. You may also obtain information about any registered font by calling **GetRFontInfo**. Both of these procedures return information in a structure of type **FontInfo**, defined in FONTB.BI as follows:

```
TYPE FontInfo
  FontNum      AS INTEGER
  Ascent       AS INTEGER
  Points       AS INTEGER
  PixWidth     AS INTEGER
  PixHeight    AS INTEGER
  Leading      AS INTEGER
  AvgWidth     AS INTEGER
  MaxWidth     AS INTEGER
  FileName     AS STRING * 66
  FaceName     AS STRING * 32
END TYPE
```

The members of type **FontInfo** hold the following information:

- **FontNum** holds the position of the font. In the case of **GetFontInfo**, this is the position in the list of loaded fonts. For **GetRFontInfo**, this is the position in the list of registered fonts.

- **Ascent** is the distance, measured in pixels, from the top of the character box to the character baseline.

- **Points** is the size of the current font, in points, as specified in the argument to the **LoadFont%** function.

- **PixWidth** is the width, in pixels, of each character in a fixed space font. **PixWidth** is set to 0 for proportionally spaced fonts.

- **PixHeight** is the height, measured in pixels, of the characters in the font.

- **Leading** is the amount of blank space, measured in pixels, at the top of the characters. This space serves as separation between successive lines of text.

- **AvgWidth** is the average width of characters, measured in pixels.

- **MaxWidth** is the width, in pixels, of the widest character in the font.

- **FileName** is the name of the disk file, including any drive and/or path information specified when the font was registered.

- **FaceName** is the name of the type face (e.g., TmsRmn).

When either of these procedures is called, your program must have access to the .FON file on disk to read needed information. The syntax for **GetFontInfo** and **GetRFontInfo** is:

```
GetFontInfo( FontData )
GetRFontInfo( n%, FontData )
```

FontData is a structure of type **FontInfo** that holds the information about the font. *n%* is an integer expression that specifies the registered font about which information is obtained.

Font Capacity

BASIC 7's default is to allow a maximum of 10 fonts to be registered and loaded at one time. You can control this value, increasing it if your program needs access to more than 10 fonts at one time or decreasing it to minimize memory use. To do so, you can use one of three procedures: **SetMaxFonts**, **GetMaxFonts**, or **GetTotalFonts**.

Use **SetMaxFonts** to change the maximum number of fonts that can be registered and loaded. The syntax for this procedure is:

```
SetMaxFonts(maxregistered%, maxloaded%)
```

maxregistered% is an integer expression specifying the maximum number of fonts that can be registered. *maxloaded%* is an integer expression that specifies the maximum number of fonts that can be loaded.

To determine the current settings for maximum fonts, use **GetMaxFonts**:

```
GetMaxFonts(maxregistered%, maxloaded%)
```

The arguments *maxregistered%* and *maxloaded%* return data from the procedure; the values of these arguments when **GetMaxFonts** is called are not important. For example, the following code increases the maximum number of registered and loaded fonts by 2:

```
...
GetMaxFonts(a%,b%)
a% = a% + 2
b% = b% + 2
SetMaxFonts(a%,b%)
...
```

To determine the number of fonts that are actually registered and loaded, use **GetTotalFonts**:

```
GetTotalFonts( registered%, loaded%)
```

After the call to **GetTotalFonts**, the arguments *registered%* and *loaded%* contain the number of currently registered and loaded fonts.

Output Length, Color, and Orientation

To accurately place font text on the screen, it can be useful to know the width (in pixels) of a specific text message when that message is displayed in the current font. You can obtain this value by using the **GetGTextLen%** function:

```
width% = GetGTextLen%( Message$)
```

This function returns an integer value that gives the width (in pixels) that *Message$* will have when displayed in the current font.

To change the color in which graphical fonts display, use the **SetGTextColor** procedure:

```
SetGTextColor( color%)
```

color% is an integer expression specifying the color value to be used for subsequent font output.

You can display font text in four orientations. To change the orientation, use the **SetGTextDir** procedure:

```
SetGTextDir( direction%)
```

direction% is an integer expression specifying the text orientation. Table 12.1 lists the values you can use for this expression.

Table 12.1 Values for **direction%**.

0	0 degrees
1	90 degrees
2	180 degrees
3	270 degrees

Font Errors

The font toolbox routines contain error-handling code that permits your program to react gracefully to font errors. When an error occurs, the variable **FontErr** contains an error code. The error codes, the corresponding constants (defined in FONTB.BI), and their meanings are listed in Table 12.2.

To handle font errors, use these codes along with BASIC 7's error-trapping abilities, which are presented in the following chapter.

Table 12.2. Error codes and their corresponding constants.

Error code	Constant	Meaning
1	**cFileNotFound**	Font file not found.
2	**cBadFontSpec**	Part of a font specification is invalid.
5	**cBadFontFile**	The specified font file has an invalid format.
6	**cBadFontLimit**	The specified font limit is invalid.
7	**cTooManyFonts**	More fonts were requested than are available.
8	**cNoFonts**	There are no loaded fonts.
10	**cBadFontType**	An attempt was made to use a vector font (non bit-mapped).
11	**cNoFontMem**	There is insufficient memory for the requested action.
200	**cFLUnexpectedOff**	An unexpected BASIC error offset occurred.

Error and Event Handling

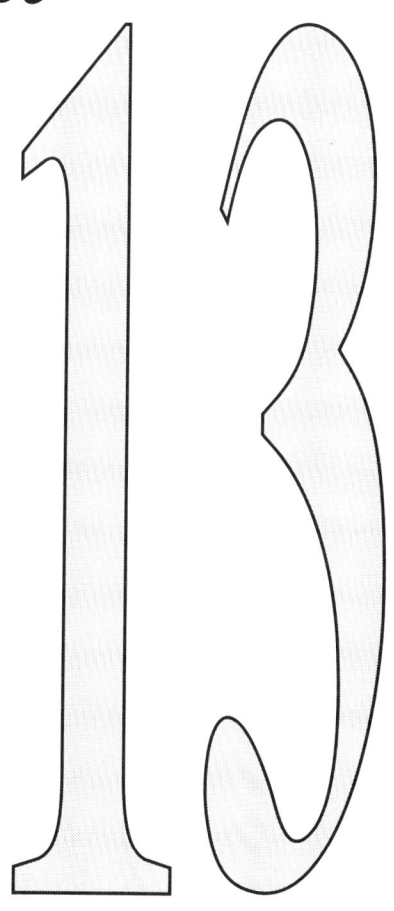

Chapter

13

237

As a programmer you have no way to prevent certain error conditions that may occur while your program is running. Fortunately, BASIC 7 has a powerful set of commands that let your program deal with most of these errors when and if they arise. Note that the errors dealt with in this chapter are *run-time* errors that occur while a program is running, and are distinct from compiler errors.

Error Handling

An *error* is a problem that occurs while a program is running, such as trying to write data to an unformatted diskette or trying to print when the printer is turned off. Left unattended, errors can cause your program to terminate, with possible loss of data. BASIC 7 provides sophisticated error-handling abilities that let your programs react gracefully to errors.

The process of error handling has two major components:

- *Trapping the error* means telling the program where execution should be routed when an error occurs. Execution is directed to error-handling code.

- *Error-handling code* deals with the error, then returns execution to the main part of the program.

Error Trapping

To enable error trapping, use the **ON ERROR GOTO** statement:

```
ON [LOCAL] ERROR GOTO line
```

line is a line number, or preferably, the line label that identifies the error-handling code. The optional **LOCAL** keyword identifies the trap as a procedure-level error trap. Without the **LOCAL** keyword the trap is a module-level error trap. (Module and procedure-level error traps are discussed in more detail later in this chapter.)

Once you enable error trapping, it's active for the duration of program execution unless explicitly turned off by a program statement. A program can contain multiple **ON ERROR GOTO** *line* statements; only the most recently executed one is active. The occurrence of any error sends program execution to the program location identified by *line*.

There are two special forms of the **ON ERROR** statement:

1. **ON ERROR RESUME NEXT** specifies that when a runtime error occurs, execution goes immediately to the statement after the statement where the error occurred.

2. **ON [LOCAL] ERROR GOTO 0** disables any module-level error trapping within the current module (if used without **LOCAL**) or within the current procedure (if used with **LOCAL**).

Error-Handling Code

You must place error-handling code in your program so that it will never be executed during normal program operation. The best location for module-level error handling code is following the program's **END** statement. The best location for procedure-level error handling code is immediately before the **END SUB** or **END FUNCTION** statement, and immediately after an **EXIT SUB** or **EXIT FUNCTION** statement. This is illustrated here:

```
SUB SubFunc

ON LOCAL ERROR GOTO SubError
...
procedure code
...
EXIT SUB

SubError:
...
error handling code
...
END SUB
```

The error-handling code determines the specific error that occurred by testing the value of the **ERR** function. **ERR** returns the error code of the most recent error. (A list of error codes and their meanings is provided in Appendix D and in the QBX Help System.) Depending upon which error occurred, the error handler can take appropriate action. This is often done with a **SELECT CASE** block that executes different statements based upon the value of **ERR**. Often the error handler prompts the user to take corrective action (such as closing a disk drive door, or turning on the printer), and then pauses for a keypress. Once the condition that caused the error is corrected, program execution must resume.

Resuming Program Execution

After the error-handling code has dealt with an error, execution must be directed back to the main program code. This is done using the **RESUME** statement, which has three forms:

1. **RESUME** or **RESUME 0** causes program execution to resume with the statement that caused the error.

2. **RESUME NEXT** causes program execution to resume with the statement immediately following the one that caused the error.

3. **RESUME** *line* causes program execution to resume at *line*, which is a label or a line number. The program location identified by *line* must be within the same procedure (for local error handlers) or in the same module (for module-level error handlers).

The appropriate form of the **RESUME** statement depends entirely upon the specifics of your program and the error that occurred. For example, use **RESUME** or **RESUME 0** when the condition causing the error has been corrected and the action can be re-tried.

The following short program demonstrates these error-handling techniques. When you run the program, leave the door to drive A open, or insert an unformatted disk in drive A.

```
' Demonstrates basic error handling.

ON ERROR GOTO ErrorHandler

CLS

' Open a file on drive A, and write some data to it.

OPEN "a:test.dat" FOR OUTPUT AS #1
WRITE #1, "Test data"
PRINT "Data written successfully."
CLOSE #1
END


ErrorHandler:

SELECT CASE ERR
   CASE 57
      PRINT "Device I/O error in drive A."
      PRINT "Correct; then press any key."
      SLEEP
      CLS
      RESUME
   CASE 71
      PRINT "Disk not ready in drive A."
      PRINT "Insert disk, close door; then press any key."
      SLEEP
      CLS
      RESUME
   CASE 72
      PRINT "Disk media error in A."
      PRINT "Replace diskette; then press any key."
      SLEEP
      CLS
      RESUME
   CASE ELSE
      PRINT "Unknown error "; ERR
      END
   END SELECT

' end of error handler.
```

Procedure- and Module-Level Error Trapping

BASIC 7 allows errors to be trapped at the procedure level as well as at the module level. This means that each procedure can include its own error-handling code to handle errors that occur while the procedure is executing. The module-level error handler need be concerned only with errors that occur while the module-level code is executing.

The process of procedure-level error trapping is a natural part of structured programming. In structured programming, each procedure deals with a specific task that may offer the possibility for certain types of errors. For example, a procedure that saves data to disk may have to handle disk-drive errors, but will never need to handle printer errors. Conversely, a procedure that sends data to the printer needs to be able to handle printer errors, but need not be concerned with disk drive errors. If you provide procedures with their own error handlers, you don't have to write a module-level error handler to address all possible errors.

To enable error handling within a procedure, first place an **ON LOCAL ERROR GOTO** statement at the start of the procedure. Next, include error-handling code at the end of the procedure, between an **EXIT SUB** or **EXIT FUNCTION** statement and the **END SUB** or **END FUNCTION** statement that marks the end of the procedure. While the procedure is executing, any module-level error trapping is suspended, and procedure-level error trapping is active. Once execution returns from the procedure, the module-level trapping is active again.

The following program demonstrates how this is done. The process of error handling in this example is rather bare-bones. Error-handling code in a real world program would have to address a greater range of possible errors. Run the program with drive A open and no paper in your printer.

```
' Demonstrates procedure-level error trapping.

DECLARE SUB PrintData ()
DECLARE SUB SaveData ()

ON ERROR GOTO ErrorHandler
DEFINT A-Z
```

```basic
        CLS

        ' Generate some data.

        DIM SHARED Array(1 TO 10)

        FOR i = 1 TO 10
          Array(i) = i
        NEXT i

        CALL SaveData
        CALL PrintData

        END

        ErrorHandler:
        PRINT "Error "; ERR
        END


        SUB PrintData

        ON LOCAL ERROR GOTO er2

        FOR i = 1 TO 10
          LPRINT Array(i)
        NEXT i

        EXIT SUB

        er2:

        SELECT CASE ERR
          CASE 27
            PRINT "Out of paper: correct, hit any key."
            SLEEP
            RESUME
          CASE ELSE
            PRINT "Error "; ERR
        END SELECT

        END SUB
```

```
SUB SaveData

ON LOCAL ERROR GOTO er1

OPEN "A:junk.dat" FOR OUTPUT AS #1

FOR i = 1 TO 10
  WRITE #1, Array(i)
NEXT i

CLOSE #1

EXIT SUB

er1:

SELECT CASE ERR
  CASE 71
    PRINT "Disk not ready; correct then press any key."
    SLEEP
    CLS
    RESUME
  CASE ELSE
    PRINT "Unknown error "; ERR
END SELECT

END SUB
```

Delayed Error Handling

There may be times when your program should detect errors, but not respond to them immediately. For example, a time-critical section of code may need to execute without interruption. In these situations, you can use the **ON ERROR RESUME NEXT** statement, which causes the error to be recorded but immediately continues execution with the statement following the one that caused the error. After the time-critical code has completed execution, you can test **ERR** to see if an error has occurred. The next code fragment shows how.

```
' Establish normal error trapping.

ON ERROR GOTO ErrorHandler
...
' Time-critical code starts here. Delay error handling.

ON ERROR RESUME NEXT
...
...
' Time critical code ends.

' Test for occurrence of error, i.e., ERR > 0.

IF ERR THEN
...
' error-handling code.
...
END IF

' Restore normal error handling

ON ERROR GOTO ErrorHandler
...
```

Simulated Errors

You can simulate the occurrence of an error using the **ERROR** statement:

```
ERROR n%
```

n% is a value between 1 and 255, inclusive, that gives the error code of the error to be simulated.

When an **ERROR** statement is executed, BASIC behaves just as if a real error *n%* has occurred: execution passes to the active error handler (if there is one), and **ERR** returns a value of *n%*. You can use **ERROR** statements to test your program's error-handling code.

BASIC does not use all of the available error codes, so you can also create user-defined errors. You can then use the error-trapping capabilities of BASIC to handle specific program conditions that may arise.

Turning Off Error Trapping

To disable module-level error trapping, execute the statement **ON ERROR GOTO 0**. To disable procedure-level error trapping, execute the statement **ON LOCAL ERROR GOTO 0** within the procedure. You can always re-enable error trapping later in the program.

When you enable error trapping, BASIC must generate extra code that checks for the occurrence of errors. This code makes your programs larger and slightly slower. In sections of code where you are confident that no error will occur, disable error trapping to decrease program size and improve execution speed. In some cases, you can avoid the need for error trapping by using appropriate programming techniques, as in the next example:

```
LINE INPUT "Enter name of file:", filename$

IF DIR$(filename$) <> "" THEN
  OPEN filename$ FOR INPUT AS #1
ELSE
  PRINT "File "; filename$; " not found."
END IF
```

Event Handling

BASIC 7 programs can trap the occurrence of certain events that may occur during program execution. Distinct from an error, an *event* is a normal occurrence that the program must respond to, such as a keypress. BASIC can trap these events:

- Data arriving at a communications port

- Keyboard input

- Passage of time

- Light-pen activity

- Background music

- Joystick-trigger activity

- User-defined events

The first three types of events are discussed in this chapter. For informaton about the other events (which are of relatively little interest to the business programmer), please refer to your BASIC 7 documentation.

Event-Handling Code

Insert event-handling code at the module level; it can't be placed within a procedure. Event-handling code must be located where it won't be executed during normal program operation; the preferred location is after the **END** statement. The event-handling code must be identified by either a line number or (preferably) a label. The only way that event-handling code can resume program execution is via the **RETURN** statement, which causes program execution to continue where it left off when the event occurred. Event-handing code can also terminate program execution by executing an **END** statement.

Trapping Keystrokes

You can trap a number of predefined keys as well as up to 11 user-defined keys. To trap the predefined keys, use this syntax:

```
ON KEY(n%) GOSUB line
KEY(n%) ON
```

line is the line label or number marking the start of the event-handling code. *n%* is the number of the key to trap, as defined in Table 13.1.

You must use both statements to trap keys; the first identifies the event-handling routine, and the second statement turns trapping on. The following statements also control the process of key trapping:

Table 13.1. Numbers cooresponding to trapped keys.

n%	key trapped
1-10	Function keys F1-F10
11-14	The Up, Left, Right, and Down Arrow keys.
15-25	User-defined keys
30,31	Function keys F11 and F12 (on 101 key keyboards only)

- **KEY(n%) STOP** suspends the trapping of key n%. If the key is pressed, it's remembered; if **KEY(n%) ON** is executed later, the remembered keypress is trapped immediately.

- **KEY(n%) OFF** disables the trapping of key n%. If the key is pressed, it's not remembered.

To trap a user-defined key, first define the specific key that will be associated with one of the key numbers 15 to 25. Use the **KEY** statement:

```
KEY n%, CHR$(kbflag%)+CHR%(code%)
```

n% is an integer value between 15 and 25. kbflag% is an integer value representing the state of the CTRL, SHIFT, and other special keys, as detailed in Table 13.2. code% is the extended key code of the actual key to be trapped. Keyboard codes are listed in Appendix B.

To trap a combination of special keys, set kbflag% equal to the sum of the codes for the individual keys. Here are some examples; the F1 key has an extended key code of 59.

```
KEY 15, CHR$(3) + CHR$(59)     ' Shift-F1
KEY 15, CHR$(4) + CHR$(59)     ' Ctrl-F1
KEY 15, CHR$(12) + CHR$(59)    ' Ctrl-Alt-F1
```

The following program demonstrates the process of trapping predefined and user-defined keys.

Table 13.2. Integer values representing special keys.

kbflag%	Special Key
0	None
1, 2, or 3	Either SHIFT key
4	CTRL
8	ALT
32	Num Lock
64	Caps Lock
128	Any extended key on the 101 key keyboard; e.g., the arrow keys not on the numeric keypad

```
' Demonstrates trapping keypresses.

CLS

' Trap the keypad arrow keys.

ON KEY(11) GOSUB UpArrow
ON KEY(12) GOSUB LeftArrow
ON KEY(13) GOSUB RightArrow
ON KEY(14) GOSUB DownArrow

' Turn trapping on.

KEY(11) ON
KEY(12) ON
KEY(13) ON
KEY(14) ON

' Trap Shift-F10

KEY 15, CHR$(3) + CHR$(68)
ON KEY(15) GOSUB ShiftF10
KEY(15) ON
```

```
' Trap Ctrl-Shift-F10

KEY 16, CHR$(7) + CHR$(68)
ON KEY(16) GOSUB CtrlShiftF10
KEY(16) ON

CLS

PRINT "Press an arrow key or Shift-F10."
PRINT "Press CTRL-SHIFT-F10 to end program."
VIEW PRINT 4 TO 24

DO
LOOP

END

UpArrow:
  PRINT "You pressed the up arrow."
  RETURN

DownArrow:
  PRINT "You pressed the down arrow."
  RETURN

LeftArrow:
  PRINT "You pressed the left arrow."
  RETURN

RightArrow:
  PRINT "You pressed the right arrow."
  RETURN

ShiftF10:
  PRINT "You pressed Shift-F10."
  RETURN

CtrlShiftF10:
  PRINT "Goodbye..."
  SLEEP 2
  VIEW PRINT
  CLS
  END
```

Trapping Communications-Port Activity

BASIC 7 can trap activity occurring at one of the computer's communications ports (also called serial ports). Once a trap is active, the receipt of data by the communications port causes execution to go to the event-handling code. In most cases, the event-handling code reads the data from the port.

The process of trapping communications-port activity is similar in most respects to the process of trapping keyboard input. The rules for the placement and the structure of event-trapping code are the same in both cases, and the statements that establish a trap are quite similar. To enable communications-port trapping, you must execute two statements:

```
ON COM(n%) GOSUB line
COM(n%) ON
```

The value of **n%** is either 1 or 2, and specifies the communications port to trap. **line** is the line label or number marking the start of the event-handling code.

The first statement identifies the event-handling routine, and the second turns trapping on. The following statements also control the process of communications-port trapping:

- **COM(n%) STOP** suspends the trapping of communications port **n%**. If the port receives data while trapping is suspended, the event is remembered; if **COM(n%) ON** is executed later, the event is processed immediately.

- **COM(n%) OFF** disables the trapping of communications port **n%**. If the port receives data, the event is not remembered.

Trapping the Passage of Time

The passage of time can be trapped in a manner similar to the process of trapping keyboard input. The "event" in this case is the passage of a specified amount of time, ranging from 1 second to 24 hours. To trap the passage of time, use this statement:

```
ON TIMER(n&) GOSUB line
TIMER ON
```

n& is a numeric expression specifying the number of seconds in the trapped interval. The allowable range is from 1 to 86,400 (24 hours). *line* is the line label or the number that marks the beginning of the event-handling code.

When timer trapping is active, execution passes to the event handling code every *n&* seconds. **TIMER OFF** disables timer trapping, and **TIMER STOP** suspends timer trapping. The process of timer trapping can be useful for such tasks as automatically saving a data file at selected intervals of time.

Be aware that the use of event trapping, as with the use of error trapping, makes programs larger and slower. Although BASIC 7's event-trapping abilities often provide the easiest solution to a problem, you can devise a bit of creative programming to perform the same task more efficiently.

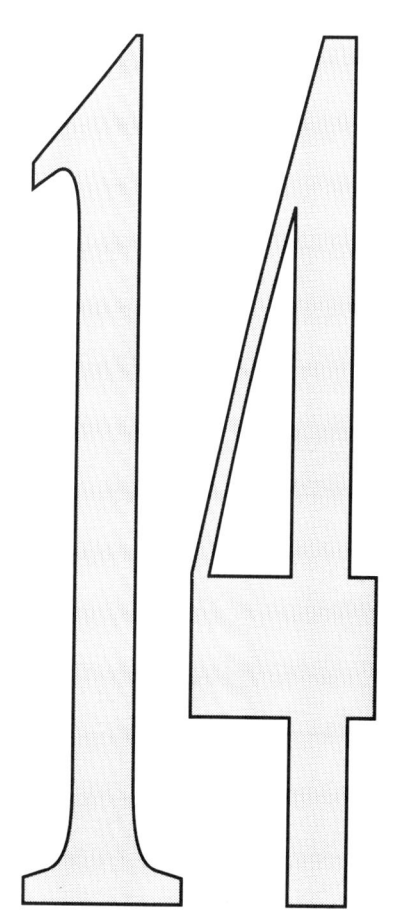

Database Programming Using ISAM

ISAM stands for *Indexed Sequential Access Method,* a powerful set of database-programming tools in BASIC 7. ISAM maintains data in the field/record structure common to most databases. When you use ISAM statements and functions, the difficult details of database maintenance are largely automated and hidden from your program.

ISAM Terms and Concepts

Before getting into the "how-to" of ISAM programming, you need to know the terms and concepts involved, and to be familiar with the way in which ISAM maintains and organizes data. The following terms will be used throughout the chapter. Many of them may be familiar to you, but their ISAM meanings may be different from their meanings when used in other contexts. In the following definitions, I use a mailing list as an illustrative example.

- A *record* is the basic unit of data storage and consists of one or more fields. Each record in a database contains the same fields. In a mailing list, each individual's complete entry comprises a record. A record is sometimes referred to as a *row.*

- A *field* is an individual data item common to all records in the database. In a mailing list, *Name, Address, City, State,* and *Zip* are fields. A field is sometimes called a *column.*

- A *table* is a collection of related data records that all have the same structure (i.e., all contain the same fields). Each row in a table contains one record; each column contains one field.

- An *index* is a component of an ISAM database that orders the records in a table in a certain fashion, based upon the data in one or more fields. Multiple indexes can be associated with a table, but only one index can be current at any time. For example, the records in a mailing list could be indexed alphabetically by name, by state, or by both.

- A *database* is an ISAM disk file that contains one or more tables, their associated indexes, and other information.

- The *NULL index* is the default index that is current when a table is first opened. The NULL index places records in order according to the order in which they were inserted into the table.

- A *combined index* places records in order based upon data in more than one field. If an index is created based upon two fields, for example, the data in the second field is used to order records that contain the same data in the first field.

- A *unique index* requires each record to contain different data in the indexed field. If you indexed a table on the Social Security Number field, you would specify a unique index because no two people have the same Social Security Number. If you later entered a number that already existed in the table, a trappable error would be generated.

- The *presentation order* is the logical order of records, and is determined by the current index.

- The *current position* in a table is the location where subsequent activity, such as deleting or modifying a record, will occur. In most situations, the current position points at a particular record in a table. This record is called the *current record* or the *focus*. The only instance when the current position does not point at a record is when the current position is located at the beginning or the end of the table.

- The *ISAM engine* is a collection of routines that perform the actual work of maintaining the database. Your program uses ISAM statements to access the ISAM routines.

- The *data dictionary* is a collection of information in an ISAM database that is used to maintain the tables and the indexes. The data dictionary is automatically maintained by the ISAM engine, and you never need to deal with it directly.

Record Structure

Each record in an ISAM table has the same field structure as all of the other records in the table. The record structure for a table is specified as a user-defined structure, using the **TYPE...END TYPE** statement. For the mailing-list table, we could use the following record structure:

```
TYPE AddressType
  Name AS STRING * 25
  Address AS STRING * 30
  City AS STRING * 12
  State AS STRING * 2
  Zip AS STRING * 5
END TYPE
```

Each structure member corresponds to a field, or column, in the table. This example uses fixed-length strings for all fields, but most other BASIC data types can be used as well. Some data types can be included in a table but cannot be used to create an index. This is summarized in Table 14.1.

When you define a user-defined structure for an ISAM table, the member names must adhere to ISAM naming conventions.

Table 14.1. The use of data types in tables and indexes.

Allowed, indexable:	INTEGER LONG INTEGER DOUBLE CURRENCY fixed-length strings (length < 256)
Allowed, not indexable:	fixed-length strings (255 < length < 32K) Static arrays (up to 64K) User-defined types (up to 64K)
Not allowed:	SINGLE Variable-length strings

ISAM Naming Conventions

The set of rules for assigning names to ISAM tables, fields, and indexes is a subset of the set of rules for naming BASIC variables. The ISAM rules impose the following limitations upon names:

- Names have a maximum length of 30 characters.

- Only alphanumeric characters are allowed (A-Z, a-z, 0-9) in the names. No type-declaration suffixes or other special characters are permitted.

- Names must begin with a letter.

- Names are not case sensitive.

ISAM Indexes

Much of the power of ISAM comes from its flexible use of indexes, so it's important that you understand how they work. When records are entered into a table, ISAM automatically maintains the NULL index, which in turn maintains the records in the order in which they were entered. Other indexes must be explicitly created by the program.

For example, after entering five records into our mailing list table, we might have the table shown in Figure 14.1 (the Address and Zip fields are omitted to save space).

Number	Name	City	State
1	Smith, Peter	Chicago	IL
2	Andrews, Jack	New York	NY
3	Miller, Henry	Los Angeles	CA
4	Jones, Fred	Miami	FL
5	Carson, Alan	Dallas	TX

Figure 14.1. An example mailing-list table.

In Figure 14.1, the Number column is *not* actually part of the table, but reflects the insertion order of records and each record's position in the NULL index. You could create an index that orders the records in the table based upon the Name field and assign a descriptive name, such as NameIndex, to the index. The indexing procedure does not change the table at all, but creates an index in which each index entry points to a record in the table. The index for the table in Figure 14.1 is shown in Figure 14.2.

If you make NameIndex the current index, the presentation order of the table changes to the order shown in Figure 14.3.

You could also create another index, named StateIndex, that orders the mailing-list records according to the contents of the State field. The resulting index is shown in Figure 14.4.

The presentation order of the same table when StateIndex is the current index is shown in Figure 14.5.

NameIndex position		Record position
1	------------>	2
2	------------>	5
3	------------>	4
4	------------>	3
5	------------>	1

Figure 14.2. An index for the table in Figure 14.1.

Number	Name	City	State
2	Andrews, Jack	New York	NY
5	Carson, Alan	Dallas	TX
4	Jones, Fred	Miami	FL
3	Miller, Henry	Los Angeles	CA
1	Smith, Peter	Chicago	IL

Figure 14.3. The table with NameIndex as the current index.

StateIndex position		Record position
1	------------>	3
2	------------>	4
3	------------>	1
4	------------>	2
5	------------>	5

Figure 14.4. The results of using the State Index index.

Number	Name	City	State
3	Miller, Henry	Los Angeles	CA
4	Jones, Fred	Miami	FL
1	Smith, Peter	Chicago	IL
2	Andrews, Jack	New York	NY
5	Carson, Alan	Dallas	TX

Figure 14.5. The table when StateIndex is the current index.

Once an index is defined, the process of maintaining it is completely automated by the ISAM engine.

Creating and Using an ISAM Database

The basic steps for creating and using an ISAM database are outlined here:

1. Create a user-defined structure that specifies the structure for the records in the table.

2. Open the ISAM database. If the database file doesn't exist, an empty database is created. If the database file exists, it's available to the program.

3. Perform database operations, including:

- Adding new records, or retrieving existing records.
- Deleting or modifying existing records.
- Creating new indexes.
- Searching for specific information.

4. Close the ISAM database.

Opening and Closing a Database

To open an ISAM database use the following variant of the BASIC **OPEN** statement:

```
OPEN database$ FOR ISAM tabletype tablename$ AS [#] filenum%
```

database$* is a string expression specifying the name of the database file. *database$ can include a disk and/or a path specification.

tabletype is the name of the user-defined structure that will be used for records in the table. *tabletype* cannot be a string expression; it must be the **TYPE** name spelled out. *tablename$* is a string expression specifying the name of the table; it must follow ISAM naming conventions. *tablename$* must be specified because a single database file can contain multiple tables.

filenum% is an integer expression between 1 and 255 that becomes associated with both the database file and the specific table that were opened. *filenum%* must be unique—it cannot be in use by any other open file, whether an ISAM or a regular BASIC file. Use **FREEFILE** to obtain available values for *filenum%*.

When you execute an **OPEN FOR ISAM** statement, the data in table *tablename$* in database file *database$* becomes available to your program. If the file *database$* does not exist, it's created by the **OPEN** statement. If the file *database$* exists but does not contain table *tablename$*, then a table of that name is created in *database$*.

Note that *filenum%* becomes associated with both the file *database$* and the table *tablename$*. If you open a different table within the same database file, you must use a different file number.

To delete a table in a database, use **DELETETABLE**:

```
DELETETABLE database$,tablename$
```

database$*** is the name of the ISAM database file containing the table to be deleted. ***tablename$ is the name of the table to be deleted.

Use **DELETETABLE** carefully—it permanently deletes a table and all associated indexes from a database.

To close an ISAM database, simply usc **CLOSE** *filenum%*. Executing **CLOSE** with no arguments closes all open files, both ISAM and otherwise.

The following short program defines, opens, and closes an ISAM database containing two tables, without adding any data.

```
' Demonstrates opening an ISAM database with 2 tables.

FileName$ = "MYDATA.DAT"

TYPE MyData1
  Field1 AS STRING * 20
  Field2 AS STRING * 12
  Field3 AS CURRENCY
  Field4 AS LONG
  Field5 AS DOUBLE
END TYPE

TableName1$ = "TABLE1"

TYPE MyData2
  Field1 AS STRING * 100
  Field2 AS DOUBLE
END TYPE

TableName2$ = "TABLE2"

OPEN FileName$ FOR ISAM MyData1 TableName1$ AS #1
OPEN FileName$ FOR ISAM MyData2 TableName2$ AS #2

CLOSE

END
```

Notes about ISAM Files

An ISAM database is a completely self-contained file. It contains not only the data (records) in its table(s), but also all indexes and other information associated with the file. Each ISAM file has some overhead, which refers to the space allocated to items other than actual data. For reasons of speed and efficiency, ISAM files are allocated in blocks of 32K in size.

When an ISAM database file is first created, initial overhead requires about 39K of disk space. A file is allocated 32K of space at a time, so the file starts out with a size of 64K even if no data has been written to it. This 64K includes about 25K of empty space that will be filled with your data and indexes as you add them to the database. When the total size exceeds 64K, another 32K is allocated.

As a database file grows, the amount of space needed for overhead remains relatively constant. The proportion of the file used for actual data increases with increasing file size. An ISAM file always grows in 32K chunks, and the maximum size is 128Mb. The ISAM engine automatically deals with such huge files, reading portions of the file into and out of memory as needed.

Obtaining Information About a File

To determine the length of an ISAM file, use **LOF**:

```
LOF( filenum% )
```

filenum% is the number associated with an open file. If the file is an ISAM table, **LOF** returns the number of records in the table. If the file is a non-ISAM file, **LOF** returns the number of bytes in the file.

To determine the type of an open file, use the **FILEATTR** function:

```
code% = FILEATTR( filenum%, attr% )
```

filenum% is the number of an open file. *attr%* is a value of either 1 or 2. If *attr%* equals 2 and the file is an ISAM table, **FILEATTR** returns 0. If *attr%* equals 2 and the file isn't an ISAM table,

Table 14.2. Codes and corresponding file modes.

Code	File mode
1	Input
2	Output
4	Random
8	Append
32	Binary
64	ISAM

FILEATTR returns the file's DOS handle. If *attr%* equals 1, **FILEATTR** returns a code that indicates the mode under which the file was opened. The codes and their corresponding modes are listed in Table 14.2.

Using Indexes

Every table has a default index, the NULL index, that orders the records according to their order of insertion. You can create additional indexes in an open table using the **CREATEINDEX** procedure:

```
CREATEINDEX[#] filenum%,indexname$,unique%,colname$[,colname$]
```

filenum% is the number associated with the table when it was opened using the **OPEN** statement. *indexname$* is the name assigned to the index. If an index with the name *indexname$* already exists, a trappable error occurs.

Set *unique%* to a non-zero value to specify that the index is unique: no two records can contain the same data in the indexed column. Set *unique%* to zero to create a non-unique index.

colname$* specifies the name of the column, or field, that the index is to be based on. *colname$ must appear in the **TYPE** statement used when the table was first created. If more than one *colname$* is given, **CREATE-INDEX** creates an index based upon the values in all listed columns.

To make a particular index current, use the **SETINDEX** statement:

```
SETINDEX [#]filenum%[,indexname$]
```

filenum% is the number associated with the table when it was opened using the **OPEN** statement. *indexname$* is the name assigned to the index when it was first created. If you omit the *indexname$* argument, the NULL index becomes current.

After you specify a new index using **SETINDEX**, the current record is the first record in that index.

To determine which index is current for a table, use **GETINDEX$**:

```
CurrentIndex$ = GETINDEX$ (filenum%)
```

filenum% is the number associated with the table when it was opened using the **OPEN** statement.

GETINDEX returns a string containing the name of the current index; it returns a null string if the NULL index is current.

To permanently delete an index from a table, use **DELETEINDEX**:

```
DELETEINDEX [#]filenum%,indexname$
```

filenum% is the number associated with the table when it was opened using the **OPEN** statement. *indexname$* is the name of the index to delete.

Whenever you add, delete, or modify records in a table, the ISAM engine automatically updates all of the table's indexes to reflect the changes. With large tables containing many indexes, this process can slow down the process of working with a table. You cannot, unfortunately, turn off indexing temporarily. You can, however, delete any indexes that aren't needed for the task at hand, and then re-create them later.

Manipulating Database Data

You can use four statements to manipulate data in a table. To add a new record to the table, use **INSERT**:

```
INSERT [#] filenum%,recordvar
```

filenum% is the number associated with the table when it was opened using the **OPEN** statement. *recordvar* is a variable of the user-defined type that defined the table when the table was first created.

INSERT places the contents of *recordvar* in the table as a new record, and then updates all indexes. The current position is not affected.

To read a record from a table, use **RETRIEVE**:

```
RETRIEVE [#] filenum%,recordvar
```

filenum% is the number associated with the table when it was opened using the **OPEN** statement. *recordvar* is a variable of the user-defined type that defined the table when the table was first created.

RETRIEVE places the contents of the current record in the variable *recordvar*. The current position is not modified, and the table itself is not changed, so there's no need to update the indexes.

To replace data in an existing record, use **UPDATE**:

```
UPDATE [#] filenum%,recordvar
```

filenum% is the number associated with the table when it was opened using the **OPEN** statement. *recordvar* is a variable of the user-defined type that defined the table when the table was first created.

UPDATE replaces the contents of the current record with the contents of *recordvar*. The current position is not modified, and all indexes are updated automatically.

To delete the current record and automatically update all indexes, use **DELETE**:

```
DELETE [#] filenum%
```

filenum% is the number associated with the table when it was opened using the **OPEN** statement.

Changing the Current Position

Many ISAM operations occur at the current position. To control which record is affected, you control which record is pointed to by the current position. To do so, you first need to understand the relationship between a table's records and its positions.

A table containing *n* records has *n+2* positions. The first position is empty, and is located just before the first record. Likewise, the last position is empty and is located just after the last record. Therefore, the current position is pointing at a record unless it is at the first or the last position in the table. The first and last positions are called the *Beginning of File* (*BOF*) and *End of File* (*EOF*), respectively. The record positions themselves are always determined by the current index, and record position 1 is the first record in the current index.

You can use four statements and two functions for manipulating the current position. They all take *filenum%* as their argument. *filenum%* is the number associated with the table when the table was opened using the **OPEN** statement.

- **MOVEFIRST** *filenum%* moves to the first record (not the first position) in the table.

- **MOVELAST** *filenum%* moves to the last record (not the last position) in the table.

- **MOVENEXT** *filenum%* moves to the next position in the table. If the last record in the table was current, **MOVENEXT** moves to the End of File.

- **MOVEPREVIOUS** *filenum%* moves to the previous position in the table. If the first record in the table was current, **MOVEPREVIOUS** moves to the Beginning of File.

- The functions **BOF(***filenum%***)** and **EOF(***filenum%***)** return true (-1) if the current position is at the Beginning of File or End of File, respectively. They return false (0) otherwise.

The following code demonstrates how to move through a table, from the first record to the last, displaying each one.

```
' Demonstrates displaying all records in an ISAM database
```

```
' in indexed order. We assume the database exists, and that
' table "Table1" exists and has an index named "Index1".

FileName$ = "MYDATA.DAT"

TYPE MyData1
  Field1 AS STRING * 20
  Field2 AS STRING * 12
  Field3 AS CURRENCY
  Field4 AS LONG
  Field5 AS DOUBLE
END TYPE

DIM Temp AS MyData1

TableName1$ = "TABLE1"

OPEN FileName$ FOR ISAM MyData1 TableName1$ AS #1

SETINDEX #1, "Index1"

' Current position is set at the first record.

WHILE NOT EOF(1)
  RETRIEVE 1, Temp
  PRINT Temp.Field1
  PRINT Temp.Field2
  PRINT Temp.Field3
  PRINT Temp.Field4
  PRINT Temp.Field5
  MOVENEXT 1
  SLEEP
  CLS
WEND
CLOSE #1
END
```

Searching for Data

You can also change the current position by using a search procedure.
The current position will point at the first record in the table that

matches a search condition you specify. These three search statements are available:

```
SEEKGT [#] filenum% ,keyval [,keyval]...
SEEKGE [#] filenum% ,keyval [,keyval]...
SEEKEQ [#] filenum% ,keyval [,keyval]...
```

filenum% is the number associated with the table when it was opened using the **OPEN** statement. *keyval* is an expression with a maximum length of 255 characters. *keyval* must have the same data type as the table column used in the current index. If you include more than one *keyval* in the search statement, ISAM assumes that the index in use is a combined index. If *keyval* is a string expression, any trailing spaces are removed.

The **SEEK..** statements cause the first matching record in the table to become the current record. Searches are always performed based on the current index. The three **SEEK** statements and their respective searches are:

SEEKGT   Searches for a record where the contents of the current index column is greater than *keyval*.

SEEKGE   Searches for a record where the contents of the current index column is greater than or equal to *keyval*.

SEEKEQ   Searches for a record where the contents of the current index column is equal to *keyval*.

If no match is found, the current position is set to End of File. You can, therefore, test **EOF()** to determine whether the search has been successful.

If the **SEEK..** statement includes more key values than the number of columns in the current index, a Syntax error occurs. If the current index is a combined index, and the number of key values is less than the number of columns in the index, no error occurs. Depending upon the **SEEK..** statement, the search fails or is performed using the supplied key values. When you don't supply enough key values for the three statements, different results can occur:

- When you supply too few key values with **SEEKEQ**, it always fails.

- When you supply too few key values with **SEEKGE**, the statement is equivalent to a **SEEKGT** with the same arguments.

- When you supply too few key values with **SEEKGT**, it will find the first record that matches the key values you supplied.

The **SEEK..** statements perform string comparisons differently from the BASIC relational operators:

1. Case is not significant. Thus, "apple" and "APPLE" are considered the same, and "aardvark" is considered to be less than "ZEBRA".

2. International characters, such as accented letters (ä, à, and å, for example) are taken into account in string comparisons. The character sort order was selected when you initially installed BASIC 7. (See Appendix E, International Character Sort Order Tables, in your *BASIC 7 Language Reference* for more information.)

You can perform string comparisons within your program using **TEXTCOMP** in the same manner that you perform searches using the **SEEK..** statements. **TEXTCOMP** is available only if the ISAM engine has been installed. The syntax for **TEXTCOMP** is:

```
TEXTCOMP(string1$, string2$)
```

string1$* and *string2$ are the strings being compared. **TEXTCOMP** returns -1 if *string1$* is less than *string2$*, 0 if the strings are equal, and 1 if *string1$* is greater than *string2$*.

Transaction Processing

Transaction processing is a powerful technique that helps your ISAM database program guard against data-entry errors. Use the ISAM transaction statements to maintain a log of all database activity. If errors are discovered, you can use the log to restore the database to its state before the errors occured. The general procedure for using transactions is:

1. Before modifying database information, start a transaction log using the **BEGINTRANS** statement. Only one transaction log can exist at a time.

2. During data operations, use the **SAVEPOINT** function to place *save points* at specific locations in the log. A save point is like a bookmark, providing a reference point for rollback operations. Save points are automatically numbered, but the numbers are not guaranteed to be sequential. Each time you call **SAVEPOINT**, it returns the number of the save point that was just placed. The use of **SAVEPOINT** is optional.

3. If errors are discovered, use **ROLLBACK** to restore the database to its previous condition. You can restore to the beginning of the transaction log or to any of the marks set with **SAVEPOINT**. You can't use **ROLLBACK** after the transaction log has been closed.

4. When you are confident that there are no errors, use **COMMIT-TRANS** to close the transaction log and write all changes to the database.

5. Optionally, use **CHECKPOINT** to force all data to be physically written to disk. ISAM may temporarily store database information in buffers in memory, so the use of **CHECKPOINT** after **COMMITTRANS** insures that all data in the transaction block is written to disk and can't be lost in the event of a power failure or other such problem.

If you close a database, the transaction log is committed even if an explicit **COMMITTRANS** is not executed. Certain error conditions that may occur during database-level or table-level operations cause an implicit **CLOSE** statement to be executed. This might add errors to the database before you have the chance to use **ROLLBACK** to correct them. For this reason it's wise to avoid performing database-level and table-level operations, such as opening tables and creating indexes, while a transaction log is open.

The **BEGINTRANS** and **COMMITTRANS** statements take no arguments. The syntax of **SAVEPOINT** is:

```
n% = SAVEPOINT
```

The value returned is an integer identifier of the save point. Save points may not be numbered sequentially, so you must record them for possible later use. You can use an array for this purpose, as shown here:

```
...
sp% = sp% + 1
SavePoints(sp%) = SAVEPOINT
...
```

The syntax of **ROLLBACK** is:

```
ROLLBACK [{savepoint|ALL}]
```

ROLLBACK restores the table to its state when the save point with number *savepoint* was placed. If no *savepoint* is specified, **ROLLBACK** proceeds to the next available save point. If **ALL** is specified, **ROLLBACK** proceeds to the beginning of the transaction log, and the table is restored to the condition it was in when the most recent **BEGINTRANS** was executed.

Using Multiple Databases

ISAM permits a single database file to contain multiple tables, so there's rarely any need to work with multiple database files at the same time. The capability to work simultaneously with up to four databases is available, however, should you needed it. ISAM's capacity for multiple files is shown in Table 14.3.

Table 14.3. ISAM's capacity for multiple files.

Databases Open	Total number of tables that can be open for all databases.
1	13
2	10
3	7
4	4 (1 per database)

ISAM Error Handling

Errors can occur during the execution of ISAM statements and functions. These errors are fully trappable using the BASIC error-handling capabilities described in Chapter 13. The ISAM error codes and their meanings are listed in the BASIC 7 documentation. Note that some of these errors are ISAM-specific, while others are regular BASIC errors that have special meaning for ISAM programs.

The ISAM Engine

The ISAM engine must be available to your program in order for the ISAM statements and functions to work. The ISAM engine comes in two forms:

- PROISAMD contains the entire set of ISAM routines.

- PROISAM contains all of the routines except those used for creating indexes and tables.

If your program will be creating tables and indexes, use PROISAMD. Many times, however, the final database program will be supplied with a predefined database that contains all of the needed tables and indexes (but no actual data). In this case, use PROISAM to conserve memory.

You can make the ISAM engine available to your program in two ways: as a terminate-and-stay-resident (TSR) utility, or as a standard library linked with the program. The availability of these options was decided when you first installed BASIC 7. (To change your ISAM engine options, run SETUP again.)

To use the TSR option, you must run a program, PROISAMD.EXE or PROISAM.EXE, prior to running the BASIC program that uses ISAM statements. Each of these programs loads the ISAM engine into memory, where it's available to your program. You must install one of the TSRs in order to execute ISAM programs from within the QBX environment. When creating standalone executable files from your BASIC programs, the advantage of using a TSR is that each .EXE file will be smaller because the ISAM routines are not included in the .EXE file itself.

To load the ISAM TSR, type **PROISAMD** or **PROISAM** at the DOS prompt. Each TSR occupies a significant amount of memory, so you may want to unload it when you finish running your BASIC ISAM program(s). To unload the TSR, type **PROISAMD /D** or **PROISAM /D** at the DOS prompt. If you are using other TSR programs, you must have installed the ISAM TSR last in order to free up its memory by unloading it.

To link ISAM routines with your programs, you must have already selected the "Full ISAM" or "Reduced ISAM" option for the library BCL70*mso*.LIB or BRT70*mso*.LIB during SETUP. Your program must be compiled and linked from the command line, and the library PROISAMD.LIB or PROISAM.LIB must be available to the linker.

Expanded Memory and ISAM

ISAM can use expanded memory that adheres to the Lotus-Intel-Microsoft 4.0 expanded-memory specification (EMS). Proper use of expanded memory can increase the speed and capacity of ISAM programs. In many cases, the default settings will enable ISAM (and QBX, if you are using it) to use the available expanded memory to best advantage. Some situations can arise, however, that require you to be aware of potential EMS conflicts:

- The program you are writing may be executed on a system with different memory availability than your system.

- If your program, or a library procedure, directly accesses expanded memory, you may need to reserve some expanded memory for ISAM.

When installing the ISAM engine as a TSR, or when using the BC command-line compiler to compile an ISAM program that will not use the TSR, you can specify one of three options:

/Ib:*pagebufs*   Specifies that *pagebufs* buffers will be set aside for ISAM. The defaults are six 2K buffers for PROISAM and nine 2K buffers for PROISAMD. These default values are the minimums needed for an ISAM program. The maximum value for *pagebufs* is 512. Buffers are taken first from expanded memory and then, if needed, from conventional memory. The best value for a particular program must be determined by experimentation.

/Ie:*mem*   Reserve *mem*K of expanded memory for non-ISAM uses. ISAM's default is to take all available expanded memory up to a maximum of 1.2Mb. Use **/Ib** in conjunction with the **/E** QBX option (discussed in Chapter 1) to apportion expanded memory between ISAM and QBX.

/Ii:*num*   Specifies the number of non-NULL ISAM indexes to be used by your program. Use this option only if your program will use more than 30 indexes. The maximum value allowed is 500.

For example, the following DOS command installs the PROISAMD TSR, reserving 500K of expanded memory for non-ISAM uses and setting a maximum of 50 indexes:

```
PROISAMD /Ie:500 /Ii:50
```

When compiling an ISAM program that will not use one of the TSRs, use the same options on the BC command line.

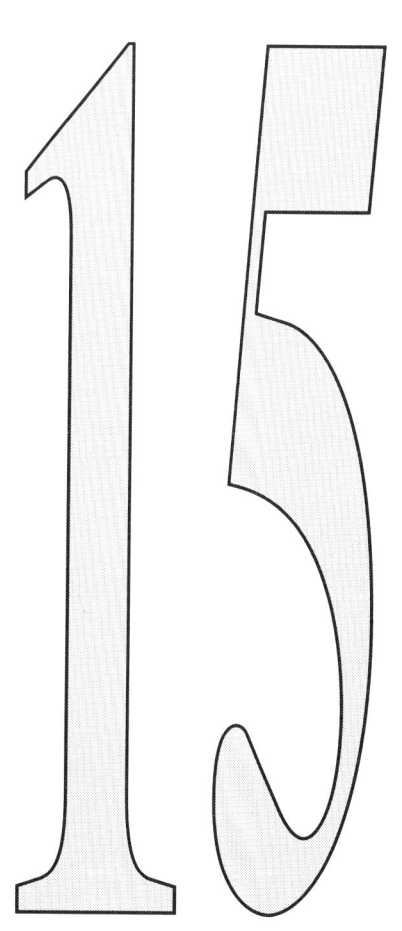

Advanced Compiler and Linker Use

Most BASIC 7 programming tasks can be handled perfectly well from within the QBX environment. In some situations, however, you must use standalone program development, using the compiler BC.EXE and the linker LINK.EXE, to create your programs. This chapter describes how to use these programs, and explains some of the programming options not available with QBX.

The Command-Line Compiler

The BASIC 7 command-line compiler, BC.EXE, is an alternative to the QBX environment for compiling your programs when you want to create a standalone .EXE file. You need to use the command line compiler if the following situations arise:

- You want to compile a program that's too large to compile within QBX.

- You want to use a specialized programming editor to write your source code.

- You want to debug the program using the CodeView debugger.

- You want to use options not available in QBX, such as create a listing file, store arrays in row order, link with stub files, use near strings, or link with more than one library.

When using the command-line compiler, follow these three program development steps:

1. Create a BASIC source-code file using an editor. You can use any editor that creates ASCII text files, such as the QBX editor or the Microsoft Editor supplied with the BASIC 7 package. If you use the QBX package, save your source-code files using the Save As command and the Text option.

2. Use BC.EXE to compile the program and create an object file,

which has an .OBJ extension. (The use of BC.EXE is described later in this section.)

3. Use the linker, LINK.EXE, to link the object file with library routines to create the final executable .EXE file. (The use of LINK.EXE is covered later in this chapter.)

Starting the Command-Line Compiler

You must provide BC with certain information, such as the name of your BASIC source file, before it can begin compiling your program. You can provide this information on the command line or in response to prompts. To respond to prompts, simply enter:

```
BC
```

at the DOS prompt. The following prompts will be displayed:

```
Source Filename [.BAS]:
Object Filename [ filename.OBJ]:
Source listing [NUL.LST]:
```

In response to the Source Filename: prompt, enter the name of your BASIC source-code file. You need not supply the .BAS extension—it's added automatically.

In response to the Object Filename: prompt, enter the name to assign to the object file. The default is the name of the BASIC source code file with an .OBJ extension added. Accept the default by pressing the Enter key. If you enter a different filename, the .OBJ extension is added automatically.

At the Source Listing: prompt, enter the name of the listing file, if you desire one. The default is NUL, meaning that no listing file is produced. A *listing file* contains the lines of your source code file, each with its relative address in the .OBJ file, plus any error messages that occurred during compilation. Enter **User** at this prompt to have the listing file displayed on the screen; enter **PRN** to have it sent to the printer.

You can enter compiler options after any prompt. For example, the following responses compile the file MYPROG.BAS with the /O option, producing the object file MYPROG.OBJ and sending the list file to the screen:

```
Source Filename [.BAS]: myprog /O
Object Filename [MYPROG.OBJ]:
Source listing [NUL.LST]: user
```

To pass options to BC on the command line, use the following form:

```
BC source [,object][,list][options][;]
```

source, *object*, and *list* are the specifications of the source file, object file, and listing file. If you omit *object* and/or *list*, and terminate the command line with a semicolon, the BC defaults will be used. If you omit the semicolon, BC prompts you for any command-line information that was omitted. For example, to compile MYPROG.BAS using the default object and listing files and the /O and /X options, enter

```
BC myprog/O/X;
```

Compiler Options

A number of options are available when you compile a BASIC 7 program. Some of these options are available when you use QBX, but BC makes all of them available. You can list options in any order on the command line or in response to a BC prompt; each option must be preceded by a slash (/) or a dash (-). A list of the options and their definitions follows.

/A	Instructs the compiler to create a listing of disassembled object code; this listing file contains the assembly language generated by the compiler for each line of BASIC source code.
/Ah	Permits dynamic arrays to occupy as much memory as

is available. Arrays can contain numeric data, records, or fixed-length strings. The default is for individual arrays to be limited to 64K each.

/C:*size*   Specifies the size, in bytes, of the receive buffer for each communications port. This option has no effect if communications-port hardware is not present. The default size is 512 bytes, and the maximum size is 32,767 bytes. A larger receive buffer means that more data can be received by a communications port before your program has to explicitly deal with it.

/D   Instructs the compiler to include debug code in the program, for runtime error checking. In addition, the **/D** option allows your program to be interrupted at any time by pressing Ctrl+Break, and inserts implicit checkpoints after every ISAM **DELETE**, **INSERT**, **UPDATE**, or **CLOSE** statement.

/E   Required if your program contains error-handling code that uses **RESUME *line*** statements.

/FPa   Enables the alternate floating-point math library. Compared with the default math library, the alternate library results in smaller .EXE files, and programs that run somewhat faster on computers without math-coprocessor chips installed. Under certain circumstances, some accuracy in calculations is lost, but the accuracy loss has no effect on most applications.

/FPi   Instructs the compiler to generate inline instructions for floating-point operations. This is the default.

/Fs   Enables far string storage. BASIC 7 offers two string storage options. *Near storage*, the default, provides a total of 64K of memory for storage of variable-length strings, simple variables, constants, and the stack. This is adequate for many programs. *Far-string storage* uses a separate storage area for variable-length strings, resulting in greater memory space for variable storage at the expense of less space for program code.

/G2   Instructs the compiler to create instructions for the 80286 chip. Programs compiled with this option are smaller and faster, but require an 80286 processor (or higher) to run.

/Ix:num   Specifies ISAM options. See Chapter 14 for details.

/Lp   Creates a protected-mode object file. This is the default if BC is running in OS/2 protected mode. Use this option only if you are running BC in real mode, and are creating a program to run in OS/2 protected mode.

/Lr   Creates a real-mode object file. This is the default if BC is running in real mode. Use this option only if you are running BC in OS/2 protected mode, and are creating a program to run in real mode.

/MBF   Converts the BASIC functions **MKS$**, **MKD$**, **CVS**, and **CVD** to the variants **MKSMBF$**, **MKDMBF$**, **CVSMBF**, and **CVDMBF**. This allows a program to read and write disk data in the older Microsoft Binary format.

/O   Compiles standalone .EXE files that don't require the Basic Run Time (BRT) module.

/Ot   Optimizes execution speed for calls to procedures in programs that contain no module-level, error-handling code, and that are not compiled with the **/D** or **/Fs** options.

/R   Stores arrays in row-major order, instead of in the default column-major order.

/S   Writes literal strings in the program code to the object file, instead of storing them in memory in the symbol table. Use this option if a program that contains many string literals generates an Out of Memory error during compilation.

/T   Turns off compiler display of warning messages.

/V   Enables event trapping, with event-checking occurring with every program statement.

/W   Same as /V, but event checking occurs only at line numbers and labels.

/X   Required if your program contains error-handling code that uses **RESUME, RESUME 0**, or **RESUME NEXT** statements.

/Z   Instructs the compiler to produce a listing of compilation errors in a file format designed for the Microsoft Editor.

/Zi   Instructs the compiler to produce an .OBJ file that includes debugging information needed to debug the program with the CodeView debugger.

Compiler Errors

When BC is compiling a program, errors that it finds (and warnings, if you don't use the /T option) are displayed on the screen in a format that pinpoints the location of the error in the source code. An example is shown in Figure 15.1. The screen display is not very useful because it disappears when you start up your editor to correct the mistakes.

You can make the error-message display more useful with one of these techniques:

```
C>bc ms_demo;
Microsoft (R) BASIC Compiler Version 7.00
Copyright (C) Microsoft Corporation 1982-1989. All rights reserved.
  003F    025C    DEM Months(1 TO 12) AS STRIG
                               ^ Equal sign Missing
                                  ^ Syntax error
  0046    02C4    READ Months(i%)
                              ^ Array not dimensioned
  00E7    02F8    Env.MainTitle.Titl = "Temperature and rainfall"
                           ^ Element not defined
                                                         ^ Type Mismatch
  0119    02F8    CALL ChartMS(Env, Months(), Weather(), 12, 1, 2, Labels())
                               ^ Parameter type mismatch
  01EF    035C    Env.YAxis.ScaleMn = 80
                           ^ Element not defined

46172 Bytes Available
40388 Bytes Free

     1 Warning Error(s)
     6 Severe  Error(s)

C>
```

Figure 15.1. The format of BC compiler error messages.

- Direct the compiler-screen output to your printer, providing a hard copy of error messages that you can refer to while making corrections.

- Direct the compiler-screen output to a disk file. If you have an editor that can edit multiple files simultaneously, you can read in the error-message file along with the source-code file, and refer to it during editing.

To do either of these techniques, use the DOS redirection command > when you invoke the compiler from the DOS prompt:

To the printer: `BC myfile; > prn`

    To a file: `BC myfile; > errors.txt`

Compiler messages will go to either the printer or the specified disk file, instead of being displayed on the screen.

The Command-Line Linker

The linker, officially known as the Microsoft Segmented Executable Linker, combines object files and libraries to create executable programs and Quick Libraries. Quick Libraries are covered in Chapter 16; this section deals with linking .EXE files.

What exactly does the linker do? The code for BASIC's intrinsic procedures, such as **CIRCLE, INSTR**, and **PRINT**, is not contained in the BC compiler or in the linker. Rather, it's contained, in compiled .OBJ code form, in one or more libraries that are created when you install BASIC 7. Libraries exist in disk files with the .LIB extension. During the linking process, the linker scans the .OBJ file created when your program was compiled, and determines which intrinsic BASIC procedures it calls. The .OBJ code for those procedures is taken from the library, and combined with your program's .OBJ code to produce the final executable file.

The Microsoft linker is a complex program that links not only BASIC programs, but programs created with other languages as well. Many of its options are never or rarely needed in BASIC program development. This section deals with those aspects of the linker that are of immediate concern to the BASIC 7 programmer.

Invoking the Linker

You can specify input to the LINK program in three ways: by responding to prompts, by placing the program on the command line, and by using a response file.

To respond to prompts, enter **LINK** at the DOS prompt. The linker presents five prompts in turn. To accept the default at a prompt, press the Enter key. You can enter LINK options at any prompt. The following prompts are presented by the linker:

```
Object Modules [.OBJ]:
Run File [filename.EXE]:
List File [NUL.MAP]:
Libraries [.LIB]:
Definitions File [NUL.DEF]:
```

Object Modules [.OBJ]: is the only prompt that requires a response. Enter the name(s) of the .OBJ file(s) to be linked. If you enter more than one filename, separate them by spaces or plus signs (+). You need not specify the .OBJ extensions.

Run File [*filename*.EXE]: is the name that the .EXE file will have. The default is the name of the first object module, with an .EXE extension.

List File [NUL.MAP]: is the name of a map file. The default is NUL, which produces no map file.

Libraries [.LIB]: is the name of one or more libraries to be linked with the object modules. List one or more libraries only if you want to link with other than the default library, which the linker uses automatically.

Definitions File [NUL.DEF]: is a module-definition file used only when linking Microsoft Windows and OS/2 programs. You don't need to make an entry here when you're linking real-mode BASIC programs.

To specify linker input on the command line, use the following format:

```
link [options] objfiles [, runfile] [,mapfile] [,libraries]
    [,deffile][;]
```

The command-line entries correspond to the prompt responses just explained. Again, the only required entry is *objfiles*. Use commas as placeholders for entries that you don't specify. Terminate the command line with a semicolon to prevent the linker from prompting you for missing, optional entries. For example, the following command links the object files MYPROG.OBJ and OLDPROG.OBJ using the library GRAPHS.LIB, and creates the .EXE file MYPROG.EXE and the .MAP file MYPROG.MAP:

```
link myprog+oldprog,,myprog,graphs.lib;
```

The third way to pass information to the linker is by means of a *response file*. A response file is simply a text file that contains the responses to the linker prompts in the same order the prompts are issued. Use a response file to save keystrokes when you are repeatedly linking and testing the same program. To use a response file, enter the link command followed by an "at" sign (@) and the name of the file.

The following response file passes the linker the same instructions in the previous command-line example:

```
myprog+oldprog

myprog
graphs.lib;
```

Note the blank line, which tells the linker to use the default for the second prompt (.EXE filename). If the link file is named MYPROG.RSP, invoke the linker using the command:

```
link @myprog.rsp
```

Linker Options

Table 15.1 explains the linker options most likely to be needed when linking BASIC programs. For information about other options, see the *BASIC 7 Programmer's Guide*. Linker options are preceded by a slash; most options have a long and a short form. The long form is indicated in Table 15.1 with square brackets.

Table 15.1. Linker options.

/BA[TCH]	Prevents the linker from prompting the user when it can't find specified .OBJ or .LIB files. This option is useful when using a batch file to perform many link tasks; it keeps the process from halting when a certain file cannot be found. When this happens, an error message is displayed, the ongoing link operation is aborted, and the batch file goes on to its next command.
	Continued

Table 15.1. Linker options (*continued*).

/CO[DEVIEW]	Required when linking programs to be debugged using the CodeView debugger. Files linked with **/CO** must have been compiled with the **/Zi** compiler option.
/E[XEPACK]	Instructs the linker to pack the executable file. Depending on the specific program, this option may result in a smaller .EXE file.
/HE[LP]	Instructs the linker to display a list of its options on the screen. When you specify **/HE**, the linker takes no other action besides listing options.
/IN[FORMATION]	Instructs the linker to display information about the linking process while it's in progress.
/NOD[:*libname*]	Instructs the linker to ignore the default library or libraries (whose names are coded into the .OBJ file), and to use only the library or libraries specified in response to the linker prompt. To ignore only a specific default library, include *libname* as part of the **/NOD** option.
/NOE[XTDICTIONARY]	Instructs the linker to ignore the extended dictionary when performing library searches. This option is required when linking with stub files (defined in the following section).
/NOL[OGO]	Suppresses the display of the linker's logo when it's invoked.
/PAU[SE]	Instructs the linker to pause during the linking process, just before it writes the .EXE file to disk. Used on diskette-only systems when you want the .EXE file written to a different diskette.
/Q[UICKLIBRARY]	Instructs the linker to produce a Quick Library. The process of creating Quick Libraries is discussed in Chapter 16.

Stub Files

Stub files are special object files or libraries that can be linked with your program to reduce the final size of the executable file. You can use stub files when you know that your program does not use certain BASIC procedures. By linking with the appropriate stub file(s), you prevent unneeded code from being linked with your program.

For example, you may be writing a program that never uses any **SCREEN** mode other than 0. By linking with the stub file NO-GRAPH.OBJ, you remove the unneeded support for graphics screen modes, resulting in a smaller .EXE file. You can use stub files when creating standalone executable programs or custom BASIC runtime modules.

Table 15.2 describes the stub files supplied with BASIC 7.

Table 15.2. The stub files in BASIC 7.

NOEVENT.OBJ*	Removes support for event trapping.
NOEMS.OBJ	Removes expanded-memory support for overlay programs; overlays will be swapped to disk, rather than to expanded memory.
NOISAM.OBJ*	Removes ISAM support from custom runtime modules.
OVLDOS21.OBJ	Required in order for a program that uses overlays to be able to run under DOS version 2.1. This stub file does not reduce .EXE file size.
SMALLERR.OBJ	Reduces the length of error messages that display for runtime errors.
87.LIB	Removes software emulation of the numeric coprocessor; a numeric coprocessor is required for any floating-point calculations.

Continued

* These stub files are applicable only when creating custom runtime modules, not for standalone executable programs.

Table 15.2. The stub files in BASIC 7 (*continued*).

NOLPT.OBJ	Removes support for printer output (device LPT*n*). Even if your program does not explicitly use **LPRINT** or other printer statements, LPT support is included if any **OPEN** statement uses a string variable for the file or device name (e.g., **OPEN filename$ FOR OUTPUT AS #1**). Linking with NOLPT.OBJ also removes support for printing the entire screen by pressing CTRL+PrintScrn.
NOCOM.OBJ	Removes support for communication ports (device COM*n*). Even if your program doesn't explicitly use the communications ports, COM support is included if any **OPEN** statement uses a string variable for the file or device name (e.g., **OPEN filename$ FOR OUTPUT AS #1**).
NOEDIT.OBJ	Reduces the ability to edit data being entered in response to an **INPUT** statement. (The Backspace and Enter keys become the only functional editing keys.)
NOFLTIN.OBJ	Removes support for floating-point input in response to **INPUT, READ**, and **VAL** statements. The only numeric input allowed is integers and long integers.
NOTRNEM*m*.OBJ	Removes support for statements that use transcendental operations. This includes **LOG, SRQ, SIN, COS, TAN, ATN, EXP**, and exponentiation (^). It also includes any **CIRCLE** statement that specifies start and/or stop angles, and any **DRAW** statement that uses the **A** or **T** commands. Note: replace *m* with **R** for real mode, and **P** for protected mode.
TSCNIO*sm*.OBJ	Removes all support for all screen output, except for text-only with no special treatment of control characters. This stub file combines the effects of all of the following graphics-related stub files. Note:replace *s* with **N** for near strings and **F** for far strings; replace *m* with **R** for real mode or **P** for protected mode.

Continued

Table 15.2. The stub files in BASIC 7 (*continued*).

NOGRAPH.OBJ	Removes support for all graphics screen modes and graphics statements. This stub file combines the effects of NOCGA.OBJ, NOHERC.OBJ, NOOGA.OBJ, NOEGA.OBJ, AND NOVGA.OBJ.
NOCGA.OBJ	Removes support for Color Graphics Adapter graphics modes, screen modes 1 and 2.
NOHERC.OBJ	Removes support for Hercules Graphics Card graphics, screen mode 3.
NOOGA.OBJ	Removes support for Olivetti graphics mode, screen mode 4.
NOEGA.OBJ	Removes support for Enhanced Graphics Adapter graphics modes, screen modes 7, 8, 9, and 10.
NOVGA.OBJ	Removes support for Video Graphics Array graphics modes, screen modes 11, 12, and 13.

To link your program with one or more stub files, follow these steps:

1. Compile the program using the BC compiler and the **/O** option.

2. Link using the **/NOE** option, and list the stub file(s) along with the program object file.

For example, to compile and link MYPROG.BAS with no support for graphics modes or LPT support, use these commands:

```
BC myprog /O;
link /NOE myprog+nograph+nolpt;
```

Overlays

Overlays is a technique used for very large programs. Some programs may be too large to load into memory as a unit. Others may fit into memory but not leave enough room for dynamic data storage. By using overlays, you can break a large program's code into sections that are loaded only as needed, so that the entire program need never reside in memory at one time.

A program that uses overlays always has a memory-resident or *root* portion that consists of part of your code and any code drawn from runtime modules. The program root remains in memory throughout program execution. There are also one or more overlays, which exist as separate sections of code stored in the program's .EXE file. Each overlay is loaded from disk (or from expanded memory, if available) into a specific region of conventional memory when it is needed. When execution passes to code contained in another overlay, the second overlay is loaded into the same memory region originally occupied by the first overlay. Only the code, never the data, is overlayed.

A penalty is paid by programs that use overlays: slower execution speed. Because additional time is required in order to swap overlays into memory, program execution is slowed compared to a non-overlay program. The process of overlay swapping is significantly faster if sufficient expanded memory is available because this removes the need for disk accesses. Of course, program size may give you no choice but to use overlays.

A BASIC program can use as many as 64 overlays, and each overlay can be up to 256K in size. That's a total of 16Mb of code—a limit that will rarely be reached by most programmers! If you think a program may require the use of overlays, you need to plan ahead.

You must write the source code for an overlay program in two or more modules. The main module (where execution starts) becomes part of the program root. Each secondary module can, at link time, be added to the root or made into a separate overlay. When writing your source code, divide your program into modules from the very start. Design the modules so that program execution passes between modules as rarely as possible, to minimize the overhead of swapping modules at runtime.

Place error and event handling code in the root section of the program. Also place procedures that are called frequently, such as keyboard or screen routines, in the root section. All modules of an overlay program must be compiled using compatible compiler options.

After you compile your program modules, use the linker to create the overlays. Let's say that you have five program modules: the main module MOD1, and four secondary modules MOD2, MOD3, MOD4, and MOD5. Each has been compiled to an .OBJ file. To place a module's code into an overlay, enclose the module's name in parentheses when invoking the linker. For example, the following linker command divides the program into a root and four overlays:

```
link mod1 + (mod2) + (mod3) + (mod4) + (mod5);
```

All program code, both root and overlay, is contained in a single disk file named MOD1.EXE. You could also enter this linker command:

```
link mod1 + (mod2+mod3) + mod4 + (mod5);
```

This command creates a root that contains the code in MOD1 and MOD4, one overlay that contains the code in MOD2 and MOD3, and a second overlay that contains the code in MOD5.

When creating overlays, you can't use the linker option **/PACKCODE**.

Using Libraries

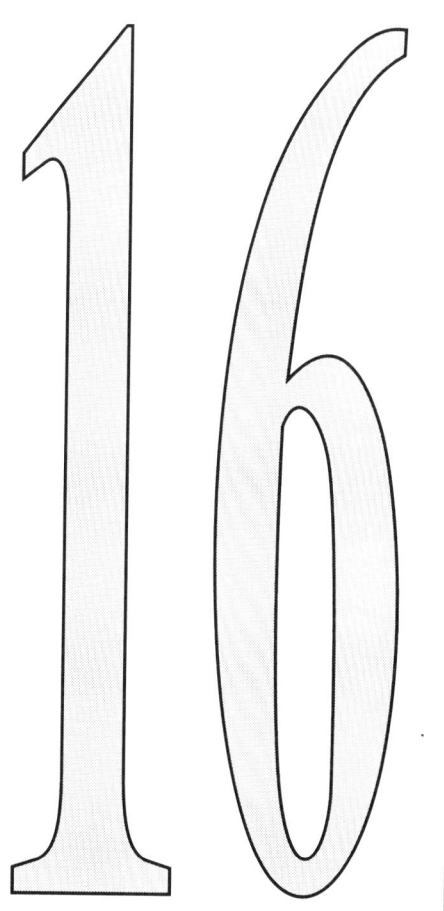

BASIC 7 provides full support for the use of libraries in program development. A *library* is a file that contains multiple BASIC and/or other language procedures in compiled object-code form. When you run your program (from within QBX) or link it (when using standalone program development), the needed procedures are made available to your program. You can use the procedures in a library with as many programs as you like.

Quick Libraries

A *Quick Library* is a special type of library intended specifically for use by the QBX environment. When a Quick Library is loaded into QBX, all of the library procedures are available to any program you are developing. BASIC 7 comes with a default Quick Library, named QBX.QLB, that contains support for the **INTERRUPT**, **INT86OLD**, and **CALL ABSOLUTE** routines. You can create your own Quick Libraries containing BASIC or other language procedures that you've written. In fact, a Quick Library is the only way to use non-BASIC routines within QBX.

Using a Quick Library

To use a Quick Library, you must load it into QBX. This can only be done when you first start QBX, by including the /L option on the command line:

```
QBX /L libname
```

libname is the name of the Quick Library to load. If you specify /L without a **libname**, the default Quick Library QBX.QLB is loaded.

When a Quick Library is loaded into QBX, all of the procedures in the Quick Library are available for use. Only one Quick Library can be loaded at a time. To view the contents of a Quick Library, exit QBX and use the utility program QLBDUMP.BAS provided with BASIC 7.

Creating a Quick Library

You can create a Quick Library using either QBX or the standalone linker. In either case, the first step is to thoroughly test and debug the code for the procedures that will be placed in the Quick Library. When you use QBX you're limited to placing BASIC procedures in a Quick Library. When you use the linker, you can also include procedures written in other languages.

When you create a Quick Library from within QBX, everything loaded in QBX is included in the new Quick Library. This includes the default Quick Library (if it's loaded) plus all procedures in all modules. Because you can't load more than one Quick Library into QBX at a time, it's often desirable to include the default Quick Library in any new Quick Library you create. To create a new Quick Library, follow these steps:

1. Start QBX, loading the default Quick Library if you want its procedures included in the new Quick Library.

2. Load the program module(s) that contain the BASIC procedures you want in the Quick Library.

3. Delete any module-level code and any procedures you don't want in the new Quick Library.

4. Select Make Library... from the Run menu. The dialog box shown in Figure 16.1 is displayed.

5. Enter the Quick Library name and select options as described below. Next, select either Make Library or Make Library and Exit.

The options in the Make Library dialog box are as follows:

• Select Code Generation for 286 if the Quick Library will be used only for programs that will run on systems with an 80286, 80386, or 80486 processor. Such programs will be smaller and execute faster, but cannot be run on PCs with an 8088/8086 processor.

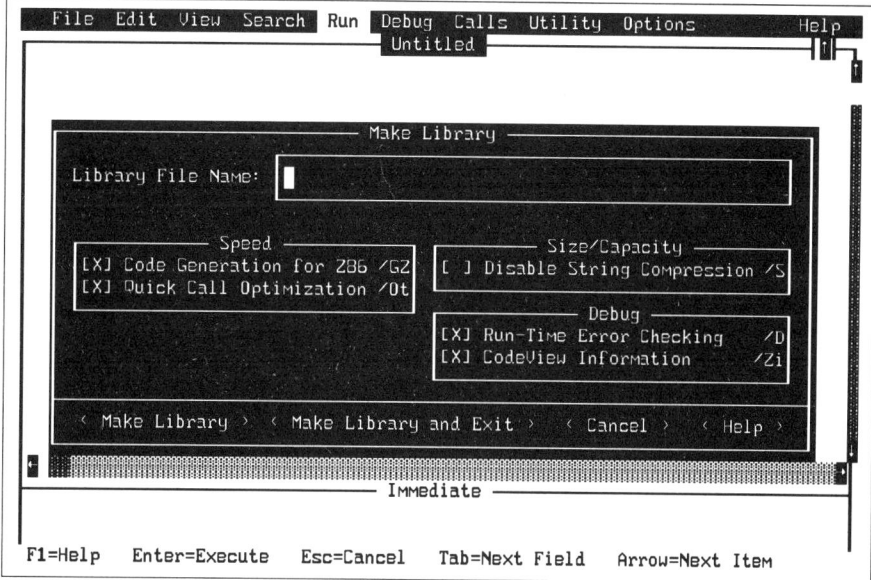

Figure 16.1. The Make Library dialog box.

- Select Quick Call Optimization for improved execution speed if the Quick Library procedures don't use local error handling.

- Select Disable String Compression if you want literal strings written to the library file without being compressed.

- Select RunTime Error Checking to include code for checking runtime errors in the Quick Library.

- Select CodeView Information to add CodeView debugging information to the object code in the Quick Library.

When QBX creates a new Quick Library, several other files are placed on your disk. One .OBJ file is created for each module that was loaded in QBX when the Quick Library was created—these .OBJ files can be deleted. Your disk will also include a standalone library with the same name as the Quick Library and the .LIB extension. This parallel library contains the same procedures that the Quick Library contains, and must not be deleted; it will be used if you create an .EXE file from within QBX.

To add one or more procedures to an existing Quick Library, start QBX and load the Quick Library. Next, load the code for the new procedures and create a new Quick Library. You can't directly delete procedures from a Quick Library. To delete procedures, you must re-load all of the source code, delete the procedures, and then create a new Quick Library.

The process of creating a Quick Library using the linker is more flexible because you can include procedures written in languages other than BASIC, such as C and assembler.

After the source code for the new Quick Library procedures is tested and debugged, compile it using whatever compiler is appropriate for the source language. The result will be one or more .OBJ files. To create the Quick Library, invoke the linker with the following syntax:

```
link /Q objfiles, qlbname, , QBXQLB.LIB;
```

/Q is the linker option that directs it to produce a Quick Library. *objfiles* is the name of one or more .OBJ files, separated by plus signs or spaces, that contain the procedures to be placed in the Quick Library. *qlbname* is the name to assign to the Quick Library. **QBXQLB.LIB** is a library containing routines that must be included in all Quick Libraries.

To include the default Quick Library procedures in the new Quick Library, include the name **QBX.LIB** at the end of the *objfiles* entry above. Here's an example: To create a new Quick Library named NEW.QLB that contains the procedures in PROC1.OBJ and PROC2.OBJ, and the procedures in the default Quick Library, use this command:

```
link /Q proc1+proc2+qlb.lib, new.qlb, nul, qbxqlb.lib;
```

The **nul** argument suppresses the creation of a .MAP file, which takes up disk space and is rarely of any use to BASIC programmers. When you use the linker to create a new Quick Library, remember to also make a parallel standalone library to enable QBX to create .EXE files. This is done by using the LIB utility, discussed later in this chapter.

Standalone Libraries

A *standalone library* is a disk file with the .LIB extension that contains procedures in compiled object-code form. When an executable file is created from your program, the linker searches one or more libraries for procedures called by your program, and includes the procedures' object code with the final .EXE file. BASIC 7 includes a number of default libraries that contain code for BASIC's intrinsic procedures. You can also create libraries that contain procedures you have written in BASIC or other languages.

Note: the BASIC 7 documentation uses the term "standalone library" with two meanings. Sometimes the term means any library that is not a Quick Library. At other times, it refers specifically to the libraries that link with a program compiled with the /O option and don't require a runtime module in order to execute.

The Default Libraries

When you installed BASIC 7 using the SETUP program, you made selections about installing default libraries. Depending upon your choices, one or more default libraries were placed in the \BC7\LIB directory. The default libraries are named BCL70*fsm*.LIB, where *f*, *s*, and *m* are as follows:

- *f* specifies floating-point support. Use E to indicate emulator math and A for alternate math.

- *s* specifies string storage. Use N to indicate near strings and F for far strings.

- *m* specifies the operating environment mode. Use R to indicate real mode and P for protected mode.

Programs are linked with the appropriate BCL70*fsm*.LIB library when they are compiled using the /O option, which creates a standalone .EXE file. If you compile without the /O option, your programs are linked with BASIC's runtime libraries. Programs linked with the runtime libraries require the presence of a runtime module when they execute. The runtime module is automatically loaded when the program is started. The differences between using and not using the /O compiler option are:

With /O   Object code for BASIC's intrinsic procedures is included in the program's .EXE file. Such programs are larger than programs compiled without /O, but require less memory at runtime because no runtime module needs to be loaded.

Without /O   Object code for BASIC's intrinsic procedures is contained in a runtime module that is loaded into memory at runtime. Individual programs are smaller than if compiled with /O.

The runtime libraries are named BRT70*fsm*.LIB. The runtime modules are named BRT70*fsm*.EXE for real mode, and BRT70*fsm*.DLL for protected mode (*f*, *s*, and *m* have the same meanings explained earlier). If you will have multiple executable BASIC programs on your system, compile them to use the runtime module in order to save disk space.

Invoking LIB

Standalone libraries are created and maintained using the LIB.EXE utility provided with BASIC 7. With LIB, you can do the following:

- Combine object files to form a new library.

- Add, delete, or replace object files in an existing library.

- Extract object files from a library.

To start LIB from the DOS prompt, use the following syntax:

```
LIB oldlib [options][commands][,listfile][,newlib][;]
```

oldlib is the name of the existing library to be operated on. If **oldlib** does not exist, LIB asks you whether it should be created. If you specify only an existing **oldlib** on the LIB command line followed by a semicolon, LIB performs an internal consistency check on the library without making any modifications. *oldlib* can include disk and/or path information; the .LIB extension is assumed. **options** to the LIB utility are discussed shortly.

commands consist of the names of object files and/or object modules, along with special symbols telling LIB what actions to take. Commands are explained later in this section.

listfile is the name of a cross-reference listing file to be created. A cross-reference listing contains a list of all public symbols and modules in the library. The default is NUL, meaning that no cross-reference file is created.

newlib is the name to assign to the modified library, if LIB is modifying an existing library. If *newlib* is not specified, the original library is renamed with a .BAK extension, and the new library is given the original name.

A semicolon at the end of the LIB command line tells LIB to use the defaults for all unspecified inputs.

LIB Options

LIB options are specified on the command line following the *oldlib* name, but before the commands. The available options are listed in Table 16.1.

LIB Commands

The LIB commands tell LIB what actions to take. These commands are associated with the name of an object file or an object module. An *object file* is a discrete disk file that contains object code, with a name and extension; the extension is usually .OBJ. Once an object file has been incorporated into a library the object file is referred to as an *object module*. An object module has a name but no extension; the name is typically the name of the source object file.

Table 16.1. LIB options.

/HELP	Instructs LIB to display information about its command syntax and options.
/I	Instructs LIB to ignore case when comparing the names of public symbols in a library. This is the default; the **/I** option is used only when combining a case-sensitive library (created with the **/NOI** option) with non-case-sensitive libraries. The resulting combined library is not case sensitive.
/NOD	Instructs LIB to not create an extended dictionary. This option is used when LIB reports an Insufficient memory or No more virtual memory error, or if the library causes a Symbol multiply defined message when using LINK.
/NOI	Instructs LIB to not ignore case in public symbols. With this option a library could contain, for example, two distinct procedures named **InvMatrix** and **INVMATRIX**.
/NOLOGO	Suppresses LIB's sign-on logo.
/PA:*num*	Specifies the page size of a new or modified library. *num* is the page size in bytes, and must be an integer power of 2 between 16 and 32,768. The default is 16. Larger page sizes allow more modules to be stored in a library, but result in more wasted disk space. Use the default page size, unless you need to put a large number of modules into a library.

A complete LIB command consists of a command symbol, followed immediately (no intervening space) by a name. The name specifies the object file, object module, or library that the command refers to. The five LIB command symbols are listed in Table 16.2.

When LIB processes commands, it never makes changes to the original target library. It first makes a copy of the original library, renames the copy with a .BAK extension, and then acts on the original. If there is a problem during the LIB session (such as a power failure), or if you interrupt activity by pressing the Ctrl+Break keys, you can always recover the original library by renaming the .BAK copy.

You can list multiple commands on the LIB command line, separated by spaces. When you give LIB multiple commands, it processes any deletion and move commands first, and then processes any addition commands. For example, the following LIB command adds the object file MOD1 to the library MYLIB.LIB:

```
LIB mylib +mod1;
```

The following LIB command deletes the module MOD1, and adds the module MOD2 to the library MYLIB.LIB:

Table 16.2. The LIB command symbols.

+	Adds a single object file, or all object modules in another library, to the target library. If you're specifying an object file, you need not include the .OBJ extension. If you're specifying a library, you must include the .LIB extension.
−	Deletes an object module from the target library.
−+	Replaces a module in the library (deletes the existing version and then adds the new version).
*	Extracts a copy of an object module from the target library; i.e., copies it from the library to an object file.
−*	Moves an object module from the target library; i.e., copies it to an object file and deletes it from the library.

```
LIB mylib +mod2 -mod1;
```

The next LIB command creates a new library named NEW.LIB that is identical to MYLIB.LIB, but with the modules MOD1 and MOD2 deleted. MYLIB.LIB is not modified:

```
LIB mylib -mod1 -mod2,,new;
```

This LIB command replaces the object module MOD1 with the contents of the object file MOD1.OBJ:

```
LIB mylib -+mod1;
```

You can also enter LIB commands in response to prompts. If you enter LIB without any commands, it prompts you as follows:

```
Library name:
Operations:
List file:
Output library:
```

Enter responses to the prompts as described for the command line. Press the Enter key to accept the default at any line except Library name:, where a response in required. The defaults for the prompts are listed in Table 16.3.

To enter more operations than will fit on one line, terminate each line with an ampersand (&). LIB will display another Operations: prompt and you can continue entering commands.

Table 16.3. Defaults for LIB prompts.

For Operations:	No change to the library file; consistency check only.
For List file:	NUL; no listing file produced.
For Output library:	The input library name.

LIB can also obtain commands from a response file. A response file is simply an ASCII text file that contains the responses to the LIB prompts, with one response to a line in the proper order. For example, the following response file adds the contents of the object files MOD1.OBJ and MOD2.OBJ to MYLIB.LIB, creating the listing file MYLIB.LST:

```
mylib
+mod1 +mod2
mylib.lst;
```

To invoke LIB with a response file, enter **LIB** followed by the at symbol (**@**) and the name of the response file.

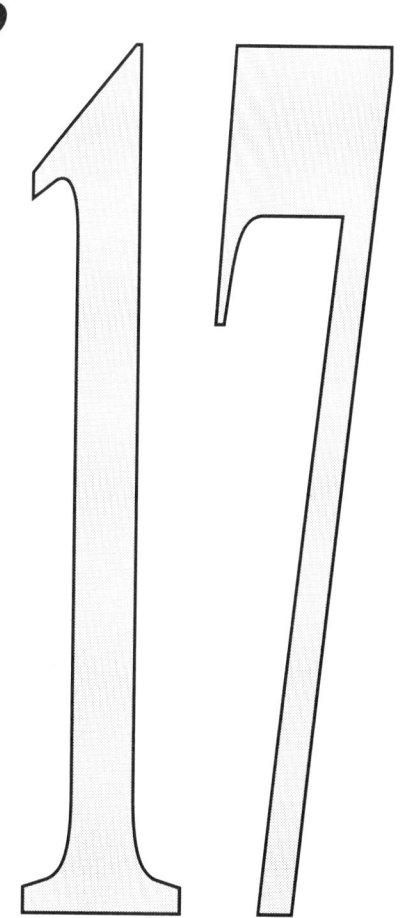

The Date/Time, Format, and Financial Libraries

BASIC 7 is supplied with two add-on libraries that provide special financial, formatting, and date/time functions. These libraries, derived from Microsoft's Excel spreadsheet, greatly simplify many business-programming tasks.

Each add-on library is provided in both Quick Library and standalone forms. The library names are:

Date/time and format: DTFMT*fm*.LIB
                         DTFMTER.QLB

Financial: FINANC*fm*.LIB
                         FINANCER.QLB

The letters *f* and *m* stand for floating-point and operating-system mode support, as selected during the BASIC 7 setup procedure. When emulator math is supported, *f* is E. When alternate math is supported, *f* is A. *m* is R for real mode and P for protected mode.

Remember that only one Quick Library can be loaded at once, so you'll need to use the methods described in Chapter 16 to create a combined date/time, format, and financial Quick Library if you want to use them both in QBX. The include files required when using the functions in these libraries are presented in Table 17.1.

Date/Time Functions

BASIC 7 uses serial numbers to represent specific dates and times. Functions are provided to convert between serial numbers and traditional

Table 17.1. Functions and corresponding include files.

To use	Include this file
date/time functions	DATIM.BI
format functions	FORMAT.BI
financial functions	FINANC.BI

date/time formats. The serial number has an integer part, which represents the date, and a decimal part, which represents the time.

Dates between January 1, 1753 and December 31, 2078 can be represented by BASIC 7 serial numbers. A serial number of 0 represents December 30, 1899. Earlier and later dates are represented by negative and positive numbers, respectively:

$$1 = \text{December 29, 1899}$$
$$33059 = \text{July 5, 1990}$$
$$-45103 = \text{July 4, 1776}$$

Times are represented by decimal values between 0, which represents 12:00:00 A.M., and 0.99999, which represents 11:59:59 P.M.:

$$0.50 \ = 12:00 \text{ noon}$$
$$0.25 \ = 6:00 \text{ A.M.}$$
$$0.875 = 9:00 \text{ P.M.}$$

Combined values represent a specific time and date:

$$33059.5 = 12:00 \text{ noon, July 5, 1990}$$

Converting Between Date and Serial Number

DateSerial# is a function that converts a date to a serial number. The date is represented as discrete values for year, month and day:

```
DateSerial#(year%, month%, day%)
```

year% is an integer expression representing a year between 1753 and 2078, inclusive. Any year in this range can be represented by its full 4-digit value. For the years 1900-2078, you can use *year%* values from 0 to 178.

month% is an integer expression between 1 and 12, inclusive. *day%* is an integer expression between 1 and 31, inclusive. If you use an invalid day (e.g., February 30), **DateSerial#** goes to the next month. For example, **DateSerial#** assigns February 31, 1990 the same serial number as March 3, 1990.

DateValue# is a function that converts a date to a serial number. The date is represented as a standard-format text string:

```
DateValue#( date$)
```

date$* is a string expression specifying a date (and, optionally, the time) between January 1, 1753 and December 31, 2078, inclusive. Valid formats include "March 7, 1947", "22/12/80", and "7-Sep-1975 12:55 PM". Time information in *date$ is ignored. If the year is omitted, the function uses the current year from the system clock.

Day& returns the day of the month for a specific serial number. Specifically, **Day&** returns a value between 1 and 31 that specifies the day of the month represented by *serialnum#*. The syntax for **Day&** is:

```
Day&( serialnum#)
```

Month& returns the month corresponding to a specific serial number. **Month&** returns a value between 1 and 12 that specifies the month represented by *serialnum#*. The syntax for **Month&** is:

```
Month&( serialnum#)
```

Weekday& returns the day of the week corresponding to a specific serial number. More specifically, **Weekday&** returns a value between 1 (Sunday) and 7 (Saturday) representing the day of the week of *serialnum#*. The syntax for **Weekday&** is:

```
Weekday&( serialnum#)
```

Year& returns the year represented by a specific serial number. **Year&** returns a value between 1753 and 2078 that gives the year of *serialnum#*. The syntax for **Year&** is:

```
Year&( serialnum#)
```

Converting Between Time and Serial Number

The function **TimeSerial#** converts a time to a serial number. The time is represented as discrete values for hour, minute, and second:

```
TimeSerial#( hour%, minute%, second%)
```

hour% is an integer expression between 0 (12:00 A.M.) and 23 (11:00 P.M.). *minute%* is an integer expression between 0 and 59. *second%* is an integer expression between 0 and 59.

The function **TimeValue#** converts a time to a serial number. The time is represented as a standard-format text string:

```
TimeValue#( time$)
```

time$* is a string expression representing a time between 00:00:00 (12:00:00 A.M.) and 23:59:59 (11:59:59 P.M.). *time$ can be in either 12- or 24-hour format, e.g., "2:30 P.M." or "14:30". *time$* can also include date information, which is ignored.

The function **Hour&** returns the hour of the day represented by a given serial number. **Hour&** returns an integer between 0 (12:00 A.M.) and 23 (11:00 P.M.) that specifies the hour of the day represented by *serialnum#*. The syntax for **Hour&** is:

```
Hour&( serialnum#)
```

The function **Minute&** returns the minute of the hour represented by a given serial number. **Minute&** returns an integer between 0 and 59 that specifies the minute represented by *serialnum#*. The syntax for **Minute&** is:

```
Minute&( serialnum#)
```

The function **Second&** returns the second represented by a given serial number. **Second&** returns an integer between 0 and 59 that specifies the second represented by *serialnum#*. The syntax for **Second&** is:

```
Second&( serialnum#)
```

Current Date and Time

The **Now#** function returns the serial number representing the date and time set on the computer's system clock. **Now#** takes no arguments.

Format Functions

BASIC 7 has five format functions. Each function takes a numeric value and returns it as a string, formatted according to your specifications. To use the format functions, your program must include the file FORMAT.BI. The five format functions work in the same manner, differing only in the data type of the numeric expression to be formatted. The functions are listed in Table 17.2.

The syntax of all of the five format functions is:

```
FORMAT X$(expression, fmt$)
```

X is the letter I, L, S, D, or C as explained in Table 17.2. *expression* is a numeric expression of the data type appropriate for *X*. *fmt$* is a string expression that specifies how *expression* is to be formatted.

The format string, *fmt$*, consists of one or more special formatting characters. The characters and their meanings are listed in Table 17.3. Note: If *fmt$* is the null string, *expression* is formatted in general format.

Table 17.2. The five format functions.

Function	Data type
FORMATI$	Integer
FORMATL$	Long integer
FORMATS$	Single precision
FORMATD$	Double precision
FORMATC$	Currency

Table 17.3. The special formatting characters.

Character	Meaning
0	A digit placeholder. The number is formatted with one digit for each 0 in *fmt$*. If *fmt$* specifies more digits than the number has, leading and/or trailing zeros are added as needed. If *fmt$* specifies too few digits to the right of the decimal point, the number is rounded off. If *fmt$* specifies too few digits to the left of the decimal point, all digits are displayed.
#	A digit placeholder. The number is formatted the same as for the 0 placeholder, except that leading and/or trailing zeros are not added.
.	Decimal point. When included, the position of the decimal point relative to the digit placeholders indicates how many digits are to be displayed on either side of the decimal point. For example, a format string of ##.### displays two digits to the left, and three to the right, of the decimal point.
%	Percentage format. The number is multiplied by 100 and displayed with a trailing percent sign (%).
,	Thousands separator. A comma included anywhere in *fmt$* with a digit placeholder on either side displays the number with thousands separators (e.g., 1,000,000). The separator symbol used is either a comma or a period, depending upon the country setting made with the **SetFormatCC** procedure.
E+ E- e+ e-	Scientific format. The number is displayed as a decimal value multiplied by a power of 10. For example, 102 in scientific format is 1.02E+2 (1.02 times 100). Use E or e to specify the case of the "E" in the display. Use digit placeholders to the left to specify digits in the value; use digit placeholders to the right to specify digits in the exponent. Negative exponents are always displayed with a minus sign. Use E+ or e+ to display positive exponents with a plus sign. Use E- or e- to display positive exponents without a sign. *continued*

Table 17.3. The special formatting characters (*continued*).

Character	Meaning
: – + $ () Space	These characters are displayed as themselves. For example, to display a number preceded by a dollar sign, you could use the format string **$##.##**.
\	Display the next character as itself, do not treat it as a formatting symbol. For example, the format string **\###.** would display a number with two digits to the left of the decimal point, preceded by a #.
""	Characters enclosed in double quotes are displayed as themselves. To include a double quote in a format string, use **CHR$(34)**. (34 is the ASCII code for the double quotation mark character.) For example, `fmt$ = CHR$(34)+"Profit = "+CHR$(34)+"$###.##"`
;	Separates the format string into sections that apply to negative, zero, and positive values. If there is one section in the format string, it applies to all values. If there are two sections, the first applies to positive and zero values and the second applies to negative values. If there are three sections, they apply to positive, negative, and zero values in turn.

Table 17.4 shows the results returned when various format strings are used to format different values. The program that produced this output is listed next.

```
' Demonstrates add-on library format functions.
' Must load DTFMTER.QLB to run in QBX.

' $INCLUDE: 'format.bi'

CONST Format = 5

DIM fmt$(1 TO Format)
```

Table 17.4. Results of various format strings.

Format String	values		
	123	123.456	1000000
0	123	123	1000000
00.00	123.00	123.46	1000000.00
##.##	123.	123.46	1000000.
#.0000E+000	1.2300E+002	1.2346E+002	1.0000E+006
$###.##;($###.##)	$123.	$123.46	($1000000.)

```
FOR i% = 1 TO Format
    READ fmt$(i%)
NEXT i%

a% = 123
a# = 123.456
a@ = 1000000

CLS

FOR i% = 1 TO Format
  LOCATE i% * 2, 1
  PRINT fmt$(i%);
  LOCATE , 24
  PRINT FormatI$(a%, fmt$(i%));
  LOCATE , 42
  PRINT FormatD$(a#, fmt$(i%));
  LOCATE , 60
  PRINT FormatC$(a@, fmt$(i%));
NEXT i%

SLEEP
END

DATA "0", "00.00", "##.##", "#.0000E+000", "$###.##;($###.##)"
```

You can use special date and time formatting characters with **FormatD$** (recall that dates and times are stored by BASIC as double-precision serial numbers). The date/time formatting characters are listed in Table 17.5.

Table 17.5. Date/time formatting characters.

s	Displays seconds as a number without leading zeros (0, 1, 2,...59).
ss	Displays seconds as a number with leading zeros (00, 01, 02,...59).
m	Following an "h", displays minutes as a number without leading zeros (0, 1, 2,...59).
mm	Following an "h", displays minutes as a number with leading zeros (00, 01, 02,...59).
h	Displays hours as a number without leading zeros (0, 1, 2,...23).
hh	Displays hours as a number with leading zeros (00, 01, 02,...23). For both hour formats, the number displayed is based on the 12-hour clock if the format contains "AM" or "PM"; otherwise, the 24-hour clock is used.
yy	Displays the year as a two-digit number (00-99).
yyyy	Displays the year as a four-digit number (1900-2040).
m	If not following an "h", displays the month as a two-digit number without a leading 0 (1-12).
mm	If not following an "h", displays the month as a two-digit number with a leading 0 (01-12).
mmm	If not following an "h", displays the month as a three-letter abbreviation (Jan, Feb, etc.).
mmmm	If not following an "h", displays the month fully spelled out (January, ...).
AM/PM am/pm A/P a/p	Display the time using the 12-hour clock rather than the 24-hour clock. For times between midnight and 12:00 noon, AM, A, am, or a is displayed. For times between 12:00 noon and midnight, PM, P, pm, or p is displayed.

The **SetFormatCC** procedure sets the country code used by the **FormatX$** functions. The syntax for **SetFormatCC** is:

```
SetFormatCC( code%)
```

code% is an integer expression specifying the country. Use the country's international telephone-dialing prefix. The country code affects only the separators used in formatting. Most European countries use the period to separate thousands, and the comma as the decimal point.

Financial Functions

The BASIC 7 financial add-on library contains a number of functions that perform commonly needed financial calculations, such as depreciation, present value, and loan payments.

Depreciation Functions

DDB# uses the double-declining-balance method to calculate the depreciation on an asset over a particular period. The syntax for **DDB#** is:

```
DDB#( cost#, salvage#, life#, period#, status%)
```

cost# is the initial cost of the asset. *salvage#* is the salvage value of the asset, i.e., its value at the end of its useful life. *life#* is the useful life of the asset. *period#* is the period over which depreciation is to be calculated. *status%* can be tested after a call to **DDB#** to determine whether the depreciation calculation failed (*status%* = 1) or succeeded (*status%* = 0).

When passing arguments to **DDB#**, be sure that *life#* and *period#* are expressed in the same units (both in months, or both in years).

SLN# calculates depreciation for a single period, using the straight line method:

```
SLN# ( cost#, salvage#, life#, status%)
```

cost# is the initial cost of the asset. *salvage#* is the salvage value of the asset, i.e., its value at the end of its useful life. *life#* is the useful life of the asset, in periods. *status%* can be tested after a call to **SLN#** to determine whether the depreciation calculation failed (*status%* = 1) or succeeded (*status%* = 0).

SYD# calculates depreciation for a specified period using the sum-of-years digits method:

```
SYD# (cost#, salvage#, life#, period#, status%)
```

cost# is the initial cost of the asset. *salvage#* is the salvage value of the asset; i.e., its value at the end of its useful life. *life#* is the useful life of the asset (the number of periods over which it is being depreciated). *life#* must use the same units (months, years) as *period#*.

period# is the period over which depreciation is to be calculated. *status%* can be tested after a call to **SYD#** to determine whether the depreciation calculation failed (*status%* = 1) or succeeded (*status%* = 0).

Annuity Functions

Annuity is a general term for any situation where fixed cash payments are made at regular intervals, with a specific interest rate, over a period of time. A car loan is one example. A regular savings plan, where you put a certain amount in your savings account every month, is another example. The financial functions that deal with annuities treat the cash you receive as positive values and the cash you pay out as negative values.

The *present value* of an annuity is its value at the present time, usually at the start of the annuity. The *future value* of an annuity is the value it will have at the end of the last annuity period. When you take out a loan, its present value is the amount borrowed, and its future value at the end of payments is zero. When you begin a savings program, its present value is zero, and its future value is the amount you want to have at the end of the annuity.

FV# calculates the future value of an annuity based on regular, constant payments and a fixed interest rate:

```
FV# (rate#, nper#, pmt#, pv#, type%, status%)
```

rate# is the interest rate per period (e.g., 0.10 for 10% interest). *nper#* is the number of payment periods in the annuity. *pmt#* is the payment to be made each period. *pv#* is the present value of the annuity.

type% specifies the type of annuity. Set *type%* to 0 if payments are made at the end of each annuity period, or to 1 if payments are made at the beginning of each annuity period.

status% can be tested after a call to **FV#** to determine whether the calculation failed (*status%* = 1) or succeeded (*status%* = 0).

FV# returns a negative number because it deals with cash paid out. When you use the **FV#** function, be sure that the *rate#* and *nper#* arguments are consistent. For example, for a five-year annuity with zero present value, 10% annual interest, and monthly payments of $100, you would use:

```
FV#(.10/12, 5*12, 100, 0, 1, status%)
```

If you were making annual payments of $1200, you would use:

```
FV#(.10, 5, 1200, 0, 1, status%)
```

IPmt# calculates the amount of the interest payment for a given annuity period, based on regular, constant payments and a fixed interest rate. Its syntax is:

```
IPmt# (rate#, per#, nper#, pv#, fv#, type%, status%)
```

rate# is the interest rate per period (e.g., .10 for 10% interest). The period for *rate#* must match the period used by *nper#* (i.e., months or years). *per#* is the payment period over which interest is to be calculated. *per#* must be in the range from 1 to *nper#*. *nper#* is the total number of payment periods in the annuity.

pv# is the present value of the annuity. *fv#* is the future value of the annuity. *type%* specifies the type of annuity. Set *type%* to 0 if payments are made at the end of each annuity period, or to 1 if payments are made at the beginning of each annuity period.

You can test *status%* after a call to **IPmt#** to determine whether the calculation failed (*status%* = 1) or succeeded (*status%* = 0).

To calculate principal payment on an annuity, use **PPmt#**.

NPer# calculates the number of periods (payments) required for an annuity based on fixed, periodic payments and a constant interest rate:

```
NPer# (rate#, pmt#, pv#, fv#, type%, status%)
```

rate# is the interest rate per period (e.g., .10 for 10% interest). The period for ***rate#*** must match the period used by ***nper#*** (i.e., both in months or both in years). ***pmt#*** is the payment made per period. ***pv#*** is the present value of the annuity. ***fv#*** is the future value of the annuity.

type% specifies the type of annuity. Set ***type%*** to 0 if payments are made at the end of each annuity period, or to 1 if payments are made at the beginning of each annuity period.

You can test ***status%*** after a call to **NPer#** to determine whether the calculation failed (***status%*** = 1) or succeeded (***status%*** = 0).

Use **NPer#** to answer questions such as: If I can put away $100 per month at 10% interest, how long will it take to save $10,000? The arguments for this problem would be:

```
NPer#(.1 / 12, -100, 0, 10000, 1, x%)
```

The answer is 72.585 months, or about 6 years.

Pmt# calculates the fixed, periodic payment for an annuity with known present and future values, based on a constant interest rate:

```
Pmt# (rate#, nper#, pv#, fv#, type%, status%)
```

rate# is the interest rate per period (e.g., .10 for 10% interest). The period for ***rate#*** must match the period used by ***nper#***. ***nper#*** is the number of annuity periods (number of payments). ***pv#*** is the present value of the annuity. ***fv#*** is the future value of the annuity.

type% specifies the type of annuity. Set ***type%*** to 0 if payments are made at the end of each annuity period, or to 1 if payments are made at the beginning of each annuity period.

You can test ***status%*** after a call to **NPer#** to determine whether the calculation failed (***status%*** = 1) or succeeded (***status%*** = 0).

Use **Pmt#** to determine the monthly payment required on a $15,000, four-year car loan at 14% interest. The arguments would be:

```
Pmt#(.14 / 12, 4 * 12, 15000, 0, 1, status%)
```

The answer is $405.17.

PPmt# calculates the amount of the principal payment for a given annuity period, based on regular, constant payments and a fixed interest rate:

```
PPmt# (rate#, per#, nper#, pv#, fv#, type%, status%)
```

rate# is the interest rate per period (e.g., .10 for 10% interest). The period for *rate#* must match the period used by *nper#*. *per#* is the payment period for which interest is to be calculated. *per#* must be in the range from 1 to *nper#*. *nper#* is the total number of payment periods in the annuity. *pv#* is the present value of the annuity. *fv#* is the future value of the annuity.

type% specifies the type of annuity. Set *type%* to 0 if payments are made at the end of each annuity period, or to 1 if payments are made at the beginning of each annuity period.

You can test *status%* after a call to **PPmt#** to determine whether the calculation failed (*status%* = 1) or succeeded (*status%* = 0).

To calculate the interest payment on an annuity, use **IPmt#**.

PV# calculates the present value of an annuity:

```
PV# (rate#, nper#, pmt#, fv#, type%, status%)
```

rate# is the interest rate per period (e.g., .10 for 10% interest). The period for *rate#* must match the period used by *nper#*. *nper#* is the total number of payment periods in the annuity. *pmt#* is the fixed payment to be made each period. *fv#* is the future value of the annuity.

type% specifies the type of annuity. Set *type%* to 0 if payments are made at the end of each annuity period, or to 1 if payments are made at the beginning of each annuity period.

You can test *status%* after a call to **PV#** to determine whether the calculation failed (*status%* = 1) or succeeded (*status%* = 0).

Use **PV#** to answer questions such as: How much money do I have to put in the bank at 8% interest to be able to withdraw $500 per month over the next 5 years, with nothing remaining at the end (i.e., future value = 0)? The correct arguments would be:

```
PV#(.08 / 12, 5 * 12, 500, 0, 1, x%)
```

The answer is $24,823.61.

Rate# calculates the interest rate per period of an annuity with a known period, future and present values, and fixed payment. The syntax for **Rate#** is:

```
Rate# (nper#, pmt#, pv#, fv#, type%, guess#, status%)
```

nper# is the number of payment periods in the annuity. *pmt#* is the payment to be made each period. *pv#* is the present value of the annuity. *fv#* is the future value of the annuity.

type% specifies the type of annuity. Set *type%* to 0 if payments are made at the end of each annuity period, or to 1 if payments are made at the beginning of each annuity period. *guess#* is your initial guess at the value of the interest rate. (0.1 is a good guess for many situations.)

You can test *status%* after a call to **Rate#** to determine whether the calculation failed (*status%* = 1) or succeeded (*status%* = 0).

The **Rate#** function operates by iteration: it starts with the *guess#* value and repeats the calculations until the answer is accurate to within 0.00001 percent. If this level of accuracy is not achieved after 20 iterations, the calculation fails and returns a *status%* of 1. If this occurs, or if you get an answer that seems way off, try a different value for *guess#*.

Use **Rate#** to answer questions such as: I want to take out a $120,000, 30-year mortgage, and can afford $950 per month payments. What is the maximum allowable interest rate? The arguments for this are:

```
Rate#(30 * 12, -950, 120000, 0, 1, .1 / 12, x%)
```

The answer is 0.00742. That number is the per-period rate, so multiply it by 12 to get an annual rate of 8.9%.

Other Functions

NPV# calculates the net present value of an investment based on a series of periodic cash flows (payments and receipts) and a fixed interest rate (also called discount rate). The syntax for **NPV#** is:

```
NPV# (rate#, valuearray#(), valuecount%, status%)
```

rate# is the interest rate, which must be fixed over the length of the period. *valuearray#()* is an array containing the cash flow values. Payments are negative values and receipts are positive values. The array must contain at least one receipt and one payment. Cash flows must be entered in the array in the same order they occurred.

valuecount% is the total number of items in *valuearray#()*. *status%* can be tested after a call to **NPV#** to determine whether the calculation failed (*status%* = 1) or succeeded (*status%* = 0).

NPV# differs from **PV#** in two ways:

1. **PV#** permits cash flow to begin at the beginning or the end of the period, and **NPV#** only allows it to begin at the end of the period.

2. **PV#** assumes a constant cash flow throughout the period, and **NPV#** allows a variable cash flow.

IRR# calculates the internal rate of return for a series of periodic cash flows that occur at regular intervals:

```
IRR# (valuearray#(), valuecount%, guess#, status%)
```

valuearray#() is an array containing the cash flow values. Payments are negative values and receipts are positive values. The array must contain at least one receipt and one payment. Cash flows must be entered in the array in the same order they occurred. *valuecount%* is the total number of items in *valuearray#()*.

guess# is your initial guess at the value of **IRR#**. (An initial guess of 0.1 is good for many situations.) You can test *status%* after a call to **IRR#** to determine whether the calculation failed (*status%* = 1) or succeeded (*status%* = 0).

The **IRR#** function operates by iteration: it starts with the *guess#* value and repeats the calculations until the answer is accurate to within 0.00001 percent. If this level of accuracy is not achieved after 20 iterations, the calculation fails and returns a ***status%*** of 1. If this occurs, or if you get an answer that seems way off, try a different value for ***guess#***.

MIRR# calculates the modified internal rate of return for a series of period cash flows that occur at regular intervals. It differs from **IRR#** in that it performs calculations based upon payments and receipts being financed at different interest rates. In other words, **MIRR#** takes into account the cost of borrowing money (***finrate#***) and the interest received on cash investments (***reinvrate#***). The syntax for **MIRR#** is:

```
MIRR# (valuearray#(), valuecount%, finrate#, reinvrate#,
       status%)
```

valuearray#() is an array containing the cash flow values. Payments are negative values, and receipts are positive values. The array must contain at least one receipt and one payment. Cash flows must be entered in the array in the same order that they occur. ***valuecount%*** is the total number of items in ***valuearray#()***.

finrate# is the interest rate paid on borrowed funds; i.e., the cost of financing. ***reinvrate#*** is the interest rate received on reinvested cash.

You can test ***status%*** after a call to **MIRR#** to determine whether the calculation failed (***status%*** = 1) or succeeded (***status%*** = 0).

The User Interface Toolboxes

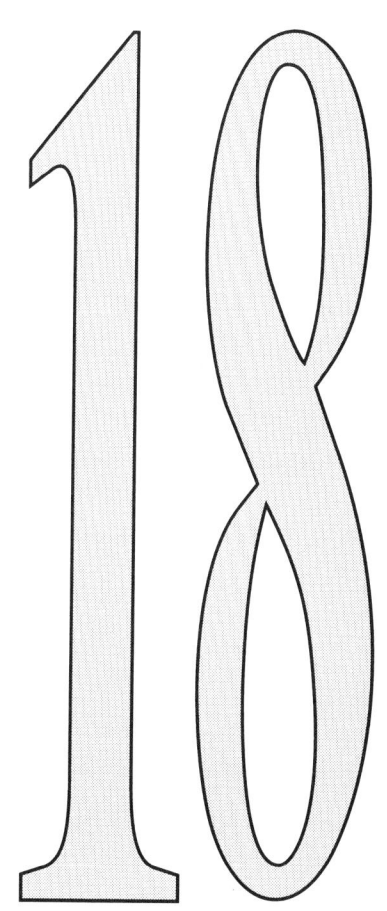

BASIC 7 comes with the source code for several collections of related routines, called *toolboxes*, that can be very useful in many programming tasks. This chapter covers the User Interface toolbox. (The Presentation Graphics and Font toolboxes were covered in Chapters 10, 11, and 12.)

Toolbox Components

The User Interface toolbox consists of five components:

1. The Menus toolbox lets you use custom, pull-down menus in your programs. The Menus toolbox consists of the BASIC source code file MENU.BAS and the include file MENU.BI.

2. The Windows toolbox is used to create text windows and dialog boxes, and consists of the BASIC source code file WINDOW.BAS and the include file WINDOW.BI.

3. The Mouse toolbox provides support for 100% Microsoft compatible mice. It consists of the BASIC source code file MOUSE.BAS and the include file MOUSE.BI.

4. The General toolbox contains several general purpose procedures that are used by both the Menus and Mouse toolboxes. The General toolbox consists of GENERAL.BAS and GENERAL.BI.

5. Assembly language routines used by the toolboxes are found in UIASM.OBJ.

This chapter describes only the Menus and Windows toolboxes, which are of primary interest to most programmers. The routines in the General and Mouse toolboxes are intended for use by the Menus and Windows toolboxes. (If you're interested in calling these routines directly, you'll find more information about them in the BASIC 7 documentation.)

In most cases you'll use the User Interface toolboxes together as a unit. Because they are supplied as four separate source files, however, you have the option to use only selected individual toolboxes. There are dependencies between the toolboxes that you must be aware of. Each toolbox requires the assembly language routines in UIASM.OBJ, and also requires that the corresponding include file be used. Four other dependencies also exist:

1. To use the Mouse toolbox, you must include the file GENERAL.BI.

2. To use the Menus toolbox, you must also use the Mouse toolbox and the General toolbox.

3. To use the Windows toolbox, you must use all other toolboxes.

4. The General toolbox is not dependent upon any other toolbox.

Using the Toolboxes

You can select from several approaches to incorporating the toolboxes into your programs.

1. When using QBX, one approach is to load the Quick Library UITBEFR.QLB, which contains all of the toolbox routines. This library is supplied with BASIC 7. If you modify the toolboxes, the User Interface Toolbox chapter in the *BASIC 7 Language Reference* contains instructions on how to create this library from the source files. When you create this Quick Library, the parallel library UITBEFR.LIB is also created. You'll need the standalone library for creating .EXE files.

2. When using QBX, an alternative approach is to load a Quick Library that contains only the assembly language routines. This library is not supplied; you must create it following the instructions in the User Interface Toolbox chapter in the *BASIC 7 Lan-*

guage Reference. Use the Load File... command to load each of the toolbox source files into QBX as a separate module. This approach is best if you want to modify the toolbox routines.

3. When using the command-line compiler and linker, link your programs with the standalone library UITBEFR.LIB.

If you are thinking about modifying toolbox routines, be aware that each toolbox contains a number of procedures that are never called directly by your program, but are used internally by other toolbox routines. You must never modify these procedures (which are identified later in the chapter), nor should your program call them directly.

A Demonstration

BASIC 7 comes with a user-interface demonstration program called UIDEMO.BAS. I strongly suggest you run this program because it provides an excellent demonstration of the toolbox capabilities. You can also examine the source code for hints about how the toolbox routines are used.

The Menus Toolbox

Menus created with the Menus toolbox are very similar to the menus found in the QBX environment. A main menu is displayed across the top of the screen; each selection on the main menu leads to a pull-down menu that contains one or more items. You can make menu selections by using the mouse, the keyboard, or the shortcut keys. Pull-down menus are numbered according to their position on the main menu, starting at 1 for the left-most menu. Items on each pull-down menu are also numbered from top to bottom, starting at 1. Item number 0 on a pull-down menu is its title, which is displayed on the main menu.

General Procedure

Any program that uses the Menus toolbox must include the following **COMMON** and **DIM** statements in the order shown, after including the file MENUS.BI:

```
COMMON SHARED /uitools/ GloMenu AS MenuMiscType

COMMON SHARED /uitools/ GloTitle() AS MenuTitleType

COMMON SHARED /uitools/ GloItem() AS MenuItemType

DIM GloTitle(MAXMENU) AS MenuTitleType

DIM GloItem(MAXMENU, MAXITEM) AS MenuItemType
```

To define and use menus, follow these general procedures:

1. Initialize the Menus toolbox with a call to **MenuInit**.

2. Use **MenuSet** to define each entry on the main menu and the pull-down menus.

3. Use **ShortCutKeySet** to define any shortcut keys that are to be associated with menu items.

4. Call **MenuColor** to define the menu's color scheme.

5. Call **MenuPreProcess** to perform needed calculations.

6. Call **MenuShow** to display the menu.

7. Call **MouseShow** to display the mouse cursor.

8. Create a program loop that calls **MenuInkey$** to detect user input and then branches accordingly.

The procedure **MenuDo** in MENU.BAS is used internally by other menu procedures. You should not use or alter this procedure.

Detecting Menu Events

Items on toolbox menus can be selected in one of three ways:

1. By clicking the menu item with the mouse.

2. By pressing **ALT+x**, where *x* is the single highlighted character in the menu item.

3. By pressing the shortcut key, if any, associated with the menu item.

Any of these actions is called a *menu event*. To respond to menu events, your program must perform two actions:

1. Determine whether or not a menu event has occurred. This is usually done with the **MenuInkey$** function, which detects all three methods of menu selection just listed.

2. If a menu event has occurred, determine which specific menu item was selected. Call **MenuCheck(0)** to determine which menu was selected, and call **MenuCheck(1)** to determine which item on the menu was selected.

Here's an example. The following code fragment shows how to use **MenuInkey$** to detect a menu event or other keyboard input:

```
...
k$ = MenuInkey$

IF k$ = "menu" THEN
  menu = MenuCheck(0)
  item = MenuCheck(1)

' Code here to direct program execution based on the
' values of menu and item.

ELSE
```

```
' Code here to deal with non-menu event input.

END IF
...
```

The procedure **MenuEvent** detects ALT-key events and mouse events, but not shortcut key events. The procedure **ShortCutKeyEvent** detects shortcut key events, but not ALT+a key and mouse menu events. Both of these procedures are called by **MenuInkey$**. There is rarely any need to call them individually.

Menu Procedures

The menu procedures are listed in Table 18.1 by function, and explained in detail in this section.

Table 18.1. Menu procedures by function.

Menu Procedure	Function
Menu system initialization	**MenuInit**
	MenuPreProcess
Define and display menus	**MenuColor**
	MenuSet
	MenuShow
Modify menu items	**MenuSetState**
	MenuItemToggle
Detect menu events	**MenuCheck**
	MenuEvent
	MenuInkey$
	MenuOff
	MenuOn
	ShortCutKeyEvent
Define shortcut keys	**ShortCutKeySet**
	ShortCutKeyDelete

The function **MenuCheck** returns a value indicating menu selections:

```
result% = MenuCheck( action%)
```

result% is any BASIC integer variable. **action%** is an integer expression with a value of 0, 1, or 2 the specifies the action that **MenuCheck** is to take. The possible actions are listed in Table 18.2.

The following code fragment shows how to use **MenuCheck** to detect a menu event.

```
MenuEvent

IF MenuCheck(2) THEN
   menu = MenuCheck(0)
   item = MenuCheck(1)
...
' Code here to handle menu selection.
...
END IF
```

Table 18.2. **MenuCheck** actions.

action%	MenuCheck action
0	Determines if a menu item was selected since the last call to **MenuCheck**. If not, **MenuCheck** returns 0. If so, **MenuCheck** returns the menu number, and sets global variables so that a subsequent call to **MenuCheck(1)** returns the item number.
1	Returns the item number of the most recent menu selection.
2	Returns true (-1) if a menu item has been selected since the last **MenuCheck** call, or false (0) if no menu selection has occurred. If true is returned, use **MenuCheck(0)** and **MenuCheck(1)** to determine which item was selected.

MenuColor assigns colors to the various menu components:

```
MenuColor ( fg%, bg%, highlight%, disabled%, crsFg%, crsBg%,
            crsHi% )
```

fg% is an integer (0-15) that specifies the menu foreground-text color. *bg%* is an integer (0-7) that specifies the menu background color. *highlight%* is an integer (0-15) that specifies the color of the access key character. *disabled%* is an integer (0-15) that specifies the text color of disabled menu items.

crsFg% is an integer (0-15) that specifies the foreground color of the menu cursor. *crsBg%* is an integer (0-7) that specifies the background color of the menu cursor. *crsHi%* is an integer (0-15) that specifies the color of the access-key character when the menu cursor is on the item.

The color of the shadows that appear "behind" menus is black, and cannot be changed. If you do not use **MenuColor** to assign colors, the following default color scheme is used:

fg% = 0
bg% = 7
highlight% = 15
disabled% = 8
crsFg% = 7
crsBg% = 0
crsHi% = 15

This default color scheme produces a monochrome menu. If your program changes colors during execution, call **MenuShow** to display the new colors.

MenuEvent detects Alt+key keypresses and mouse menu events (but not shortcut keys). Its syntax is simply:

```
MenuEvent
```

When it's called, **MenuEvent** checks to see if an Alt key is pressed, or if the mouse button was pressed while the mouse cursor is on the main menu. If so, the internal routine **MenuDo** is called. **MenuDo** retains control until one of two things happens:

1. A menu item is selected.

2. The user exits the menu system by pressing the Esc key or by releasing the mouse button when the cursor is positioned outside the main menu.

After you call **MenuEvent**, call **MenuCheck** to determine if a menu selection was made, and which item was selected. See the sample code under **MenuCheck** for an example.

MenuInit initializes the global menu arrays and the mouse driver:

```
MenuInit
```

MenuInit must be the first menu routine called by your program. **MenuInkey$** is a function that checks for user input:

```
variable$ = MenuInkey$
```

*variable$* is any BASIC string variable. When you call **MenuInkey$**, it performs a standard BASIC **INKEY$**, as well as a **MenuEvent** procedure and a **ShortCutKeyEvent** procedure. When you call **MenuInkey$**, one of two conditions will hold:

1. If either a menu event or a shortcut-key event has occurred, **MenuInkey$** returns "menu". You must call **MenuCheck** next to determine which menu selection was made.

2. If no menu or shortcut-key event occurred, **MenuInkey$** returns the value returned by **INKEY$** (which is the null string if no key was pressed).

MenuItemToggle toggles the state of a specific menu item between 1 (enabled) and 2 (enabled with a check mark). The syntax for **MenuItemToggle** is:

```
MenuItemToggle( menu%, item%)
```

menu% is an integer expression specifying the left-right position of the menu. *item%* is an integer expression specifying the position of the item on the menu.

You do not have to call **MenuPreProcess** after a call to **MenuToggleItem**.

MenuOff and **MenuOn** turn menu-event processing off and on. Their syntax is:

```
MenuOff
MenuOn
```

When menu event processing is off, any menu events (either keyboard or mouse) are ignored. The menu remains displayed. These procedures operate by changing the global variable **GloMenu.MenuOn** to either true or false.

MenuPreProcess performs internal calculations and builds indexes that are required by the menu toolbox. The result is that the menu procedures run faster. The syntax for **MenuPreProcess** is:

```
MenuPreProcess
```

You must call **MenuPreProcess** each time **MenuSet** is called one or more times, when a menu item's state is changed to or from the empty state, or when any changes (other than item selection changes) are made to the menu.

Use **MenuSet** to define individual menu items:

```
MenuSet(menu%, item%, state%, text$, accessKey%)
```

menu% is an integer expression specifying the pull-down menu the item is on. Menus are numbered from left to right. *item%* is an integer expression specifying the item on the pulldown menu. Use *item%* = 0 to specify the menu title. Actual menu selections are numbered from top to bottom.

state% is an integer expression that specifies the state of the menu item, as described in Table 18.3.

text$* is a string expression that specifies the menu item. Maximum length is 15 characters for titles and 30 characters for menu selections. Specify *text$ = "-" to display a horizontal bar across the menu.

Table 18.3. Various states of menu items.

state%	Menu item is
-1	Empty. Not displayed and not selectable.
0	Disabled. Cannot be selected, and is displayed in the color specified by the *disabled%* color set with **MenuColor**.
1	Enabled. The normal state.
2	Enabled and displayed with a check mark.

accessKey% is an integer expression specifying the position in *text$* of the single character that can be used to select the menu item. The character is displayed in the color specified by the *highlight%* argument passed to **MenuColor**.

MenuSet must be called once to define each individual item on your menu system. After defining your menus with **MenuSet**, call **MenuPreProcess** to perform needed calculations and call **MenuShow** to display the main menu. After you define a menu, you can modify the state of individual items using **MenuSetState**.

Use **MenuSetState** to change the state of existing menu items:

```
MenuSetState( menu%, item%, state%)
```

menu% is an integer expression specifying which pull-down menu the item is on. Menus are numbered from left to right. *item%* is an integer expression specifying the item on the pull-down menu. Use *item%* = **0** to specify the menu title. Actual menu selections are numbered from top to bottom.

state% is an integer expression that specifies the state of the menu item, as described in Table 18.3.

After you call **MenuSetState**, you must call **MenuPreProcess** if the item's state has been changed to or from the "empty. Not displayed" state.

MenuShow displays the main menu across the top of the screen:

```
MenuShow
```

Call **MenuShow** to display the main menu after you define the menu items with **MenuSet** and then call **MenuPreProcess**. Call **MenuShow** to redisplay the main menu anytime you change one of its components.

ShortCutKeyDelete deletes the shortcut key associated with a specific menu item. The syntax for this proccdurc is:

```
ShortCutKeyDelete( menu%, item%)
```

menu% is an integer expression specifying the left-right position of the menu. *item%* is an integer expression specifying the position of the item on the menu.

Use **ShortCutKeyEvent** to determine if keyboard input matches one of the defined shortcut keys:

```
ShortCutKeyEvent( k$)
```

k$ is a string variable containing a character that has been entered from the keyboard. **ShortCutKeyEvent** checks *k$* against the list of currently defined shortcut keys. If a match is found, the proper menu and item are selected (highlighted). If no match is found, execution returns with no action occurring. You must next call **MenuCheck** to determine which menu item was selected.

Use **ShortCutKeySet** to define shortcut keys that can be used to select menu items:

```
ShortCutKeySet( menu%, item%, key$)
```

menu% is an integer expression specifying the left-right position of the menu. *item%* is an integer expression specifying the position of the item on the menu.

key$* is a string specifying the key to assign to the specified menu item. *key$ can designate any single character or extended character, with the exception of Alt+key combinations. To define *key$*, use **CHR$()** with the key's scan code(s). For example, definitions for the function keys F1 through F10 are listed in Table 18.4.

Table 18.4. Definitions for function keys.

CHR\$(0) + CHR\$(59) = F1	**CHR\$(0) + CHR\$(64)** = F6
CHR\$(0) + CHR\$(60) = F2	**CHR\$(0) + CHR\$(65)** = F7
CHR\$(0) + CHR\$(61) = F3	**CHR\$(0) + CHR\$(66)** = F8
CHR\$(0) + CHR\$(62) = F4	**CHR\$(0) + CHR\$(67)** = F9
CHR\$(0) + CHR\$(63) = F5	**CHR\$(0) + CHR\$(68)** = F10

The Windows Toolbox

You can use the routines in the windows toolbox to create a variety of pop-up windows. These windows can greatly enhance the user interface of your programs. These windows are very much like the windows used in the QBX environment and include:

- Text windows for displaying and entering text.

- Alert boxes that require a user response.

- Dialog boxes with edit fields, option buttons, and command buttons.

- List boxes with vertical and/or horizontal scroll bars.

General Procedure for Using Windows

Any program that uses the Windows toolbox must include the file WINDOW.BI followed by the **COMMON** and **DIM** statements in the order shown in Table 18.5.

The Windows toolbox routines are dependent upon the Menus toolbox, so you must also include the **COMMON** and **DIM** statements required by the Menus toolbox (described earlier in this chapter). The general procedure for using windows is outlined here:

1. Initialize the Menu toolbox with a call to **MenuInit**. (Recall that the Windows toolbox is dependent on the Menu toolbox, so this call is necessary even if your program won't use menus per se.)

2. Initialize the Windows toolbox with a call to **WindowInit**.

3. Use window procedures to define and display one or more windows. Multiple windows can be displayed, but only one is active at any time.

4. Perform window actions including:

   • Displaying text

   • Processing window button presses

   • Performing text editing

   • Moving and resizing windows

   • Closing old windows and opening new ones

Table 18.5. **COMMON** and **DIM** statements.

```
COMMON SHARED /uitools/ GloWindow()        AS WindowType
COMMON SHARED /uitools/ GloButton()        AS ButtonType
COMMON SHARED /uitools/ GloEdit()          AS EditFieldType
COMMON SHARED /uitools/ GloStorage         AS WindowStorageType
COMMON SHARED /uitools/ GloWindowStack()   AS INTEGER
COMMON SHARED /uitools/ GloBuffer$()

DIM GloWindow(MAXWINDOW)                    AS WindowType
DIM GloButton(MAXBUTTON)                    AS ButtonType
DIM GloEdit(MAXEDITFIELD)                   AS EditFieldType
DIM GloWindowStack(MAXWINDOW)              AS INTEGER
DIM GloBuffer$(MAXWINDOW + 1, 2)
```

Window Properties

Each window you create has several properties that can be set independently of any other window:

- The window's screen position and size

- The window colors

- Whether the window can be closed, moved, and/or resized by the user

- The window's title, if any

- The characters used for the window border

- Whether the window is *modal*, meaning that the user must respond to a prompt in the window before exiting the window

Characters in a window's border indicate whether the window can be closed, moved, and/or resized:

- A window that can be moved is displayed with a dotted background in its title bar. To move the window, drag the title bar with the mouse.

- A window that can be closed is displayed with an equal sign as the upper-left character of the border. Click the equal sign to close the window.

- A window that can be resized is displayed with a plus sign as the lower-right character of the border. Drag the plus sign to resize the window.

Each window you open has a *handle*, which is an integer value that uniquely identifies that window. Each item within a window, such as a button or an edit field, also has a handle. Alert windows (explained later) do not have handles, nor do they offer the options of moving, resizing, and closing.

Window Procedures

The following procedures in WINDOW.BAS are used internally by other window procedures. You must not call these procedures directly or modify them.

```
BackgroundRefresh
BackgroundSave
ButtonShow
FindButton
FindEditField
WhichWindow
WindowPrintTitle
WindowRefresh
WindowSave
WindowShadowRefresh
WindowShadowSave
```

The Windows toolbox procedures are listed by category in Table 18.6, and described in detail in this section.

The function **Alert** displays a window with a text message, and 1 to 3 buttons from which the user must select. The syntax for **Alert** is:

```
choice% = Alert( style%, text$, r1%, c1%, r2%, c2%, b1$, b2$,
                 b3$ )
```

choice% is any BASIC variable. After execution returns from **Alert**, *choice%* is set to 1, 2, or 3, indicating which button the user selected. *style%* is an integer specifying the display style to be used for *text$*. The choices for *style%* are listed in Table 18.7.

text$ is a string expression specifying the text message to be displayed in the window. Use the vertical bar character (|) to start a new line.

r1% and *c1%* are integer expressions specifying the absolute screen row and column position for the upper-left corner of the win-

Table 18.6. Windows toolbox procedures.

Category	Procedure
Window system initialization	**WindowInit**
Defining, opening, and closing windows	**Alert** **ListBox** **WindowClose** **WindowColor** **WindowOpen** **WindowSetCurrent**
Obtaining information about windows	**MaxScrollLength** **WindowBorder** **WindowCols** **WindowCurrent** **WindowNext** **WindowRows**
Displaying text and lines in windows	**WindowCls** **WindowLine** **WindowLocate** **WindowPrint** **WindowScroll**
Using window buttons	**ButtonClose** **ButtonInquire** **ButtonOpen** **ButtonSetState** **ButtonToggle**
Using edit fields	**EditFieldClose** **EditFieldInquire** **EditFieldOpen**
Detecting window events	**Dialog** **WindowDo**

Table 18.7. The *style%* integer choices.

style%	Display
1	Truncated. Lines of text longer than the window are truncated.
2	Character wrapping. Lines of text longer than the window are wrapped to the next line.
3	Word wrapping. Lines of text longer than the window are wrapped to the next line; wrapping occurs only at spaces.
4	Centered. Text is centered; if too long, it's truncated.

dow. *r2%* and *c2%* are integer expressions specifying the absolute screen row and column position for the lower-right corner of the window.

b1$*, *b2$, and *b3$* are string expressions specifying the text for the buttons. To use fewer than three buttons, specify the null string ("") for the unused buttons. If you don't specify any buttons, a single "OK" button is automatically provided.

The alert window must be wide enough to display the text for all three buttons on the bottom row. If it is not, or if any other problem occurs, **Alert** returns 0. Alert windows are modal, so the user must make a selection from the window before proceeding. Since only one alert window can be displayed at any time, no handle is required.

The following code displays the alert window shown in Figure 18.1.

```
...
a$ = "Your printer is not responding."
x% = Alert(4, a$, 9, 15, 12, 65, "Retry", "Cancel", "Help")
...
```

The procedure **ButtonClose** removes a button from the current window; the button is erased from the screen and removed from global arrays. The syntax for **ButtonClose** is:

```
ButtonClose( button% )
```

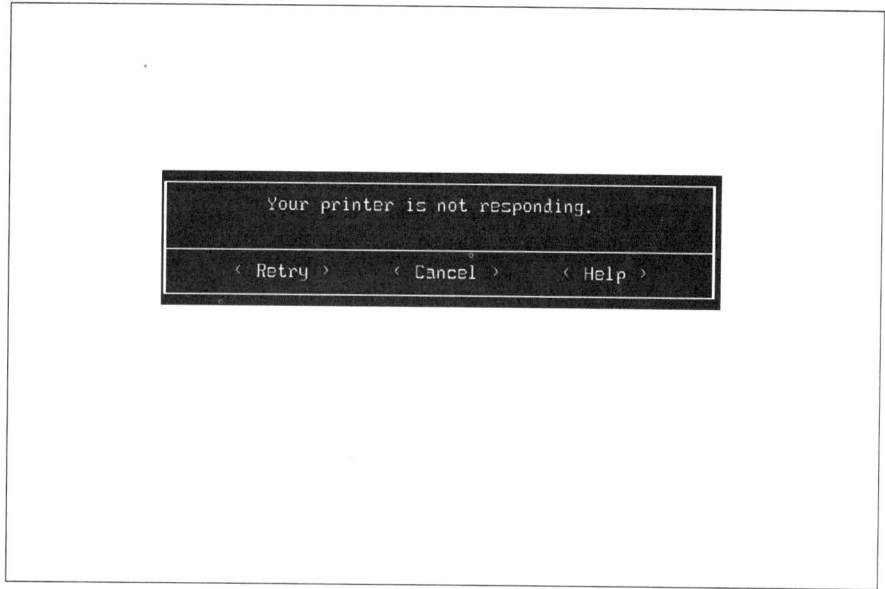

Figure 18.1. An alert window.

button% is the integer value associated with the button when it was created using **ButtonOpen**. If ***button%*** = 0, all buttons in the current window are closed.

ButtonInquire is a function that returns the state of a specified button in the current window. The syntax for **ButtonInquire** is:

```
state% = ButtonInquire( button%)
```

state% is any BASIC variable. Possible button states are explained in the information provided about the **ButtonOpen** procedure. ***button%*** is the integer value associated with the button when it was created using **ButtonOpen**. Use **ButtonInquire** with type 1, 2, 3, 6, or 7 buttons as opened with **ButtonOpen**.

ButtonOpen is a procedure that opens a button in the current window. You can open buttons only in windows that are not resizable. The syntax for this procedure is:

```
ButtonOpen( button%, state%, text$, r1%, c1%, r2%, c2%, type%)
```

button% is an integer value between 1 and the constant

MAXBUTTON. It indicates the number of the button being opened. *state%* is an integer that determines the state of the button. The meaning of *state%* depends upon the type of button (and does not apply to type 4, area button), as shown in Table 18.8.

text$ is the text to be displayed with the button. This argument does not apply to button types 4, 6, or 7. *r1%* and *c1%* are integers specifying the row and column position of the upper-left corner of the button, relative to the current window.

r2% and *c2%* are integers specifying the row and column position of the lower-right corner of the button, relative to the current window. These arguments apply only to button types 4, 6, and 7, and are ignored (but must be included) for other types. *type%* is an integer specifying the button type. Valid button types are listed in Table 18.9.

Each button within a window must have a unique handle, but the same handle can be shared by buttons in different windows. An *area button* is not displayed in the window. It is simply an area of the window defined as a button: if you click there with the mouse, an event occurs. Figure 18.2 illustrates three button types. The following code produced the figure. Note that this code only displays the buttons; it does not respond to any user input.

Table 18.8. The effect of the button type on *state%*.

Type	State	Meaning
1	1	Normal
	2	Default choice (brackets are highlighted)
	3	Chosen (displayed in reverse video)
2, 3	1	Normal
	2	Selected (checked)
6, 7	n	Initial position of the scroll bar's elevator box. n can be anywhere between 1 and the maximum position.

Table 18.9. Valid button types.

type%	Description
1	Command button
2	Check box
3	Option button
4	Area button
6	Vertical scroll bar
7	Horizontal scroll bar

```
' Demonstrates button types.
'$INCLUDE: 'general.bi'
'$INCLUDE: 'mouse.bi'
'$INCLUDE: 'menu.bi'
'$INCLUDE: 'window.bi'

COMMON SHARED /uitools/ GloMenu           AS MenuMiscType
COMMON SHARED /uitools/ GloTitle()        AS MenuTitleType
COMMON SHARED /uitools/ GloItem()         AS MenuItemType
COMMON SHARED /uitools/ GloWindow()       AS windowType
COMMON SHARED /uitools/ GloButton()       AS buttonType
COMMON SHARED /uitools/ GloEdit()         AS EditFieldType
COMMON SHARED /uitools/ GloStorage         AS WindowStorageType
COMMON SHARED /uitools/ GloWindowStack()  AS INTEGER
COMMON SHARED /uitools/ GloBuffer$()

DIM GloTitle(MAXMENU)             AS MenuTitleType
DIM GloItem(MAXMENU, MAXITEM)     AS MenuItemType
DIM GloWindow(MAXWINDOW)          AS windowType
DIM GloButton(MAXBUTTON)          AS buttonType
DIM GloEdit(MAXEDITFIELD)         AS EditFieldType
DIM GloWindowStack(MAXWINDOW)     AS INTEGER
DIM GloBuffer$(MAXWINDOW + 1, 2)

CLS
```

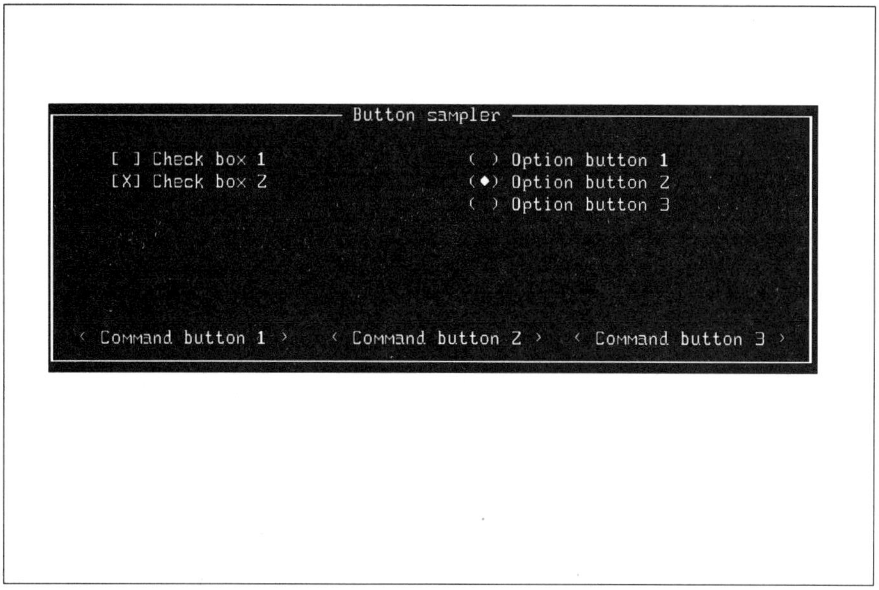

Figure 18.2. Three types of buttons that can be displayed in a window.

```
MenuInit
WindowInit
MouseShow

WindowOpen 1, 6, 5, 15, 75, 0, 7, 0, 7, 15, FALSE, FALSE,
FALSE, TRUE, 1, "Button sampler"

ButtonOpen 1, 1, "Check box 1", 2, 6, 0, 0, 2
ButtonOpen 2, 2, "Check box 2", 3, 6, 0, 0, 2
ButtonOpen 3, 1, "Option button 1", 2, 40, 0, 0, 3
ButtonOpen 4, 2, "Option button 2", 3, 40, 0, 0, 3
ButtonOpen 5, 1, "Option button 3", 4, 40, 0, 0, 3
ButtonOpen 6, 2, "Command button 1", 10, 3, 0, 0, 1
ButtonOpen 7, 1, "Command button 2", 10, 27, 0, 0, 1
ButtonOpen 8, 1, "Command button 3", 10, 50, 0, 0, 1

SLEEP

MouseHide
COLOR 15, 0
CLS
END
```

ButtonSetState sets the state of buttons already open in the current window. The syntax for this procedure is:

```
ButtonSetState( button%, state%)
```

button% is the value associated with the button when it was opened. *state%* is the new state of the indicated button. The meaning of *state%* depends upon the type of button (and does not apply to type 4, the area button), as shown in Table 18.8.

Use **ButtonSetState** to change the state of a button (e.g., to turn the check mark in an option button on or off) in response to user input.

The procedure **ButtonToggle** toggles the state of a button between state 1 (normal) and state 2 (selected). **ButtonToggle** applies only to type 1, 2, and 3 buttons. Its syntax is:

```
ButtonToggle( button%)
```

button% is the value associated with the button when it was opened.

Dialog is a function that determines the button, edit field, or window event that occurred during the execution of **WindowDo**. The syntax for **Dialog** is:

```
event% = Dialog( op%)
```

event% is any BASIC variable. *op%* is a code that determines the information returned by **Dialog**. Use *op%* = 0 to determine what event occurred, then use other values of *op%* to determine where the event occurred. The relationship between the return value, *op%*, and window events is shown in Table 18.10.

EditFieldClose is a procedure that closes a specified edit field in the current window. Its syntax is:

```
EditFieldClose( field%)
```

field% is the number associated with the edit field when it was opened with **EditFieldOpen**. If *field%* = 0, all edit fields in the current window are closed.

Table 18.10. The relationship between *op%* and window events.

op%	*event%*	Meaning
0	0	No event occurred.
	1	A button was pressed.
	2	An edit field was selected.
	3	A different window was selected.
	4	The current window's close box was selected.
	5	The current window was resized and therefore needs to be refreshed.
	6	The Enter key was pressed.
	7	The Tab key was pressed.
	8	The Shift+Tab keys were pressed.
	9	The Esc key was pressed.
	10	The Up Arrow key was pressed.
	11	The Down Arrow key was pressed.
	12	The Left Arrow key was pressed.
	13	The Right Arrow key was pressed.
	14	The Spacebar key was pressed.
	15	The Current window was moved.
	16	The Home key was pressed.
	17	The End key was pressed.
	18	The PgUp key was pressed.
	19	The PgDn key was pressed.
	20	A menu item was chosen.

continued

Table 18.10. The relationship between *op%* and window events (*continued*).

op%	event%	Meaning
1	*n*	Returns the number of the button just pressed.
2	*n*	Returns the number of the edit field just selected.
3	*n*	Returns the number of the window just selected.
17	*n*	Returns the row position of the cursor within a type 4 button field.
18	*n*	Returns the column position of the cursor within a type 4 button field.
19	-2	The down or right direction box was selected on a scroll bar.
	-1	The up or left direction box was selected on a scroll bar.
	n	Selected a position in a scroll bar's grayed area. *n* can range from 1 to the maximum number of scroll bar positions.

EditFieldInquire is a function that returns the string currently associated with a specified edit field. Its syntax is:

```
text$ = EditFieldInquire( field%)
```

text$ is any BASIC string variable. After the call to **EditFieldInquire** occurs, *text$* contains the string currently associated with the edit field. *field%* is the number associated with the edit field when it was opened.

EditFieldOpen is a procedure that opens an edit field in the current window:

```
EditFieldOpen( field%, text$, row%, col%, fg%, bg%, visLen%,
maxLen%)
```

field% is the unique number to be associated with the edit field. It can be any value between 1 and the constant **MAXEDITFIELD**.

text$* is a string expression specifying the text to be initially placed in the edit field for editing. Set *text$ = "" for an initially empty edit field.

row% and *col%* are integer expressions specifying the row and column positions of the upper-left corner of the edit field, relative to the current window. *fg%* and *bg%* are integer expressions specifying the foreground (0-15) and background (0-7) colors of the edit field.

visLen% is an integer expression specifying the length, in characters, of the edit field visible on the screen. *maxLen%* is an integer expression specifying the maximum length, in characters, of the edit field. If *maxLen%* is greater than *visLen%*, the contents of the edit field will scroll right and left as needed. The maximum value for *maxLen%* is 255.

An edit field by itself does not include a label or an enclosing box. You must place these items separately using the **WindowPrint** and **WindowBox** procedures. While an edit field is active, the basic editing keys (arrows, Home, End, Backspace, Del) can be used for editing; press the Enter key to accept the edit-field entry.

ListBox is a function that displays a list of text items and allows the user to select one. The syntax for **ListBox** is:

```
choice% = ListBox( text$(), maxRec% )
```

choice$* is any BASIC integer variable. *text$() is an array of strings containing the text items to be displayed in the list box. *maxRec%* is an integer expression specifying the maximum number of items displayed in the list box.

A list box displays a window containing the list of text items, a scroll bar, an OK button, and a Cancel button. The user can use the mouse or the keyboard to scroll through the list and select an item. Selecting OK returns the number of the selected item in *choice%*; selecting Cancel returns 0.

MaxScrollLength is a function that returns the maximum number of positions in a scroll bar in the current window. Its syntax is:

```
positions% = MaxScrollLength( button% )
```

positions% is any BASIC integer variable. *button%* is the integer value associated with the scroll bar when it was opened using **ButtonOpen**.

You need to know how many positions a scroll bar has so that your program can properly increment or decrement the cursor position in response to scroll-bar input.

WindowBorder is a function that returns information about a window's border. The border of a window determines some of the window's characteristics, such as whether it can be closed. The syntax for this function is:

```
border$ = WindowBorder( WindowType% )
```

border$ is any BASIC string variable. *WindowType%* is an integer specifying a window type. After the call to **WindowBorder**, *border$* contains a 14-character string. This string contains the window's border characters as described in Table 18.11.

Table 18.11. Window border characteristics.

Position in *border$*	Border Character	Special effect
1	Upper-left corner	Equal sign makes window closeable.
2	Top line	Dot-pattern character (ASCII 176) makes window moveable.
3	Upper-right corner	
4	Left-side line	
5	Middle fill	
6	Right-side line	
7	Lower-left corner	
8	Bottom line	
9	Lower-right corner	Plus sign makes window resizable.

continued

Table 18.11. Window border characteristics (*continued*).

Position in *border$*	Border Character	Special effect
10	Left-side intersection	
11	Middle line	
12	Right-side intersection	
13	Shadow flag	An "S" in this position displays the window with a three-dimensional shadow.
14	Title flag	A "T" in this position displays a title across the top of the window if **WindowOpen** specifies a title with length > 0.

WindowBorder is used internally by the Windows toolbox procedures in conjunction with the toolbox's 24 predefined window types. You will rarely, if ever, call **WindowBorder** directly. If you wish to create your own customized window types, examine the code in **WindowBorder**, modify it as needed, and then recompile WINDOW.BAS to make the new window types available to your programs.

WindowBox is a procedure that draws a box in the current window:

```
WindowBox(r1%, c1%, r2%, c2%)
```

r1% and *c1%* are integer expressions specifying the row and column position of the top-left corner of the box, relative to the current window. *r2%* and *c2%* are integer expressions specifying the row and column position of the lower-right corner of the box, relative to the current window.

The box is drawn with a single-line border. Use **WindowBox**, for example, to place a box around edit fields.

WindowClose is a procedure that closes a specific window:

```
WindowClose(handle%)
```

handle% is the integer assigned to the window when it was opened using **WindowOpen**. All buttons and edit fields associated with the window are closed as well. If *handle%* = 0, all windows are closed.

WindowCls is a procedure that clears the current window. All text in the window is cleared to the window background color. The syntax for **WindowCls** is:

```
WindowCls
```

The procedure **WindowColor** modifies the colors of text in the current window:

```
WindowColor(textfg%, textbg%)
```

textfg% and *textbg%* are integer expressions specifying the foreground (0-15) and background (0-7) colors of window text. **WindowColor** affects subsequently printed text, not existing text.

WindowCols is a function that returns the number of interior columns in a window. (*Interior columns* are columns where text can be displayed.) Use **WindowCols** to determine the size of a window after it has been resized. The syntax for **WindowCols** is:

```
columns% = WindowCols(handle%)
```

columns% is any BASIC integer variable. *handle%* is the integer value associated with the window when it was opened.

WindowCurrent is a function that returns the handle of the current window:

```
curhandle% = WindowCurrent
```

curhandle% is any BASIC integer variable. Use **WindowCurrent** when you need the handle of the current window for use by another procedure, such as **WindowClose**.

WindowDo is a procedure that waits for a window event to occur:

```
WindowDo(currentButton%, currentEdit%)
```

currentButton% is an integer indicating the number of the button where the text cursor will be placed. ***currentEdit%*** is an integer indicating the number of the edit field where the text cursor will be placed.

There can be only one cursor at a time, so if you specify nonzero values for both arguments to **WindowDo**, the cursor will be placed on the specified edit field. Use 0 for both arguments if the window doesn't contain any buttons or edit fields.

WindowDo takes control of program execution and waits for some window event to occur (a button press, etc.). While **WindowDo** is active, the user can use Tab and Shift+Tab to move the cursor between window items, select and deselect options, edit text in edit fields, and move and resize windows. As soon as an event occurs, execution returns; you then use **Dialog** to determine the nature and the location of the event.

WindowInit is a procedure that initializes the global Windows toolbox arrays. It must be the first window procedure called by your program. The syntax is:

```
WindowInit
```

WindowLine is a procedure that draws a horizontal line across the current window:

```
WindowLine( row%)
```

row% is an integer specifying the row where the line is to be placed, relative to the top of the window.

WindowLocate is a procedure that sets the position of the text cursor in the current window:

```
WindowLocate( row%, col%)
```

row% and ***col%*** are integer expressions specifying the cursor position relative to the top-left corner of the window. The cursor indicates the location where text is placed by the **WindowPrint** procedure.

WindowNext is a function that returns the next available window handle:

```
nextHandle% = WindowNext
```

nextHandle% is any BASIC integer variable. **WindowNext** returns the next available (unused) window handle. Use **WindowNext** when your program needs to open a window but doesn't know how many other windows are already open.

WindowOpen is a procedure that defines and opens a window:

```
WindowOpen(handle%, r1%, c1%, r2%, c2%, textFg%, textBg%,
          fg%, bg%, highlight%, move%, close%, size%, modal%,
          borderchar%, title$)
```

handle% is an integer specifying the window's handle. It can be any value between 1 and the constant **MAXWINDOW**. Each window must have a unique handle.

r1% and *c1%* are integer expressions specifying the row and column position of the window's upper-left corner, relative to the screen. *r2%* and *c2%* are integer expressions specifying the row and column position of the window's lower-right corner, relative to the screen.

textFg% and *textBg%* are integer expressions specifying the foreground (0-15) and background (0-7) colors to be used for text displayed in the window. *fg%* and *bg%* are integer expressions specifying the foreground (0-15) and background (0-7) colors to be used for the window itself. *highlight%* is an integer expression (0-15) specifying the color to be used for highlighted buttons.

Set *move%* to true (-1) or false (0) to specify whether or not the window can be moved. A window that can be moved is displayed with a dotted background in its title bar.

Set *close%* to true (-1) or false (0) to specify whether or not the window can be closed. A window that can be closed is displayed with an equal sign as the upper-left character of the border.

Set *size%* to true (-1) or false (0) to specify whether or not the window can be resized. A window that can be resized is displayed with a plus sign as the lower-right character of the border.

Set *modal%* to true (-1) or false (0) to specify whether or not the window is modal. Use *borderchar%* to specify the border type: 0 = none, 1 = single line, 2 = double line. *title$* is the window's title, which is displayed at the top of the window. Set *title$* = "" for a window with no title.

The procedure **WindowPrint** displays text in the current window:

```
WindowPrint(style%, text$)
```

text$ is the text to be displayed. Printing begins at the window position specified with **WindowLocate**. *style%* specifies the style to be used for the displayed text. The options are listed Table 18.12.

Table 18.12. Options for style of displayed text.

style%	Meaning
1	Truncated printing. Text lines longer than the window's width are truncated, and the text cursor is moved to the first position in the next line.
2	Character wrapping. Text lines longer than the window's width are wrapped to the next line. The text cursor is moved to the first position on the next line, and the window is scrolled if necessary.
3	Word wrapping. Text lines longer than the window's width are wrapped to the next line, with wrap breaks occurring only at spaces. The text cursor is moved to the first position on the next line, and the window is scrolled if necessary.
4	Truncated centering. Each line of text is centered, and is truncated on both the left and right if it's too long.
-1	Same as style 1, but the text cursor is positioned immediately after the last character displayed.
-2	Same as style 2, but the text cursor is positioned immediately after the last character displayed.
-3	Same as style 3, but the text cursor is positioned immediately after the last character displayed.

WindowRows is a function that returns the number of interior rows in a window. (*Interior rows* are rows where text can be displayed.) Use **WindowRows** to determine the size of a window after it has been resized. The syntax for **WindowRows** is:

```
rows% = WindowRows( handle%)
```

rows% is any BASIC integer variable. *handle%* is the integer value associated with the window when it was opened.

WindowScroll is a procedure that scrolls text in the current window:

```
WindowScroll( lines%)
```

lines% is an integer expression specifying the number of lines to scroll. Positive values of *lines%* scroll text up and negative values scroll text down. If *lines%* = 0, the window is cleared.

WindowSetCurrent is a procedure that makes a specified window current:

```
WindowSetCurrent( handle%)
```

handle% is the value associated with a window when it was opened. When a window is made current, it is displayed "on top" of all other windows.

OS/2 Programming

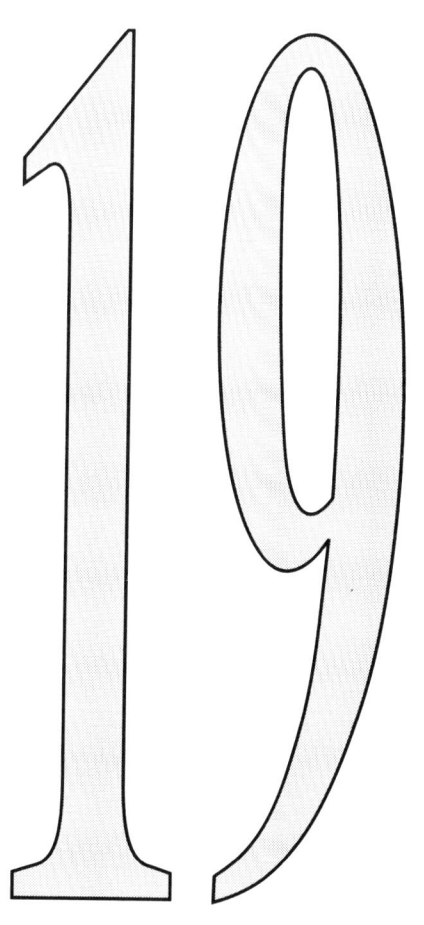

You can use BASIC 7 to write programs that run in real mode or in protected mode. A *real-mode program* runs under DOS or in the DOS compatibility box of the OS/2 operating system. A *protected-mode program* runs full screen or in a text window under OS/2. You can't create programs that use the Presentation Manager graphical interface, nor can you create bound programs. (A *bound program* is a single .EXE file that can execute in either real or protected mode.)

OS/2 protected-mode programming is a complex topic. This chapter is not intended to be a guide to the OS/2 operating system, or to provide general information about protected-mode programming. You should have some familiarity with these topics before you attempt to write and compile a protected-mode program using BASIC 7. For more information, refer to the OS/2 documentation or to one of the many OS/2 books that have been published.

To create a protected-mode BASIC program follow these steps:

1. Write the program, taking into account the language limitations that exist in protected mode, and calling OS/2 functions as needed.

2. Compile the program, specifying that a protected-mode object file is to be produced.

3. Link the program, using appropriate **LINK** options.

4. If necessary, debug the program using the protected-mode version of CodeView.

Writing OS/2 Source Code

The process of writing BASIC source code that is to be compiled into a protected-mode program is very similar to the process of writing real-mode source code. The most important differences are explained in this section.

Limitations of Protected Mode

Table 19.1 describes BASIC statements that have limitations or are not available when you create a protected-mode program. Note that some of the unavailable statements have OS/2 equivalents that can be called instead.

Table 19.1. BASIC statements not available to protected-mode programs.

Statement	In protected mode:
BLOAD, BSAVE	Memory referenced by a **BLOAD** or **BSAVE** statement must be writable or readable by the program. If write or read permission is not available, BASIC may generate a Permission denied error, or OS/2 may generate a permission exception.
CALL	**CALL** can be used to access OS/2 functions and routines in dynamic link libraries. The four include files, BSExxxx.BI, contain function declarations and data structure definitions for the OS/2 routines.
CALL ABSOLUTE	The memory referenced by a **CALL ABSOLUTE** statement must be accessible by your program. One safe technique is to use memory allocated for an array.
CALL INT86	Not available.*
CALL INT86X	Not available.*
CALL INT86OLD	Not available.*
CALL INTERRUPT	Not available.*
COLOR	Ignored in **SCREEN** mode 1.
DEF SEG	Use with caution, and avoid if possible. See warnings in BASIC 7 documentation.

continued

Table 19.1. BASIC statements not available to protected-mode programs (*continued*).

Statement	In protected mode:
INP	Not available.
IOCTL, IOCTL$	Not available.[*]
ON *event*	**ON PEN, ON PLAY, ON STRIG** are not available.
OUT	Not available.
PALETTE [USING]	Not available.
PEEK	Your program must have read permission for any address referred to by **PEEK**.
PEN	The **PEN** function and the **PEN ON, PEN OFF**, and **PEN STOP** statements are not available.
PLAY	Not available.
POKE	Your program must have write permission for any address referred to by **POKE**.
SCREEN	Only modes 0, 1, and 2 are available; the active page and visual page arguments to **SCREEN** are ignored.
SETMEM	Can be called but performs no action (returns a dummy value).
SOUND	Not available.
STICK	Not available.
STRIG	Not available.
VARSEG	Returns the selector of the specified array or variable.
WAIT	Not available.

[*] Can be replaced with equivalent OS/2 functions.

Protected-Mode Statements

The following statements are supported only in protected mode.

ON SIGNAL specifies an event trap that is activated when an OS/2 protected-mode signal is received. The syntax for **ON SIGNAL** is:

```
ON SIGNAL( n%) GOSUB line
```

n% is an integer expression specifying the OS/2 signal to be trapped. The available signals are listed in Table 19.2.

line is a line number or label identifying the first line of the code to be executed when the specified signal is received. The trap code must end with a **RETURN** statement.

Executing **ON SIGNAL GOSUB** identifies the trap routine, but does not activate trapping. Use the following statements to activate, suspend, and cancel control trapping:

- **SIGNAL(*n%*) ON** turns on trapping of signal *n%*.

- **SIGNAL(*n%*) STOP** suspends trapping of signal *n%*. If the signal is received, it's remembered. If **SIGNAL(*n%*) ON** is later received, the remembered signal is trapped immediately.

Table 19.2. Available OS/2 signals.

n%	Signal
1	Key combination Ctrl+C
2	Pipe connection broken
3	Program terminated
4	Key combination Ctrl+Break
5	Process flag A
6	Process flag B
7	Process flag C

- **SIGNAL(*n%*) OFF** disables trapping of signal *n%*. If the signal is received, it's not remembered.

An implicit **SIGNAL STOP** is executed when execution passes to the trap-handling code. This prevents any interuption by another signal of the execution of the signal handler. An implicit **SIGNAL ON** is executed when execution returns from the trap code.

Using OS/2 Functions

The OS/2 operating system includes a large number of built-in functions that your program can call to perform various tasks. (Details about the functions themselves is beyond the scope of this book.) If you have information about some of the functions, you can call them from your protected-mode BASIC program. Support is not provided for OS/2 functions that BASIC cannot use (multiple thread capabilities) or for functions that duplicate BASIC statements (keyboard input).

Support for OS/2 functions is provided in four include files that come with BASIC 7. These files are listed in Table 19.3.

To use an OS/2 function, include the appropriate file with the **$INCLUDE:** statement, and then call the function using the same syntax as the syntax used for a BASIC function. This syntax is re-

Table 19.3. Include files and OS/2 functions.

Include file	Supports these functions
BSEDOSPC.BI	Semaphores, process control, pipes, queues, signals, errors, session manager
BSEDOSFL.BI	Device drivers and file management
BSESUBMO.BI	Mouse
BSEDOSPE.BI	Module management, resource management, language (country codes), date/time, timer, memory management, information segments

quired even if you are not interested in the OS/2 function's return value. (Some of the OS/2 functions require data types that are not part of BASIC. The include files listed in Table 19.3 provide standard methods. See the OS/2 Programming chapter in the *BASIC 7 Programmer's Guide* for further information.)

Compiling and Linking Protected-Mode Programs

The QBX environment can run only in real mode, but you can use it to compile a protected-mode program. To do so, select Make EXE File from the Run menu, and then select the OS/2 Protected Mode option. The resulting .EXE file runs under protected mode.

If you're working in protected mode, you can use the Programmer's Workbench (PWB) to edit and compile your program. PWB provides an editing environment similar to but not as powerful as QBX. For example, PWB does not check syntax while you edit, nor does it interpret your program while you write it. To compile and link your program, PWB uses the command-line compiler and linker. (See the *Getting Started* booklet in your BASIC 7 documentation for further information on PWB.)

Whether you use PWB or another editor, you can compile a protected-mode program using the command-line compiler, BC.EXE. BC can run in either real or protected mode. If you run BC in protected mode, its default is to compile for protected mode. If you run BC in real mode, its default is to compile for real mode, and you must use the **/Lp** compiler option to create a protected-mode .OBJ file.

To link a protected-mode program, the proper libraries must be available. If you compiled the program using the **/O** option, the required library is BCL70*fs*P.LIB. If you compiled without the **/O** option, the necessary library is BRT70*fs*P.LIB, and the required runtime module is BRT70*fs*P.DLL. In all of these cases, f and s stand for the math and string options selected when the library was created. f is either E or A when emulator or alternate math were selected, respectively. s is either N or F when near or far strings were selected, respectively.

Running and Debugging Protected-Mode Programs

A BASIC 7 protected-mode program is installed and run under OS/2 in the same manner that is used for any other non-Presentation Manager OS/2 program. Your OS/2 documentation contains instructions on how to do this, including how to install a program in the Start Programs window.

When a protected-mode program runs, it needs access to one or more dynamic link libraries, which are disk files with the .DLL extension. If your BASIC program was compiled without the /O option, it needs to access the runtime module in the file BRT70*fs*P.DLL. This file must be in one of the directories specified in the LIBPATH command in your CONFIG.SYS file.

To debug a protected-mode program, use the protected-mode version of the CodeView debugger, CVP.EXE.

Installing BASIC 7

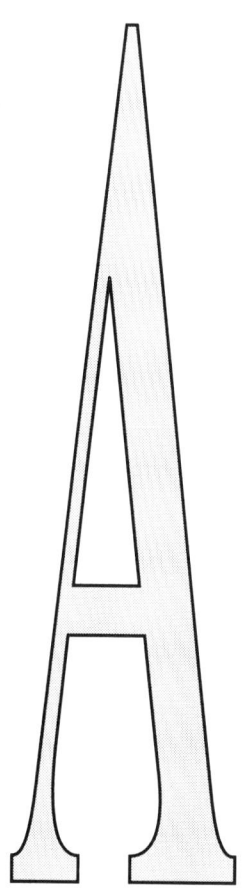

The process of installing BASIC 7 on your system is made relatively painless by an excellent setup utility that does most of the work for you. A number of installation options are available and you must know which of the options you will need in order to respond to prompts displayed by the setup program. This chapter outlines the setup procedure and explains the options. Don't worry about selecting the wrong options—you can always remove unneeded options, or run Setup again to add additional options.

Note: You *must* use the setup program to install BASIC 7. You can't simply copy files from the BASIC 7 diskettes to your hard disk. Remember to make backup copies of the original diskettes and keep them in a safe place.

To use the BASIC 7 Professional Development System, you need:

- An IBM XT, AT, or compatible computer.

- A minimum of 640K memory.

- A hard disk drive.

- DOS version 3.0 or later, or OS/2 version 1.1 or later

The amount of hard disk space required depends upon the options selected during setup. As much as 14Mb can be needed, but more typical installations require only about half of that amount. The Setup program calculates the needed space and, before actually copying any files, tells you if your disk doesn't have enough space available. You'll need a high-density diskette drive for installation, unless you requested a BASIC 7 package with 360K diskettes.

To begin the Setup procedure, insert the setup disk (disk 1) in a diskette drive. At the DOS prompt, type *x:setup*, where *x* is the letter of the diskette drive. The Setup Main menu screen will appear, as shown in Figure A.1.

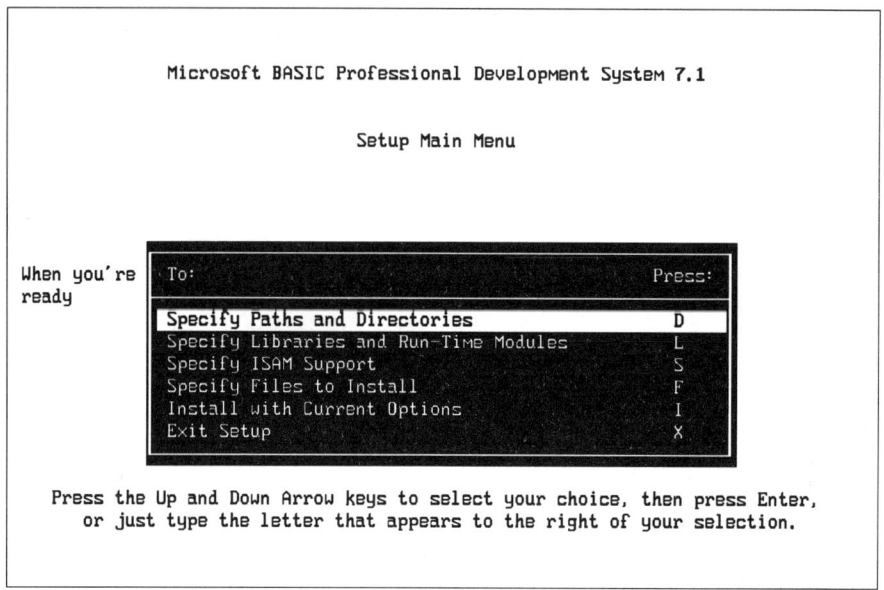

Figure A.1. The Setup Main menu.

The Setup procedure consists of two stages:

1. Use the first four selections on the Main menu to specify installation options. During this stage, Setup is not copying any files and is only obtaining information about options.

2. After you specify all options, select Install with Current Options to begin the actual installation process. During this stage, Setup prompts you to swap diskettes.

The entire installation procedure can take from as little as 20 to 25 minutes on a fast 80386 computer, to more than an hour on slower machines. Set aside a block of time to install BASIC 7. You can interrupt the installation process if necessary, but then you'll have to start over from scratch.

When you select Specify Paths and Directories from the Setup Main menu, the screen in Figure A.2 is displayed. The top section of the screen displays the default path and directories that Setup will use

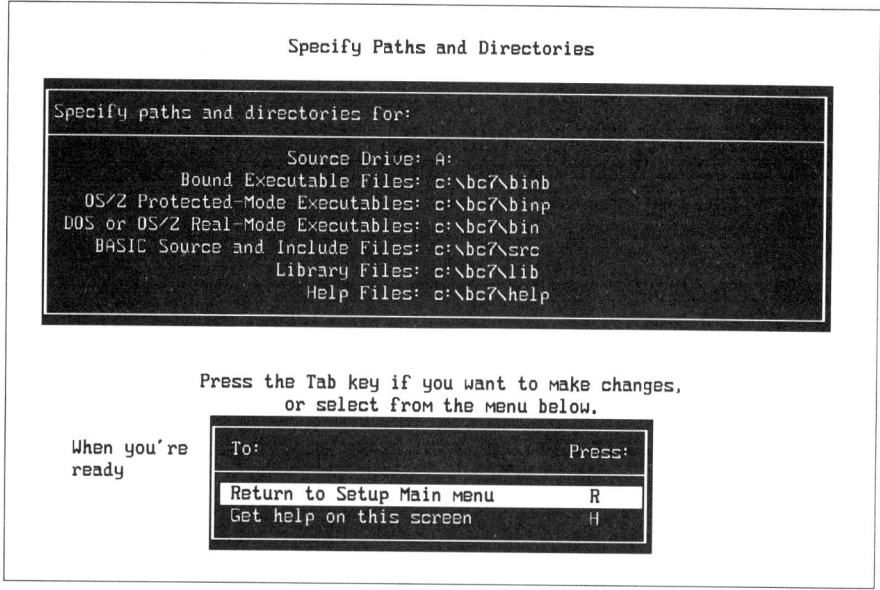

Figure A.2. The setup Specify Paths and Directories screen.

for the BASIC 7 files. Unless you have a specific reason not to, accept the defaults.

When you select Specify Libraries and Run-Time Modules from the Main menu, you are led through three screens. Screen 1 is shown in Figure A.3.

On this screen, specify which compiler options will be installed. You can select one or both options in each group.

In the EXE Type box, select the types of .EXE file you'll be able to create. Select Stand-Alone EXE to create .EXE files that are linked with the BASIC library routines and don't require the runtime module. .EXE files compiled with this option are larger, but initialize faster and require less memory when running. Select EXE Requiring BRT Module to create .EXE files that are not linked with the BASIC library routines. These programs must access the runtime module on disk when executed. Programs compiled with this option are smaller, but initialize slower and require more memory when running.

In the Math Package box, select options that affect floating-point math. Select 80x87 or Emulator Math if you don't know whether the

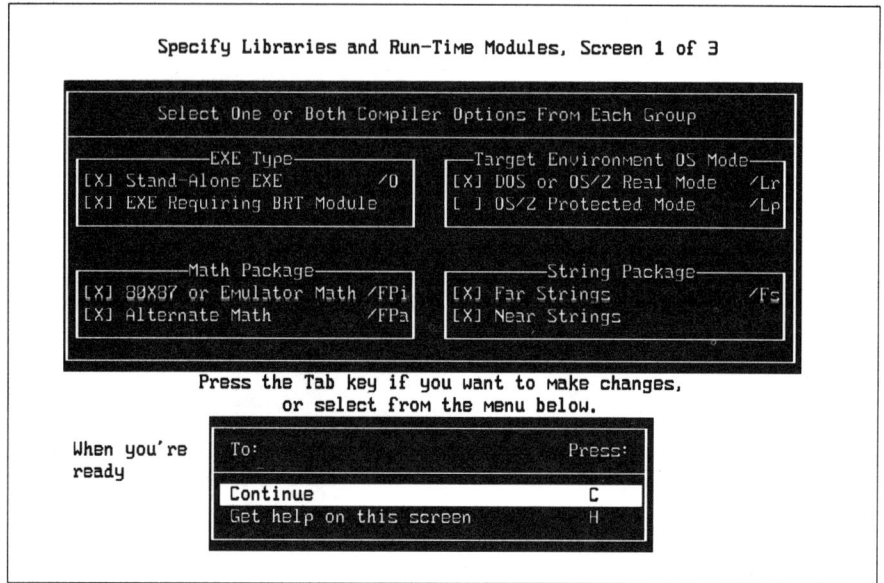

Figure A.3. The first Specify Libraries and Run-Time Modules screen.

system your programs will run on will have a numeric coprocessor installed. The resulting programs will use the coprocessor if present, and emulate it in software if not. Full precision is maintained in calculations. Select Alternate Math if you expect your programs to run on a system without a coprocessor. This option results in a smaller program that runs faster on systems lacking a coprocessor. The tradeoff is a slight loss of precision when compared to the 80x87 or Emulator Math option. (This loss of precision is irrelevant for most applications.)

In the Target Environment box, specify the operating system the programs will be running under. Select DOS or OS/2 Real Mode to be able to create programs that execute under the DOS operating system or in the OS/2 operating system's DOS Compatibility Box. Select OS/2 Protected Mode to create programs that execute in the OS/2 operating system's protected mode.

Under String package, select options that affect the storage of strings. Select the Far Strings option to obtain maximum program-storage space for string and numeric variables, at the expense of decreased space for program code. Select the Near Strings option to obtain maximum space for program code at the expense of decreased variable-storage space.

On the second Specify Libraries and Run-Time Modules screen, shown in Figure A.4, select the screen and graphics support that will be available to your BASIC programs. If, for example, you will be creating only text-mode programs that use no graphics, select only the first option in this list.

The third and final Specify Libraries and Run-Time Modules screen is shown in Figure A.5. On this screen, select the support for the various options provided by stub files. For a complete description of the stub files options, see Chapter 15.

Select Specify ISAM Support from the Setup Main menu to display two screens, the first of which is shown in Figure A.6. ISAM, the Indexed Sequential Access Method for database programming, is covered in detail in Chapter 14. Several Setup options are available:

- ISAM Routines in TSR places ISAM routines in a TSR (terminate-and-stay-resident) program that must be loaded into memory before your ISAM program executes.

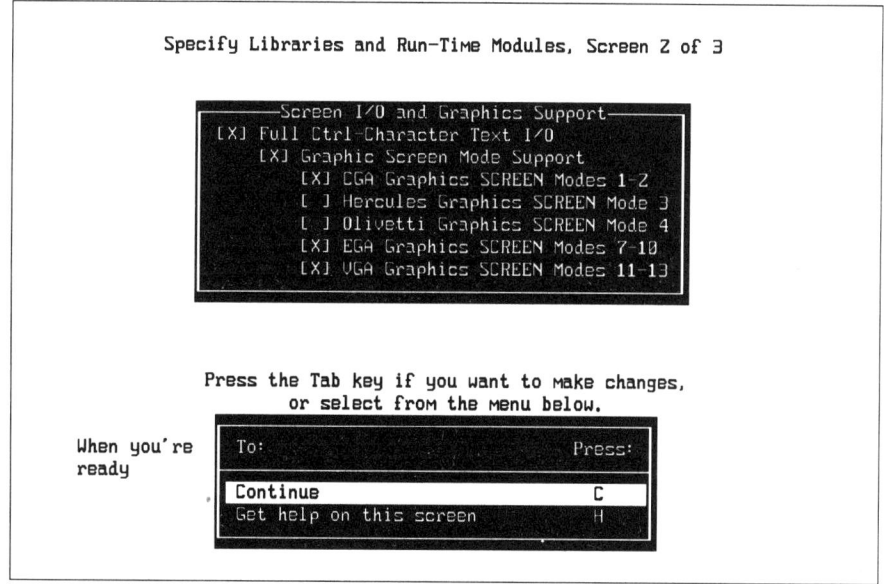

Figure A.4. The second Specify Libraries and Run-Time Modules screen.

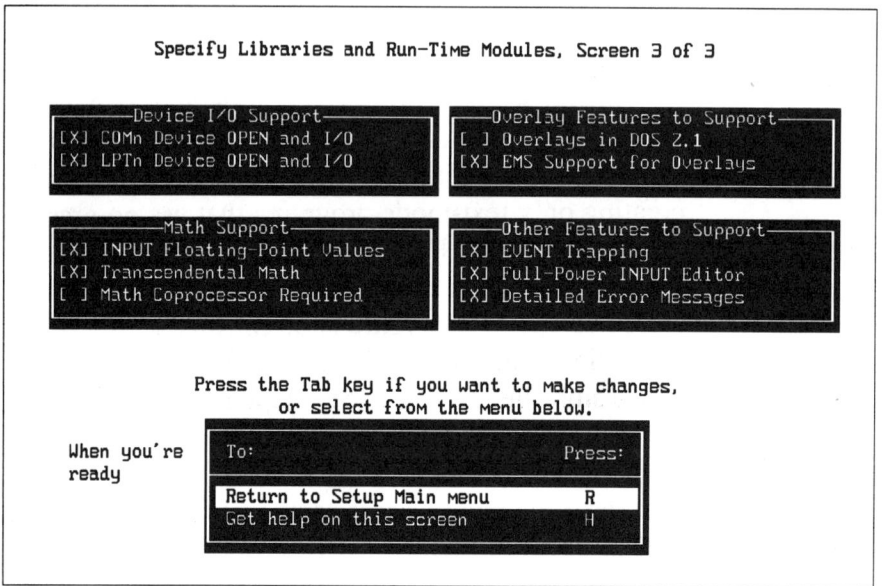

Figure A.5. The third Specify Libraries and Run-Time Modules screen.

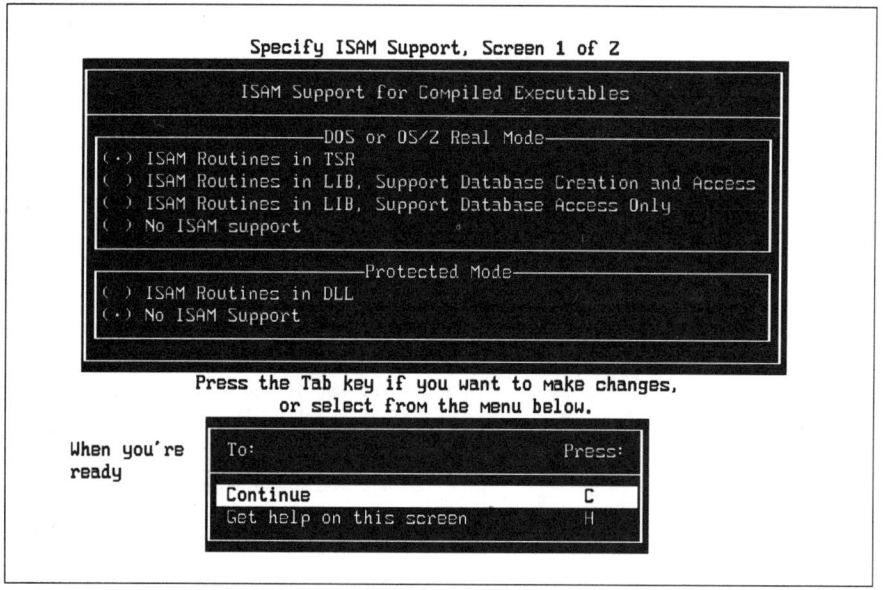

Figure A.6. The first Specify ISAM Support screen.

- ISAM Routines in Lib, Support Database Creation and Access places all ISAM routines in a library, from where they are linked directly with your program.

- ISAM Routines in Lib, Support Database Access Only places a subset of ISAM routines into a library. Select this option if your ISAM program will access, but will not create or modify, ISAM databases.

- No ISAM support does not install ISAM routines.

The second Specify ISAM Support screen, shown in Figure A.7, lets you specify the language whose character set will be used for sorting ISAM databases. A database created with one language specification cannot be used by an ISAM program compiled with a different language option.

After you select the ISAM options, your Setup Main Menu screen will appear as shown in Figure A.8. Note that a bullet appears next to

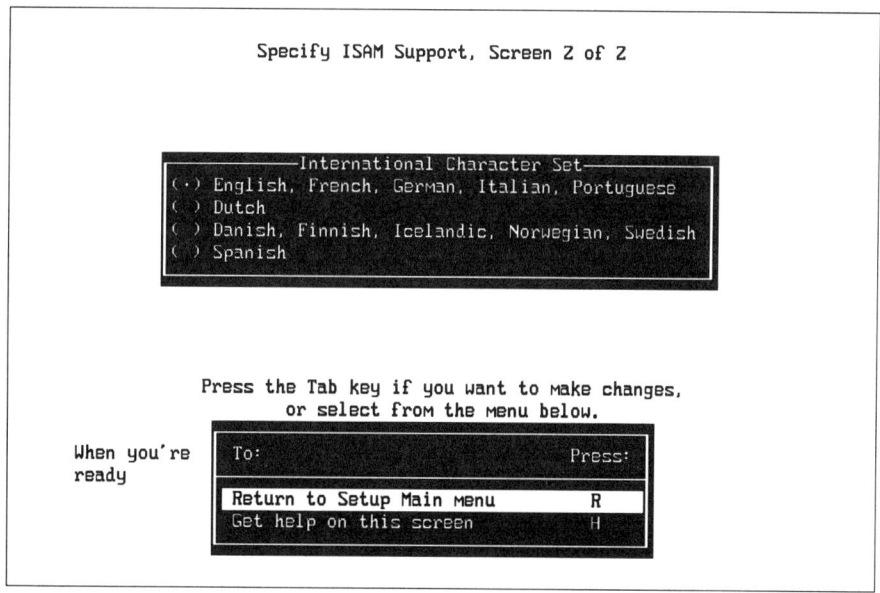

Figure A.7. The second Specify ISAM Support screen.

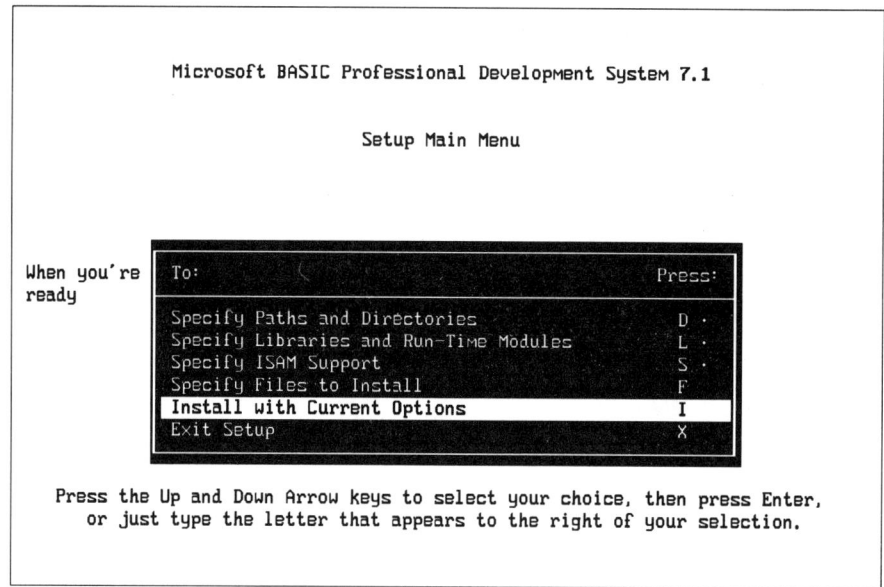

Figure A.8. The Setup Main Menu after all needed installation options have been specified.

cach of thc first four mcnu sclections, indicating that all needed options have been selected.

The next step is to select Install With Current Options. One final screen is displayed, asking you whether the component libraries should be deleted or retained. To make a selection here, you need to understand one aspect of how the installation process works.

The BASIC 7 diskettes contain a large number of libraries and object files that support various features of the language. During the setup process the needed component libraries and object files are copied to your hard disk. The Setup program then uses these components to build combined libraries containing the options that you specified. Once this is done, the component libraries are not needed in order to compile and run BASIC programs. You will need them only if you later decide to modify a combined library. They occupy a significant amount of disk space, so you should specify that they be deleted unless you're sure you'll need them. You can also copy them from the installation disks at a later date.

After you make this selection, the actual installation process begins. You will be prompted to insert different diskettes while BASIC 7 files are copied to your hard disk. When all of the files have been copied, Setup builds the combined libraries, and (if you requested it) deletes the component libraries. BASIC 7 is now installed and ready for use.

Keyboard Codes

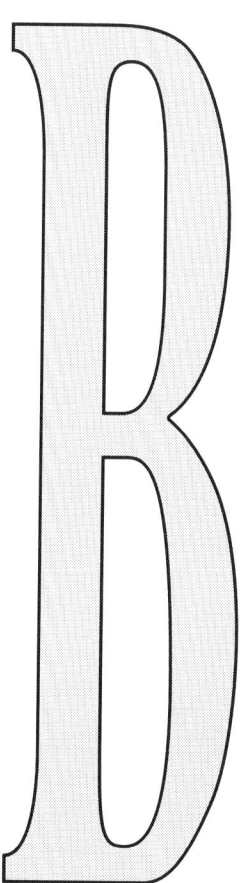

The keyboard codes are the numeric values returned by the BASIC **INKEY\$** function. For many keys (but not all), the code is the same as the character's ASCII code. If a key has been pressed, **INKEY\$** returns a code containing either one or two characters; the codes containing two characters are called *extended codes*. The first character of an extended code is always NUL (ASCII value 0), and the second character identifies the key. The identity of a keystroke returned by **INKEY\$** is determined by the code's length and its ASCII value. This is illustrated by the following code fragment:

```
CONST TRUE = -1, FALSE = 0

DO
  Key$ = INKEY$
LOOP WHILE Key$ = ""

IF LEN(Key$) = 2 THEN
  extendedKey% = TRUE
  keyCode% = ASC(RIGHT$(Key$,1))
ELSE
  extendedKey% = FALSE
  keyCode% = ASC(Key$)
END IF
```

After this code executes, the identity of the key that was pressed can be determined from the values of the variables **extendedKey%** and **keyCode%**.

Table B.1 lists the codes for every key on the IBM keyboard when pressed alone or in combination with the Shift, Alt, or Ctrl key. Nonextended codes are listed as the ASCII value of the single character returned; extended codes are listed as a 0 followed by the ASCII code of the second character. If no code is listed for a particular combination, that combination does not return a code.

Table B.1. Codes for all IBM keyboard keys.

Key	alone	Shift	Ctrl	Alt
Esc	27	27	27	27
1	49	33		0 120
2	50	64	0 3	0 121
3	51	35		0 122
4	52	36		0 123
5	53	37		0 124
6	54	94	30	0 125
7	55	38		0 126
8	56	42		0 127
9	57	40		0 128
0	48	41		0 129
-	45	95	31	0 130
=	61	43		0 131
Backspace	8	8	127	
Tab	9	0 15		
a	97	65	1	0 30
b	98	66	2	0 48
c	99	67	3	0 46
d	100	68	4	0 32
e	101	69	5	0 18
f	102	70	6	0 33

continued

Table B.1. Codes for all IBM keyboard keys (*continued*).

Key	alone	Shift	Ctrl	Alt
g	103	71	7	0 34
h	104	72	8	0 35
i	105	73	9	0 23
j	106	74	10	0 36
k	107	75	11	0 37
l	108	76	12	0 38
m	109	77	13	0 50
n	110	78	14	0 49
o	111	79	15	0 24
p	112	80	16	0 25
q	113	81	17	0 16
r	114	82	18	0 19
s	115	83	19	0 31
t	116	84	20	0 20
u	117	85	21	0 22
v	118	86	22	0 47
w	119	87	23	0 17
x	120	88	24	0 45
y	121	89	25	0 21
z	122	90	26	0 44
F1	0 59	0 84	0 94	0 104

continued

Table B.1. Codes for all IBM keyboard keys (*continued*).

Key	alone	Shift	Ctrl	Alt
F2	0 60	0 85	0 95	0 105
F3	0 61	0 86	0 96	0 106
F4	0 62	0 87	0 97	0 107
F5	0 63	0 88	0 98	0 108
F6	0 64	0 89	0 99	0 109
F7	0 65	0 90	0 100	0 110
F8	0 66	0 91	0 101	0 111
F9	0 67	0 92	0 102	0 112
F10	0 68	0 93	0 103	0 113
F11	0 133	0 135	0 137	0 139
F12	0 134	0 136	0 138	0 140
`	96	126		
,	44	60		
.	46	62		
/	47	63		
;	59	58		
'	39	34		
\	92	124	28	
[	91	123	27	
]	93	125	29	
Spacebar	32	32	32	32

continued

Table B.1. Codes for all IBM keyboard keys (*continued*).

Key	alone	Shift	Ctrl	Alt
Enter	13	13	10	
Up Arrow	0 72	55		
Down Arrow	0 80	50		
Right Arrow	0 77	54		
Left Arrow	0 75	52		
Home	0 71	55	0 119	
End	0 79	49	0 117	
PgUp	0 73	57	0 132	
PgDn	0 81	51	0 118	
Ins	0 82	48		
Del	0 83	46		

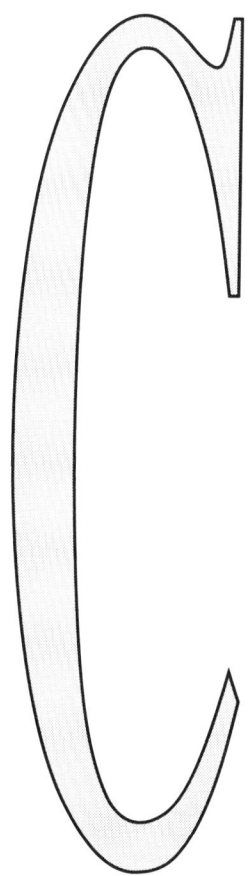

ASCII Character Codes

The *ASCII codes* are the numeric values used internally to represent letters, punctuation marks, and other characters. The BASIC functions **ASC** and **CHR$** translate between characters and their ASCII codes. For example, because the ASCII code for upper case A is 65, we have the following translations:

ASC("A") = 65
CHR$(65) = "A"

The ASCII codes range from 0 to 255. The codes and their corresponding characters are shown in Table C.1. They can be divided into three sections:

- Most of the characters with codes between 0 and 31 have dual meanings. On IBM-compatible video hardware, they display as special symbols, such as smiley faces and arrows. They also have special control-key meanings—e.g., line feed, bell, and tab.

- The characters with codes between 32 and 127 are the standard ASCII characters. This range includes all letters, numerals, and punctuation marks. These characters display on all monitors, and print on all printers.

- The characters with codes greater than 127 are the extended ASCII set. You can use them in your BASIC programs, but they may not display and print on all hardware combinations.

Table C.1. The complete ASCII character set.

ASCII	Dec	Hex	Control		ASCII	Dec	Hex
	0	00	NUL	(Null)	\<space>	32	20
☺	1	01	SOH	(Start of heading)	!	33	21
●	2	02	STX	(Start of test)	"	34	22
♥	3	03	ETX	(End of text)	#	35	23
♦	4	04	EOT	(End of transmission)	$	36	24
♣	5	05	ENQ	(Enquiry)	%	37	25
♠	6	06	ACK	(Acknowledge)	&	38	26
•	7	07	BEL	(Bell)	'	39	27
◘	8	08	BS	(Backspace)	(	40	28
○	9	09	HT	(Horizontal tab)	)	41	29
◙	10	0A	LF	(Linefeed)	*	42	2A
♂	11	0B	VT	(Vertical tab)	+	43	2B
♀	12	0C	FF	(Formfeed)	,	44	2C
♪	13	0D	CR	(Carriage return)	–	45	2D
♫	14	0E	SO	(Shift out)	.	46	2E
☼	15	0F	SI	(Shift in)	/	47	2F
►	16	10	DLE	(Data link escape)	0	48	30
◄	17	11	DC1	(Device control 1)	1	49	31
↕	18	12	DC2	(Device control 2)	2	50	32
‼	19	13	DC3	(Device control 3)	3	51	33
¶	20	14	DC4	(Device control 4)	4	52	34
§	21	15	NAK	(Negative acknowledge)	5	53	35
▬	22	16	SYN	(Synchronous idle)	6	54	36
↨	23	17	ETB	(End transmission block)	7	55	37
↑	24	18	CAN	(Cancel)	8	56	38
↓	25	19	EM	(End of medium)	9	57	39
→	26	1A	SUB	(Substitute)	:	58	3A
←	27	1B	ESC	(Escape)	;	59	3B
└	28	1C	FS	(File separator)	<	60	3C
↔	29	1D	GS	(Group separator)	=	61	3D
▲	30	1E	RS	(Record separator)	>	62	3E
▼	31	1F	US	(Unit separator)	?	63	3F

continued

Table C.1. The complete ASCII character set (*continued*).

ASCII	Dec	Hex	ASCII	Dec	Hex	ASCII	Dec	Hex
@	64	40	`	96	60	Ç	128	80
A	65	41	a	97	61	ü	129	81
B	66	42	b	98	62	é	130	82
C	67	43	c	99	63	â	131	83
D	68	44	d	100	64	ä	132	84
E	69	45	e	101	65	à	133	85
F	70	46	f	102	66	å	134	86
G	71	47	g	103	67	ç	135	87
H	72	48	h	104	68	ê	136	88
I	73	49	i	105	69	ë	137	89
J	74	4A	j	106	6A	è	138	8A
K	75	4B	k	107	6B	ï	139	8B
L	76	4C	l	108	6C	î	140	8C
M	77	4D	m	109	6D	ì	141	8D
N	78	4E	n	110	6E	Ä	142	8E
O	79	4F	o	111	6F	Å	143	8F
P	80	50	p	112	70	É	144	90
Q	81	51	q	113	71	æ	145	91
R	82	52	r	114	72	Æ	146	92
S	83	53	s	115	73	ô	147	93
T	84	54	t	116	74	ö	148	94
U	85	55	u	117	75	ò	149	95
V	86	56	v	118	76	û	150	96
W	87	57	w	119	77	ù	151	97
X	88	58	x	120	78	ÿ	152	98
Y	89	59	y	121	79	ö	153	99
Z	90	5A	z	122	7A	Ü	154	9A
[	91	5B	{	123	7B	¢	155	9B
\	92	5C	¦	124	7C	£	156	9C
]	93	5D	}	125	7D	¥	157	9D
^	94	5E	~	126	7E	Pt	158	9E
_	95	5F	△	127	7F	ƒ	159	9F

continued

Table C.1. The complete ASCII character set (*continued*).

ASCII	Dec	Hex	ASCII	Dec	Hex	ASCII	Dec	Hex
á	160	A0	∟	192	C0	α	224	E0
í	161	A1	⊥	193	C1	β	225	E1
ó	162	A2	⊤	194	C2	Γ	226	E2
ú	163	A3	├	195	C3	π	227	E3
ñ	164	A4	─	196	C4	Σ	228	E4
Ñ	165	A5	┼	197	C5	σ	229	E5
ª	166	A6	╞	198	C6	μ	230	E6
º	167	A7	╟	199	C7	τ	231	E7
¿	168	A8	╚	200	C8	Φ	232	E8
⌐	169	A9	╔	201	C9	Θ	233	E9
¬	170	AA	╩	202	CA	Ω	234	EA
½	171	AB	╦	203	CB	δ	235	EB
¼	172	AC	╠	204	CC	∞	236	EC
¡	173	AD	═	205	CD	φ	237	ED
«	174	AE	╬	206	CE	ε	238	EE
»	175	AF	╧	207	CF	∩	239	EF
█	176	B0	╨	208	D0	≡	240	F0
█	177	B1	╤	209	D1	±	241	F1
█	178	B2	╥	210	D2	≥	242	F2
│	179	B3	╙	211	D3	≤	243	F3
┤	180	B4	╘	212	D4	⌠	244	F4
╡	181	B5	╒	213	D5	⌡	245	F5
╢	182	B6	╓	214	D6	÷	246	F6
╖	183	B7	╫	215	D7	≈	247	F7
╕	184	B8	╪	216	D8	°	248	F8
╣	185	B9	┘	217	D9	•	249	F9
║	186	BA	┌	218	DA	·	250	FA
╗	187	BB	█	219	DB	√	251	FB
╝	188	BC	▄	220	DC	η	252	FC
╜	189	BD	▌	221	DD	²	253	FD
╛	190	BE	▐	222	DE	■	254	FE
┐	191	BF	▀	223	DF		255	FF

BASIC Runtime Errors

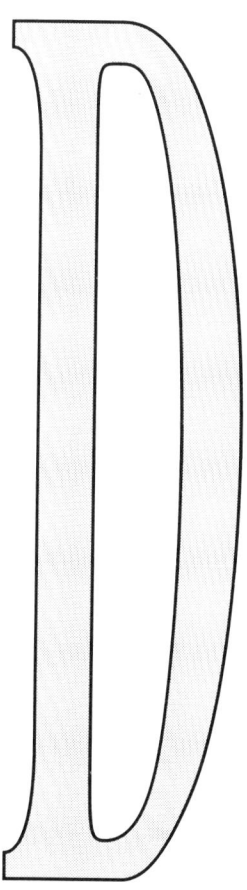

Table D.1 provides a list of the BASIC runtime errors and their associated number code (returned by the **ERR** function). For more details about individual errors, see Appendix D in the *BASIC Language Reference*.

Table D.1. BASIC runtime errors and code numbers.

Code number	Runtime error
1	**NEXT** without **FOR**
2	Syntax error
3	**RETURN** without **GOSUB**
4	Out of **DATA**
5	Illegal function call
6	Overflow
7	Out of memory
8	Label not defined
9	Subscript out of range
10	Duplicate definition
11	Division by zero
12	Illegal in direct mode
13	Type mismatch
14	Out of string space
16	String formula too complex
17	Cannot continue
18	Function not defined
19	No **RESUME**

continued

Table D.1. BASIC runtime errors and code numbers (*continued*).

Code number	Runtime error
20	**RESUME** without error
24	Device timeout
25	Device fault
26	**FOR** without **NEXT**
27	Out of paper
29	**WHILE** without **WEND**
30	**WEND** without **WHILE**
33	Duplicate label
35	Subprogram not defined
37	Argument-count mismatch
38	Array not defined
40	Variable required
50	**FIELD** overflow
51	Internal error
52	Bad filename or number
53	File not found
54	Bad file mode
55	File already open
56	**FIELD** statement active
57	Device I/O error
58	File already exists
59	Bad record length

continued

Table D.1. BASIC runtime errors and code numbers (*continued*).

Code number	Runtime error
61	Disk full
62	Input past end of file
63	Bad record number
64	Bad filename
67	Too many files
68	Device unavailable
69	Communication-buffer overflow
70	Permission denied
71	Disk not ready
72	Disk-media error
73	Feature unavailable
74	Rename across disks
75	Path/File access error
76	Path not found
80	Feature removed
81	Invalid name
82	Table not found
83	Index not found
84	Invalid column
85	No current record
86	Duplicate value for unique index
87	Invalid operation on null index
88	Database needs repair

Index